Personal Recollections and Observations of
General Nelson A. Miles

MAJOR-GENERAL NELSON A. MILES.

PERSONAL RECOLLECTONS

AND OBSERVATIONS OF

GENERAL NELSON A. MILES

EMBRACING A BRIEF VIEW OF THE CIVIL WAR

OR

FROM NEW ENGLAND TO THE GOLDEN GATE

AND THE STORY OF HIS INDIAN CAMPAIGNS
WITH COMMENTS ON THE

EXPLORATION, DEVELOPMENT AND PROGRESS

OF

OUR GREAT WESTERN EMPIRE

VOLUME 2

COPIOUSLY ILLUSTRATED WITH GRAPHIC PICTURES BY
FREDERIC REMINGTON
AND OTHER EMINENT ARTISTS

Introduction to the Bison Book Edition by Robert Wooster

University of Nebraska Press
Lincoln and London

First Bison Book printing: 1992
Most recent printing indicated by the last digit below:
10   9   8   7   6   5   4   3   2   1

Library of Congress Cataloging-in-Publication Data
Miles, Nelson A., 1839–1925.
Personal recollections and observations of General Nelson A. Miles, embracing a brief
view of the Civil War; or From New England to the Golden Gate and the story of his Indian campaigns with comments on the exploration, development, and progress of our great
western empire / introduction to the Bison Book edition by Robert Wooster; copiously illustrated with graphic pictures by Frederic Remington and other eminent artists.
p.   cm.
Originally published: Chicago: Werner, 1896.
ISBN 0-8032-8180-3 (vol. 1).—ISBN 0-8032-8181-1 (vol. 2).—ISBN 0-8032-8182-X (Set)
1. Miles, Nelson A., 1839–1925.   2. Indians of North America—Wars—1866–1895.
3. West (U.S.)—Description and travel—1860–1880.   4. Indians of North America—West
(U.S.)   5. Generals—United States—Biography.   I. Title.
E83.866.M64   1992
355.3′32′092—dc20
[B]
91-39603   CIP

Reprinted from the original edition published in 1896 by the Werner Company, Chicago.
For this Bison Book edition General Miles's memoirs have been divided into two volumes.
Volume 2 begins with Chapter XXV.

♾

✦ ✦ ✦ DEDICATED

To the memory of the heroes and patriots who have made the soldier's sacrifice while protecting the innocent against savage ferocity, maintaining their country's honor and perpetuity, and advancing the lines of civilization.

INTRODUCTION

By Robert Wooster

Civil War hero and conqueror of Puerto Rico, Lieutenant General Nelson Appleton Miles was best known for his military success against the American Indians. Despite his brilliant combat record, however, contemporary observers frequently lampooned the general. Contentious and egotistical, he was rendered an easy mark by his affinity for pomp and circumstance. "Seize Gin'ral Miles' uniform," teased Finley Peter Dunne, whose satiric narrator Mr. Dooley delighted readers across the country, "we must strengthen th' gold reserve." "A brave peacock," scoffed Theodore Roosevelt.[1]

Yet Miles was one of the most important figures of the late-nineteenth-century United States. Born in 1839 at Westminster, Massachusetts, he was a raw young man with a rudimentary education and almost no military training when he volunteered for the Union army after the Battle of First Bull Run. A wartime hero, Miles emerged from the civil conflict as a major general of volunteers. He spent a year at Fortress Monroe, Virginia, where he oversaw the imprisonment of Jefferson Davis, former president of the Confederacy. Miles was then transferred to North Carolina, where he served as assistant commissioner in the Freedmen's Bureau.

Securing a colonelcy in the regular army, Miles was in 1869 appointed to command the Fifth Infantry Regiment. He went on to compile a splendid record fighting Indians across the West; indeed, no other officer could match his success against the Southern Cheyennes, Comanches, Sioux, Northern Cheyennes, Nez Perces, Bannocks, and Apaches. In 1895 he became commanding general of the army; from that position he masterminded the invasion of Puerto Rico during the war against Spain. Appointed lieutenant general in 1900, Miles resigned from the army three years later at the mandatory retirement age of sixty-four.

Departure from regular military service hardly slowed this most ambitious man. Following an unsuccessful bid to secure the Democratic Party's 1904 presidential nomination, he served a brief stint as adjutant general of the Massachusetts state militia. An ardent advocate of Prohibition and nativism, Miles was a leader of an anti-Catholic group known as the Guardians of Liberty. The general also acted as historical advisor for an early western movie starring Buffalo Bill Cody and offered to lead a military expedition into Russia during the First World War. Frequently called to testify before Congress, he opposed Secretary of War Lindley Garrison's plan for a "Continental Army," criticized the League of Nations, and supported Billy Mitchell's advocacy of air power. Even death came with a dose of Milesian drama. On May 16, 1925, he took his grandchildren to see the Barnum and Bailey Circus. As he rose to stand at allegiance for the national anthem, he died of a heart attack.

In 1896, Nelson Miles was delighted at the completion of his memoirs. Published by the Werner Company of Chicago, the lavishly illustrated 591-page tome featured prints of fifteen paintings by Frederic Remington, a friend and public ally of General Miles. Da Capo Press issued a limited edition reprint in 1968, but this Bison Book edition makes the book more generally available to modern readers. The University of Nebraska Press has divided the manuscript into two volumes. The first described Miles's career through his campaigns against the Bannock Indians in 1878 and his role in the surrender of Sitting Bull. The present volume includes his analysis of Indians and Indian policy, his observations about the West and Alaska, and an account of his campaigns against Geronimo.

Miles completed this work just as he assumed his office as commanding general of the United States Army. Insatiably ambitious, he hoped to enter the political arena after his military days had ended. Assisted by former aides Captain Marian Maus and Lieutenant Henry T. Allen, old scout Ben Clark, and secretary Noble E. Dawson, Miles assembled a collection of extracts from official reports, quotations from contemporary social scientists, and historical and personal observations. Miles avoided his more controversial experiences, not wanting to antagonize potential readers. For example, the early chapters, in the first volume of the Bison Book reprint, omit references to his actions during Reconstruction. Readers of this second volume will note that Miles ended discussions of his own career with the late 1880s. This decision allowed the general to ignore his much-disputed service in the Wounded Knee campaign and the Pullman Strike of 1894.

Miles did, however, emphasize three issues of lifelong interest. The first affirmed the immense potential of the American West. This seemed a logical outgrowth not only of the region's resources but of personal habit. For years Miles had trumpeted the virtues of whatever area he happened to be stationed in, hoping that local politicians might reciprocate by favoring his career advancement. "It is a mistake," he concludes, "to suppose that the West is crude or uncultivated. The strongest, most resolute, enterprising and ambitious of our men have gone West."[2]

A second theme concerned Indians and Indian policy. Consistent with his previously published articles, congressional testimony, and private letters, *Personal Recollections and Observations* advocated substantial change while reflecting the paternalism common to mainstream reformers. The Indians "stood . . . in the position of unruly children to indulgent parents for whom they have very little respect, at times wrongly indulged and again unmercifully punished." Nothing could stop Americans from claiming the continent from these peoples, thus bringing about a "wonderful change."[3]

Yet the United States had broken many treaties and, by allowing the Bureau of Indian Affairs to remain within the authority of the corruption-riddled Department of the Interior, allowed naive and venal agents to carry out policy. Miles urged that the Indian bureau be transferred to the Department of War. Officers who had been entrusted with the command of huge armies and millions of dollars in public property should, he argued, be allowed to administer Indian affairs. In turn, the Indians should be encouraged to abandon their tribal habits for the ways of white Protestant farmers.

Miles devoted nearly one hundred pages to the wars against the Apaches. This decision is not surprising when balanced against the enormous controversies the campaigns engendered. His chief rival for Indian-fighting honors, George Crook, had during the 1870s forced an uneasy truce as commander of the Department of Arizona. During his second tour of duty there, Crook found the final conquest of Geronimo and other independent-minded Apaches more difficult. The commanding general, Phil Sheridan, questioned Crook's reliance on hired Apache auxiliaries and suggestions that a negotiated peace be pursued. When Crook offered his resignation on April 1, 1886, Sheridan seized the opportunity to replace him with Brigadier General Miles.

Eager to outshine Crook, Miles promised to use his regulars to crush Geronimo and the remaining Apaches. But despite four months of hard campaigning and the presence of nearly four thousand soldiers, several dozen Apaches continued to defy U.S. authority. To secure additional advantages, Miles determined to remove the inhabitants of the San Carlos Reservation to Florida, thus reducing what had once been for Geronimo a convenient source of rest, recruitment, and supplies. The general also enlisted the services of Lieutenant Charles B. Gatewood, a veteran of the Arizona campaigns widely associated with the methods of George Crook.

Washington continued to insist upon Geronimo's unconditional surrender. Miles, on the other hand, stressed that some form of negotiated peace was essential if Geronimo were ever to be captured. Telegraph wires buzzed with military communications even as Geronimo and his followers, exhausted by the months of hard pursuit and fearing the presence of about two hundred Mexican soldiers along the border, met with Gatewood in late August. Stunned by the lieutenant's news about the removal of their loved ones at San Carlos, they took comfort when he suggested that their lives might be spared.

But they must see Miles before making any final decision. The general, who had avoided such a meeting until surrender seemed assured, spoke with Geronimo on September 3 and 4. The site—a frequent Indian haunt called Skeleton's Canyon, which Miles described as "well suited by name and tradition to witness the closing scenes of such an Indian War"[4]—seemed appropriate to the dramatic occasion. Geronimo, eyes burning, was nervous about his fate; Miles, his bearing reflective not only of his military exploits but also of his egotistical nature, scratched out pictures in the dirt which suggested that all the Chiricahuas would be reunited in Florida until the president decided their fate. United States soldiers, Miles informed Geronimo, were not in the habit of summarily executing their prisoners.

The surrender concluded, Miles raced back to Fort Bowie. On September 7, his superior, Major General Oliver O. Howard, informed Washington that Geronimo had surrendered unconditionally. Sheridan then instructed Miles to hold the Apaches in Arizona for civil trial. Miles questioned this decision, arguing that he could not guarantee the confinement of the prisoners at Bowie. On the 8th, President Grover Cleveland decided that the Indians should be kept in Arizona. But it was too late; Geronimo and his followers, along with two of the Apache scouts who had been essential to the entire campaign, had been loaded onto railroad cars and whisked east. Furious Washington officials stopped the train at San Antonio, but Cleveland, after weighing his options, decided that the prisoners must go to Florida in accord with Miles's promise.[5]

Government officials accused Miles of having exceeded his authority in offering Geronimo any terms. Howard, a Civil War comrade who had broken with Miles in the controversial aftermath to the campaigns against Chief Joseph, asked that he be allowed "to enforce obediance" over his subordinate. But in a claim supported by the diary of Lieutenant Leonard Wood, Miles maintained that he did not know of Cleveland's final decision until well after the Apaches had left Fort Bowie. Mounting pressure led Miles to strike back wildly, sending his wife on an eastern tour to drum up sympathy and devising a special telegraphic cipher with Governor Edmund G. Ross of New Mexico so as to receive confidential information concerning Cleveland, Secretary of War William Endicott, Interior Secretary L. Q. C. Lamar, Sheridan, and Adjutant General Richard C. Drum.[6]

The public relations moves backfired, and two congressional investigations reflected poorly upon the general's conduct. During the late 1880s, Crook and Howard mounted a determined effort to transfer the Apaches from their squalid quarters in Florida to the Indian territory. Although Miles himself had suggested the latter as a compromise site in the late summer of 1886, in time he instinctively challenged any suggestions made by his rivals. The Apaches thus languished in Florida and Alabama until 1894, when they were finally moved to a more suitable location at Fort Sill, Oklahoma.

Naturally, *Personal Reminiscences and Observations* portrays the campaign and the resulting controversies in a light most favorable to Nelson A. Miles. Particularly revealing is his use of narratives by Marion Maus and Leonard Wood rather than Gatewood, whose role was much more crucial to Geronimo's surrender but whose association with Crook might have lent credence to the theory that even Miles relied upon Crook's methods. But the book received little notice in the popular press, and both *Harper's Weekly* and *The Army and Navy Journal* declined to print excerpts from the original manuscript.[7] Even worse, the Werner Company, without permission from Remington or Miles, authorized a reprint of several illustrations in a separate publication. The two men secured a court injunction against the distribution of the rival work, and the Werner Company had by 1898 gone bankrupt.[8]

Undaunted, Miles continued his literary efforts. In 1898 Doubleday and McClure Company published his *Military Europe: A Narrative of Personal Observation and Personal Experience*, an account of the general's 1897 tour of the continent. *The Forum* carried his articles, "Our Coast Defences" and "The Political Situation in

Europe and the East." And following the war against Spain, Miles wrote the intro-duction for *Harper's Pictorial History of the War with Spain*. Essays on the Panama Canal, Japan, his treatment of Jefferson Davis, and various patriotic and Civil War themes appeared in the coming years.

Concerned that *Personal Recollections and Observations* had not adequately cov-ered his career, Miles set out to correct the record with a second set of memoirs. *Serving the Republic: Memoirs of the Civil and Military Life of Nelson A. Miles, Lieutenant-General, United States Army*, was published in 1911 by Harper and Brothers. *Cosmopolitan* produced a series of excerpts from the new volume. But Miles shied away from the personal experiences and insights necessary to such a genre, and *Serving the Republic* failed to gain wide readership.[9]

These experiences are in many ways symbolic of Miles's career. A brilliant combat commander who managed to gain the army's highest rank despite his lack of formal military training, Miles saw himself as the victim of a long series of conspiracies orchestrated by his enemies. By writing his memoirs, he might take his case directly to the American people. But he never grasped the subtle intricacies and nuances of the written word, a failing at least partially attributable to his limited education. *Personal Recollections and Observations*, in substance as well as in intent, thus reveals much about the character of Nelson A. Miles. It is important not only as a primary source document on the Civil and Indian wars, but also because it illustrates what the nation's highest ranking army officer thought the American public wanted to read. Understanding Miles's career—his military successes as well as his public relations fiascos—does much to help subsequent generations assess the army he represented.

NOTES

1. Finley Peter Dunne, *Mr. Dooley in Peace and in War* (1898; rpt. New York: Greenwood Press, 1968), p. 32; Henry F. Pringle, *Theodore Roosevelt: A Biography* (New York: Harcourt, Brace and Co., 1931), p. 446.

2. *Personal Recollections and Observations*, 589.

3. Ibid., 342.

4. Miles to Adjutant General, Division of the Pacific, Sept. 24, 1886, Senate Executive Document 117, 49th Congress, 2 session, serial 2449, p. 19. As in many sections of the text of *Personal Recollections and Observations*, Miles relied heavily on earlier material. See p. 520.

5. For a good summary of the correspondence, see Senate Executive Document 117.

6. Howard to Adjutant General, Sept. 9, 1886, Nelson A. Miles Collection, U.S. Army Military History Research Institute, Carlisle Barracks, Pa. (USAMHI); Diary, Sept. 8, 1886, box 1, Leonard Wood Papers, Library of Congress, Washington, D.C.; Miles to Ross, Oct. 1, 4, 1886, Miles Collection, USAMHI; Miles to Ross, Nov. 1, 1886, Edmund G. Ross Collection, Center for Historical Research, Kansas State Historical Society, Topeka; Ross to Miles, Aug. 14, Oct. 3, Nov. 15, 1886, box 3, Nelson A. Miles Papers, Library of Congress (LC).

7. H. Nelson to Miles, Aug. 5, 1895, box 8, Miles Papers, LC; Miles to Church, Oct. 2, 1895, box 2, William C. Church Papers, LC; Clark to Miles, Aug. 26, 1895, box 1, Miles Papers, LC.

8. *New York Times*, Nov. 17, Dec. 11, 1898; B. Colby to Miles, Feb. 23, 1900, box 1, Miles Papers, LC; John Tebbel, *A History of Book Publishing in the United States*, vol. 2: *The Expansion of an Industry* (New York: R. R. Bowker, 1975), pp. 447–48; *Publishers Weekly* (Dec. 3, 1898), p. 1034; (Dec. 17, 1898), p. 1105.

9. Butt to Clara, April 28, 1910, in *Taft and Roosevelt: The Intimate Letters of Archie Butt, Military Aide* (Garden City, New York: Doubleday, Doran and Co., 1930), p. 340; *New York Times Review of Books*, Nov. 19, 1911; *The Independent* 71 (Nov. 30, 1911), p. 1206.

ILLUSTRATIONS

TABLE OF CONTENTS

CHAPTER XXX.

A CHAPTER OUT OF EARLY HISTORY.

CHAPTER XXXI.

DEPARTMENT OF THE COLUMBIA.

CHAPTER XXXII.

CHIEF MOSES AND HIS TRIBE.

CHAPTER XXXIII.

OUR ALASKAN POSSESSIONS.

CHAPTER XXXIV.

FROM INDIAN TERRITORY TO ARIZONA.

CHAPTER XL.

END OF THE APACHE WAR.

CHAPTER XLI.

HOW THE REGULARS ARE TRAINED.

CHAPTER XLII.

THE ARID REGION AND IRRIGATION.

CHAPTER XLIII.

TRANSPORTATION.

CHAPTER XLIV.

CALIFORNIA.

CHAPTER XXV.

RESULTS OF SIX YEARS OF INDIAN CAMPAIGNING.

REDEEMED TERRITORY — ITS VAST AREA — ZONES OF EMIGRATION — INDICATIONS OF CHARACTER
FROM NATURAL SURROUNDINGS — THE TRANS-CONTINENTAL RAILWAYS — LAND AND ITS
FERTILITY — DESTINY OF THE WEST — YELLOWSTONE VALLEY — THE PROBLEM OF
IRRIGATION — A WESTERN "CITY" — THE PLACE AND WORK
OF OUR SOLDIERS IN WESTERN PROGRESS.

BETWEEN the years 1874 and 1880, a belt of country extending from the Rio Grande or the Mexican boundary on the south, to the Canadian boundary on the north, and averaging some four hundred miles in width from east to west, was redeemed from a wild state and its control by savage tribes, and given to civilization. This vast region comprised a territory nearly eight times as large as all New England. Take out of it as many square miles as there are in New England, and add to this New York, New Jersey, Delaware, Maryland, Pennsylvania, Virginia, West Virginia, North Carolina, South Carolina and Georgia, and there would still remain more than enough territory to carve out other States such as Alabama, Mississippi, Tennessee and Kentucky. Or, again, take all New England, New York, Pennsylvania, Ohio, Indiana, Illinois and Iowa—the belt containing the greatest wealth and densest population of the United States—out of this great territory, and there will still be an abundance remaining out of which to form several other States.

This vast country, over which in 1874 roamed powerful bands of Indian warriors and countless numbers of wild game, was in six years, by the operations of the United States Army, freed for all time from the desolating influence of the savage, and made habitable for civilized man. And these results are due to the heroic services, the splendid fortitude and courage and noble sacrifices, of men like Lewis, Custer, Thornburgh, Hale, Bennett, Keogh, Yates, Tom Custer, Crittenden, Biddle, McKinney, and hundreds of others, officers and soldiers, who placed themselves between war and peace, between danger and security, guarding the newly-constructed railways and protecting the towns as they rose on the plains. They freely offered their lives, and actually cleared this vast region during that brief time, giving it to civilization forever. It is to be hoped that the services and sacrifices of these men will at least be remembered by the people who occupy this country and enjoy its benefits.

It is somewhat singular how prone man is to follow in his migrations the zone where his fathers lived. Ohio and Kentucky were settled largely by the middle Atlantic States; Texas from the southern States; Iowa, Kansas and Nebraska by the Middle States; Michigan, Wisconsin and Minnesota by people from the northern zone of our country; and the settlements in western Texas, western Kansas, western Nebraska, the Dakotas and Montana exhibit the same phenomenon of growth to-day. The people of each are wedded to their own zone and climate, and are enthusiastic in the development of their own district of country. If we may judge by the comparative vigor and enterprise of the aboriginals in the countries occupying the different belts, we may estimate the character of the descendants of the people that have supplanted them, and measure their future activity and intelligence.

The southwest country has been noted ever since civilized man has been there for its active, intelligent and enterprising spirit; and its present population has forever supplanted the Comanches and Kiowas as possessors of the soil. The white settlers who have gone into that region have manifested great resolution and energy in the development of its natural resources, building a network of railways, opening mines and establishing factories, blocking out plantations and building homes. Along the middle belt we see the enterprise and intelligence that have made Pennsylvania, Ohio, Indiana, Illinois, Iowa, Missouri, Kansas, Nebraska, Colorado, Utah, Idaho and California what they are to-day.

In the extreme north the Dakotas and Montana will also develop in the near future a strong, hardy, heroic race. That country is being filled by people from along the line of New England, New York, Ohio, Michigan and Minnesota, as well as by a foreign population accustomed to the rigorous climate of northern Europe, such as the Scotch, Irish, English, North Germans, Swedes, Norwegians and even the Russians.

Every individual coming from Europe and settling in that country becomes an agent or missionary for the planting of still other colonies. A man or woman who has worked there long enough to be enabled to save fifty dollars, can take that sum to almost any bank along the line of the Great Northern or Northern Pacific, give the name of his relative in the home country, whatever part of Europe that may be, and the person named will be transported to the place where the money has been deposited without giving himself any further concern, the banks and transportation companies attending to the entire transaction. In this way vast numbers of people are already occupying that country, and while it results in but little advantage to the present generation, the next, by attending the public schools and acquiring a knowledge of the English language, and an interest and pride in our institutions, will become Americanized and help make in the great population now growing up in those western States a sure foundation for the future prosperity of the commonwealth. Un-doubtedly, as the Dakota Indians were among the most stalwart, bold and enterprising of the native races, so that same climate will have its effect upon the descendants of the people settling there at the present time, and will place them among the strongest and most independent of our citizens. There is something in the climate that engenders a spirit of independence, energy and fortitude.

During the last two decades that great belt of country stretching from the Rio Grande to the Canadian boundary has been crossed by not less than twelve great railway systems that have lateral and trans-continental connections, to-wit: the Kansas Pacific, the Union Pacific, the Chicago and Northwestern, the Atchison, Topeka and Sante Fé, the Northern Pacific, the Great Northern, the Burlington, the Elk Horn, the Rock Island, the Denver, Texas and Gulf, the Southern Pacific, and the Texas Pacific, together with all their branches and tributaries. The smoke of the Indian villages has been replaced by the foundries and furnace fires of civilization; the signal-lights no longer flash from the hills, but in their places the headlight of the locomotive and the electric light dispel the shadows of town, city, and plain, and illumine the pathway of progress and civilization.

As has well been said by an eminent writer, this is "the land of large-ness." Mountains, rivers, railways, ranches, herds, crops, business transac-tions, ideas, all are Cyclopean. It is said that western stories are often on such a large scale that it takes a dozen eastern men to believe one of them; but large as they are they still possess all the elements of verity. The States and Territories are large. New Mexico is larger than the United Kingdom of Great Britain and Ireland. That part of the country, freed from the ravages of the Indians by the campaign of 1874 and '75, is alone larger than all New England, together with New York, New Jersey and Delaware.

The amount of useless land, though large in the aggregate, is much less than is commonly supposed, and in comparison with the wealth-producing lands is almost insignificant. The vast region east of the Rocky Mountains, though not long since known as "The Great American Desert," really does not contain a large percentage of useless land. We have seen cattle come out of the Bad Lands in the spring as fat as if they had been fed all the winter. The United States surveyor generaly states that the proportion of waste lands in the Dakotas, owing to the absence of swamps, mountains, and overflowed and sandy tracts, is less than in any other territory of the same size in the Union. The Staked Plains of Texas has been spoken of as a "desert"; but a Texas writer who has lived there for years says: "While it is true that this vast territory which we are describing is mainly a grazing country, it is

MARCHING ON THE STAKED PLAIN.

also true that it abounds in fertile valleys and rich locations of large extent which are well watered and as fertile as any in the Union." That portion of the Staked Plains which is mountainous is rich in minerals, and land often appears worthless which upon trial proves to be fertile. Water is all that is needed to make most of our western "deserts" blossom as the rose. The important question of irrigation is attracting the attention of the entire western people.

The unrivaled resources of the West, together with the unequaled enterprise of its citizens, are a sure prophecy of wealth. Already have some of these new States outstripped their older sisters at the East. The West is destined to equal them in agriculture, stock-raising, and eventually in manufacturing. With many times the room and resources of the East, the West will have twice its population and wealth, together with all the intelligence which under popular government accompanies them.

It is not within the scope of my plan to discuss any of the individual enterprises that have marked the development of this wonderful territory, although the temptation to do so is great. The pony express, the building of the trans-continental railways, the great irrigation schemes, the mammoth mining enterprises, are all subjects of absorbing interest, and present materials that would fill many volumes.

In the light of information that I have obtained during the last eighteen years, my opinion has not changed as to the great future of that country, although statistics and records are most valuable in forming

M—19.

correct conclusions, especially as to the natural limitations. Statistics have shown that it was not safe to rely entirely upon the natural elements in agriculture in that belt of country which I have described, and which was formerly known as the "Plains" country. In Montana, the Dakotas, Nebraska, and western Kansas, in some seasons excellent crops will be produced, and then will come a time when in a few days they are cut down and withered by hot, dry winds that absorb every particle of moisture. Undoubtedly irrigation could be made the salvation of this belt of country, as it has of the arid territory west of it. Irrigation is the surest method of producing sufficient moisture to insure crops in almost any part

SCENE IN THE YELLOWSTONE VALLEY.

of the country, and especially in that region. It has in fact been found beneficial in almost every district of the United States.

If we will take account of the moisture that comes from the rainfall in that section of country, the melted snow of the springtime, and the moisture received from the perpetual snows of the mountains, added to the flow of water down the Missouri through its tributaries—the Yellowstone, the Little Missouri, the Platte, the Kaw, and those great rivers, the Arkansas and the Red, which empty into the Mississippi,—we will understand why for so many years it has been necessary for Congress to appropriate many millions of dollars to confine the overflow of the Mississippi along its lower portion, and the question arises, if a portion of that enormous sum had been, or can be, expended in the construction of water storages to retain the water in early seasons in artificial lakes, and allow it to be carried over arid fields and plains where it would produce an abundance of every kind of agricultural substance, and then slowly find its way toward the Gulf, would it not benefit both sections of the country equally?

In describing the quick growth of the far West, I can think of no better example than the Yellowstone Valley, a region with which I am familiar.

An exhaustive description of its topographical features would require more space than is available for that purpose in this volume. The following brief summary of the subject, partially quoted from articles on the subject by Mr. E. V. Smalley, will give the reader a general conception of the character of the country, and of the progress of settlement along the river up to the time of my departure for my new command on the Pacific Coast in 1881. The readiest route in every respect for entering the valley is the eastern one, which insures railroad travel to the Missouri River. The traveler at St. Paul taking the trains on the Northern Pacific Railroad which leave morning and evening, finds himself twenty-four hours later at Bismarck, now the capital of North Dakota, on the Missouri River. He has traveled in that interval four hundred and seventy-one miles, which has been comfortably passed in elegant sleeping cars and day coaches, which have carried him through the greatest wheat-raising country of America, crossing one hundred miles of the fertile valley of the Red River of the North, and traversing the rich and almost boundless prairies of Dakota.

The steamboat route was the favorite method of traveling during the few months of the year that it was available. The Yellowstone River is fed in the summer months by the melting snows of the Rocky Mountains, and of the lofty ranges which lie at the head waters of its larger tributaries, the Tongue and Big Horn Rivers. From the middle of May until the first of September there is usually sufficient water in the Yellowstone for purposes of navigation. At best, however, the channel is narrow and winding, and the current runs at an average rate of five miles per hour. The Missouri has an almost equally rapid stream, and the voyage from Bismarck to Fort Buford, opposite the mouth of the Yellowstone, although a distance of only three hundred and eighty miles, is seldom accomplished in less than four or five days. Excepting in clear moonlight weather no progress is attempted at night, the boats being tied to trees on the bank during the interval of darkness, which fortunately, however, is very brief in this high latitude. Fort Buford, in latitude forty-eight degrees north and longitude one hundred and four degrees west, is a military post designed to receive a garrison of four companies and to serve as a depot for the upper Missouri and Yellowstone Valleys. Directly across the Missouri from the post, the Yellowstone pours into the stream a vast volume of muddy, yellow water, and at its mouth it is apparently the larger river of the two. It was named by the early French explorers the "Rochejaune," of which its present name is the translation. Its title was derived from the prevailing reddish-yellow color of the stone which crops out along its shores. After the middle of July the condition of the channel is precarious—not to mention the almost inevitable risk the traveler runs of being discovered by the tiny and song-less mosquito, which is a curious and pertinacious and multitudinous feature of the Missouri River part of the journey. It is not necessary here to dwell upon the characteristics of the scenery along the two rivers. The description we are at present aiming at precludes the use of so-called fine writing. Suffice it to say that both in Dakota on the Missouri, and in Montana on the Yellowstone, the heart of the intending settler will be gladdened with the sight of broad prairie lands, rich river bottoms and fertile, undulating plains, the immensity of which surpasses the power of human description, all holding forth in the summer sunshine a smiling invitation to the agriculturist, and all open to the actual settler by the free gift of the government. These facts, which are purposely stated inside the bounds of truthful privilege, have not we believe a parallel in any other habitable country of the globe.

After the long steamboat ride the traveler naturally feels an eager desire to reach the point of disembarkation. That feeling is enhanced by the prospect of emerging from the wilderness, to set foot in some place dignified with the appellation of "city." It sometimes happens, however, that words of strict technical import acquire through custom and usage meanings wholly at variance with their primitive significance. Thus the word "city" has become in American parlance a relative term. In the Eastern States where a definite ratio of population to the acre determine the eligibility of a town, a city is an almost exceptional thing. In the West, where the acreage is vastly disproportioned to the population, a city is the simplest thing imaginable. Given a cluster of men established with a view to permanence at any point showing promise of development, and it is as easy to call the aggregation a "city" as it would be to call it a camp or a village or town. So when writers in the West speak of cities, readers in the East must not construe their meaning according to their own stand-ards. This, however, be it understood is not by way of apology. A county town in the West may be the capital of a region rather more than one-third larger in area than the whole State of Pennsylvania. It may be, and usually is, a lively, bustling and eminently successful little town. There are skilled artisans of almost every handicraft, in addition to a fair allowance of merchants, lawyers in abundance and physicians. Some of the stores will be found to contain, in great variety of course, every staple of merchandise purchasable in Eastern cities, besides countless articles of mere luxury. Prices are quite reasonable considering the cost and difficulties of transportation. Such a town rapidly growing, is usually regarded as destined in time to justify its name of "city." The place, notwithstanding that it may derive its support thus far mostly from its proximity to a vast rich region not yet developed, may contain in its list of industrial enterprises, carpenters, blacksmiths, painters, dining-halls and saloons of every grade, excellent drug stores, depots of fancy notions, a free school, a courthouse, a jail, and every comfortable thing in fact requisite to maintain a town on an independent footing, as well as a first-class hotel suitable for the accommodation of tourists and business men temporarily sojourning there. Moreover, it may well be an orderly place in which riotous demonstrations are promptly and inflexibly repressed. Often the presentation of a pistol in a threatening manner subjects the offender to a heavy fine, and even the wanton discharge of firearms in the streets is a punishable offence. For the frontier settlement is apt to rapidly assert itself as a type of a better civilization, despite the primeval and savage associations which still attach to it like the touch of a bloody finger.

Around a nucleus like this may lie the splendid stock-raising plains in which the famous Montana cattle thrive, finding pasture the year round. For sheep raising also the advantages are equally great. Agriculture on any important scale is perhaps as yet almost an untried experiment, but the natural fertility of the soil, the general moisture of the atmosphere, and the comparative ease of artificial irrigation, if needed, have long indicated that the Yellowstone Valley is likely in the future to compete in productiveness with any section in the United States. The climate is on an average about the same as that of the northwestern part of New York State—the extreme ranges of the mercury being greater in Montana, but owing to the purity and dryness of the atmosphere not much more appreciable as a cause of discomfort to animal or plant. This matter of atmosphere is something that must be experienced to be appreciated. To invalids it is especially grateful. The predominance of ozone renders it exhilarating to sound lungs, and invigorating to weak ones if not too far gone in disease.

The north shore of the Yellowstone is only inferior to the south shore in the fact of its possessing fewer water courses than the latter. It is probable that artificial irrigation will be necessary in many places, but it will not be universally or generally required, and there is everywhere an abundance of water for the purpose. In some seasons crops are raised throughout the valley which astonish the farmers themselves. Sometimes

"CASTLE" GEYSER, YELLOWSTONE PARK.

4,000 bushels of oats are produced on less than a hundred acres of land. In the Yellowstone Valley the productiveness of the soil was at first untested and the surface was only tickled in a desultory way. Wherever any experiments are made in real agriculture the result is unqualified success. The soil in the valley is an alluvial deposit of rich, black and somewhat heavy earth on the bottoms near the stream, and a warm sandy loam on the bench lands which rise in terraces further back, and which are generally recognized as the lands capable of the widest range of production.

The region alluded to, taken as an example of far western growth, is one that the writer has himself marched over and camped upon in campaigns that are described in this volume. A few years ago it was so remote as to be almost inaccessible, and so wild as to be quite unknown. The Dakotas owned it in apparent perpetuity, and gave it up at last with great reluctance.

It was so within memory, with all the vast domain west of the Missouri. All that we now call the "West" has practically become ours only since our energies were turned in that direction after the close of the great war. The unorganized march of our ex-soldiers passed westward against an opposition that was stubborn and almost ceaseless, but they were aided always on their front by the officers and soldiers whose campaigns, so far as I have personally known them, are described in these chapters.

The six years of campaigning I have alluded to were not all that were consumed in the struggle that peradventure is not even yet entirely ended. They were merely the most active and fruitful ones, opening almost at once the enormous area I have alluded to on previous pages. Wherever the struggle has ceased there has at once come the change I have described as local to the great valley of the Yellowstone in far Dakota.

The picture is not an ideal or an imaginary one, and I have in my mind the very scenes described. Looking backward but a few years, I, myself having witnessed all the processes intervening between the tepee and the town, am astonished at the change. In the weariness of the march, the loneliness of the camp and the excitement of the fight, the soldier of the western campaigns was not aware of the flood of energy behind him, whose barriers he was breaking, and which followed instantly when he led the way. As I have said before, the Indian was never destined to remain in the position of barring the way of a mighty civilization. The wrongs he has suffered are inexcusable, and his destiny is one of the saddest in human history. He might have yielded most that he has lost and still have been treated fairly, still have had the promises made him fulfilled. But between him and all broken contracts and all changing policies, the soldier of the little army of the United States has been required to stand. That stand is now a matter of history. The result alone is seen — a result before which we stand surprised, while old-world statesmen discredit and even deny.

Yet all that is here stated is but a discussion of mere beginnings. It was once prophesied that these United States would yet hold a hundred millions of free men living under the laws of Alfred.   To those who have watched the growth of the mighty West for a quarter of a century, the estimate seems to fall far short.   That multitude, and more, are destined to live beyond the Mississippi, undivided from their brethren, and still under the code, the spirit, the customs and the faith that had their origin among the fathers of the race.

It may seem pertinent to this chapter to devote a little space to the social life and amusements of our army on the frontier, and a brief outline of some of the social features of that life may be of interest.   The officers and their families at these posts, sometimes hundreds of miles from the nearest railroad, without churches, libraries, art galleries, clubs or theaters, deprived even of the daily paper, and rarely seeing new faces, are forced to find in themselves and in each other something to replace the multifarious forms of social and intellectual activity usual in all civilized communities.

Not having the various outside interests, which in a city often keep apart the nearest neighbors, intercourse is free and informal, and the closest and most enduring friendships are often formed.   As the deadliest enmity is sometimes found between those whom Nature has the most closely united, so it sometimes happens that bitter animosities and feuds are engendered in these little clusters of humanity, so dependent on each other for companionship.   These cases are fortunately exceptional, the prevailing tone being that of simple cordiality and kindness, even where no great congeniality exists.

Fort Keogh, Montana, where I was in command for several years, might be considered a typical frontier post from the date of its establishment in 1876 until the completion to that point of the Northern Pacific Railroad in 1882.   During the first year the post was known simply as the Tongue River Cantonment, the command being quartered in rude shelters constructed in quite a primitive manner.   This cantonment was situated at the mouth of the Tongue River, on the south bank of the Yellowstone; Bismarck, North Dakota, distant three hundred miles, being the nearest available railroad station.   When all the postal connections were closely made, mail from St. Paul or Chicago was received in about six days; but in winter this time was sometimes increased to several weeks.

During the summer of 1877 the comparatively commodious quarters of Fort Keogh were built near the cantonment, and the garrison moved into them in November.   The social circle was enlarged by the arrival of officers' families; the upper story of a large storehouse was turned into a hall for entertainments, pianos and comfortable furniture appeared, the

SURRENDER OF CHIEF JOSEPH.

"FROM WHERE THE SUN NOW STANDS I FIGHT NO MORE AGAINST THE WHITE MAN."—SEE PAGE 275.

valuable library of the Fifth Infantry was unpacked, and the fine band of the same regiment contributed to make of the post an oasis of civilization.

For a short season each year the Yellowstone River was navigable for small stern-wheel steamers. The arrival of these were occasions of unusual interest, the first steamer of the season being watched for with special anxiety, and great was the excitement and delight when her whistle was heard or her smoke discovered down the stream. Goods and supplies often ordered months before were received, new faces were added to the circle, or familiar ones reappeared, and there was a decided break in the monotony of many months. The departure of the last steamer in the fall was always an occasion of sadness, bearing away as it did children going to school, officers and their families changing stations, and sometimes summer visitors who had come to experience the novelty of life at an army post in the far West.

An amateur theatrical company was organized, which transported in imagination the spectators from the banks of the Yellowstone to other lands and other times. Scene painters as well as actors were provided by "home talent," and their efforts may have been a little crude, but their performances met with much applause and served to beguile the long winter evenings. A play that needed long and careful preparation and many rehearsals was liable to suddenly lose the male members of the cast, as detachments from the garrison were frequently sent out as scouts and on expeditions of different kinds against the Indians, their absence ranging from a few days to weeks or even months.

Owing to the situation of the post in a prairie country, and to other favoring circumstances, equestrianism held an important place among the recreations. The garrison for several years consisted entirely of mounted troops, being composed of the Fifth Infantry, mounted on choice ponies that had been captured at different times from the Indians, and a squadron of the Second Cavalry. Many of the officers also owned fine private horses, and a pack of excellent hounds for chasing game was kept at the post. The surrounding country was an ideal one for horseback riding, the wide, level river bottoms and the rolling prairies being alike covered with firm, elastic turf, save where broken here and there by the underground cities of the prairie dog.

In that region is found much of the "Bad Lands" formation peculiar to Montana. These Bad Lands may be described as follows: Riding over the prairie one sees towering in the distance what appears to be a confused mass of ruined masonry. Reflecting back the rays of the sun, walls of red brick, broken turrets of bluish stone and crumbling battlements are flung together in bewildering confusion. Approaching nearer the contours change, and the ruined city proves to be a stupendous mass of variegated clay, almost a group of small mountains heaped upon the prairie, and worn by the weather into a chaos of precipices, chasms and fissures. Here and there the fantastic labyrinth is penetrated by bridle paths, trodden only a few years ago by herds of elk and buffaloes, and leading to lofty points of observation, crowned perhaps by bits of prairie, or to little secluded valleys and patches of grazing land.

Most of the ladies at Fort Keogh became expert horsewomen. To see one of these parties dashing after the hounds across the broad valley lands of the Yellowstone was an exhilarating sight. The prairies were untouched by fence or plow, though buffalo trails were numerous, a herd of these animals having been in sight of this post as late as January, 1881. A wolf or deer was occasionally started and taken by these parties,

INDIAN MEDICINE MAN.

but the game most easily found and taken was the hare, better known as the jack rabbit. Small riding parties were sometimes organized, and congenial people visited together the various points of interest in the vicinity, exploring the recesses of the broken country and riding through the Indian villages, redolent always of kinnikinic, and often vibrant with wild song and dance, or with the incantations of the medicine man, or the harangues of the tribe orator.

The Indians sometimes came to the post in full war paint and feathers, and gave an Omaha dance, weird and grotesque in the extreme with its mimic warfare and accompaniment of tom-toms. The Omaha dance is meant to be complimentary and must be recognized by substantial gifts, but it would be terrifying to the timid except for the sense of security afforded by a strong garrison. In winter skating and sleighing parties were most enjoyable.

Fort Keogh is now in the heart of a flourishing grazing and farming community, and only two miles from a thriving western town and county seat. All the conditions have changed. The life which I have meagerly outlined, leaving imagination to supply the rest, has vanished, or like so many other phases pertaining to the frontier is swiftly drifting into the to-morrow that returns not again.

CHAPTER XXVI.

The Indian Problem.

Conclusions of Personal Experience—End of the Indian Troubles Not Yet
Near—Original Causes of These—Indians in Motive Like Other Men—History of the Indian in the United States—The Two Modes of Solving
the Question—The Author's Plan for the Benefit of the
Indian and the Securing of Permanent Peace.

DURING my experience along the frontier of the Southwest and the Northwest, I had opportunities of seeing much of the savage natures of the Indians, of hearing much of their depredations and atrocities, and the expression that "the only good Indian is a dead Indian" was not an uncommon one. At the same time I had opportunities of seeing the better elements of their nature, the good qualities that some possessed, and noted the same differences in them that we find in other people under similar or like circumstances.

I have had occasion to speak of the wrongs that I noticed committed against the Indians in New Mexico. Another incident illustrates the difficulty of the good purposes of the government being fulfilled. Upon one occasion a commissioner was sent from Washington to meet a large tribe of Arapahoes on the plains near the Arkansas River, where they had been gathered for council. All the Indians being gathered in, the council opened with great ceremony and ostentation, and the commissioner was treated with great distinction as coming from the Great Father at Washington. The commissioner explained to the Indians that the Great Father was President of the whole country; that he had the same interest in the welfare of the Indians that he had in all the other inhabitants of the United States, regardless of color, race or condition; that the Great Father had commissioned him to express his good will toward them and his deep interest in their welfare, and also the hope that they might be industrious and prosperous, and he further hoped that they might gather large quantities of robes and furs and receive good returns for them, in order that they might supply the wants of themselves and families; that they might live in peace and friendship with their white neighbors, and that they would refrain from going to war; that they would be ever faithful and loyal to the general government and to the end that they and their families might live in peace and happiness all their lives. Unfortunately, the commissioner had employed as his interpreter at this council a man who had lived many years with the Indians, and who was employed by a firm known as Bent, at Bent's store on the Arkansas River, who was accustomed to purchase robes and furs and give to the Indians very small returns. When he came to that part of the message of the Great Father, instead of interpreting what the commissioner really said, he thought he would do a little business for the trader, and said that "the Great Father hoped that they would gather large quantities of buffalo robes and furs, and be careful to bring them all to Bent's store and sell them cheap;" and for many years the Indians supposed that the President at Washington had sent this absurd message.

Again, at another time a steamer load of annuity goods was sent up the Missouri River to near Fort Peck in Montana, and instead of being distributed to the Indians, a store was opened and the entire amount bartered to the Indians for furs and robes, and the next year the same steamer carried down the river a load of these valuables obtained by fraud.

Sometimes, indeed, intertribal jealousies and hatreds have involved the whites in unintentional and unpremeditated aggression upon, or conflict with, some particular band or tribe. A case in point is related by Washington Irving in his "Adventures of Captain Bonneville" as occurring in 1832 in the valley called Pierre's Hole, adjoining that named Jackson's Hole, where the Bannock Indian outbreak has been threatened as this book is being put in type. The valley so named is about thirty miles long and fifteen wide, overlooked to the east by the lofty mountains called the Three Tetons, southwest of the Yellowstone National Park. Pierre's Hole had been selected as the annual rendezvous for that year, and in it was congregated the motley populace connected with the fur trade—traders, trappers, hunters, half-breeds; also Nez Percés, Flatheads and other Indians with their families, assembled from all quarters awaiting their yearly supplies, preparatory to starting away in all directions for the ensuing year's hunting and trapping. When the gathering dispersed, one band of fourteen trappers, led by a brother of the famous Captain Sublette, set out in company with two other bands from whom they were to separate later, numbering forty altogether, for the southwest. On the following morning, just as they were breaking camp, they observed a long line of Blackfeet Indians approaching, about one hundred and fifty in number—men, women and children. Having perceived the trappers before they were themselves discovered, these Indians came down from the mountain defile yelling and whooping into the plain.

"One of the trappers of Sublette's brigade," says Irving, "named Antoine Godin, now mounted his horse and rode forth as if to hold a conference. He was the son of an Iroquois hunter who had been cruelly murdered by the Blackfeet at a small stream below the mountains, which still bears his name. In company with Antoine rode forth a Flathead Indian, whose once powerful tribe had been completely broken down in their wars with the Blackfeet. Both of them therefore cherished the most vengeful hostility against these marauders of the mountains. The Blackfeet came to a halt. One of the chiefs advanced singly and unarmed, bearing the pipe of peace. The overture was certainly pacific; but Antoine and the Flathead were predisposed to hostility, and pretended to consider it a treacherous movement.

"'Is your piece charged?' said Antoine to his red companion.

"'It is.'

"'Then cock it and follow me.'

"They met the Blackfeet chief half way, who extended his hand in friendship. Antoine grasped it.

"'Fire!' cried he.

"The Flathead leveled his piece and brought the Blackfeet chief to the ground. Antoine snatched off his scarlet blanket, which was richly ornamented, and galloped off with it as a trophy to the camp, the bullets of the enemy whistling after him."

What wonder that a bloody and immediate battle ensued between the Blackfeet and the trapper bands, in which the latter got much the worst of it until reënforcements came from the collection of whites still remaining at the rendezvous, eight miles further up the valley.

Such were the wars and feuds among the tribes, and from such seemingly trifling causes came results at times of far-reaching and tragic importance to the white people.

During the winter of 1878–9 the Indian problem was exciting much interest, and at the request of Mr. Allen Thorndyke Rice I wrote the following article on the subject, which appeared in the "North American Review" for March 1879. The article presents the views I entertained at that time and many of the suggestions therein contained have since been adopted.

THE INDIAN PROBLEM.

Strange as it may appear, it is nevertheless a fact that, after nearly four hundred years of conflict between the European and American races for supremacy on this continent, a conflict in which war and peace have alternated almost as frequently as the seasons, we still have presented the question, "What shall be done with the Indian?" Wise men differ in opinion, journalists speculate, divines preach, and statesmen pronounce it still a vexed question.

If the graves of the thousands of victims who have fallen in the terrible wars of the two races had been placed in line, the philanthropist might travel from the Atlantic to the Pacific, and from the Lakes to the Gulf, and be constantly in sight of green mounds. And yet we marvel at the problem as if some new question of politics or morals had been presented.

The most amusing part of the quandary, however, is that it should be regarded as something new and original. After every generation had, in its time, contended on deadly fields with the hope of settling the question, after the home governments had enacted laws, and the colonies had framed rules, every succeeding administration of our government has been forced to meet the difficulty, every Congress has discussed the "Indian Question," and we are still face to face with the perplexing problem. The real issue in the question which is now before the American people is, whether we shall ever begin again the vacillating and expensive policy that has marred our fair name as a nation and a Christian people, or devise some way of still improving the practical and judicious system by which we can govern a quarter of a million of our population, secure and maintain their loyalty, raise them from the darkness of barbarism to the light of civilization, and put an end forever to these interminable and expensive Indian wars.

In considering the subject it might be well to first examine the causes which governed so long the condition of affairs, and if in doing so the writer shall allude to some of the sins of his own race, it will only be in order that an unbiased judgment may be formed of both sides of the question.

It will be remembered that one class or race is without representation, and has not the advantages of the press or telegraph to bring it into communication with the intelligence of the world, and that it has seldom been heard except in the cry of alarm and conflict along the Western frontier. If we dismiss from our minds the prejudice we may have against the Indians, we shall be able to more clearly understand the impulses that govern both races. Sitting Bull, the great war chief of the Dakota nation, uttered one truth of his times when he said that "there was not one white man who loved an Indian, and not an Indian but who hated a white man."

Could we but perceive the true character of the Indians, and learn what their dispositions are when not covered by the cloak of necessity, policy and interest, we should find that they have always regarded us as a body of false and cruel invaders of their country, while we in turn are too apt to consider them as a treacherous and bloodthirsty race, who should be destroyed by any and all means. If we now fairly consider the cause of this feeling, we may more readily understand its result.

The more we study the Indian's character, the more we appreciate the marked distinction between the civilized being and the real savage. Yet we shall find that the latter is, after all, governed by the impulses and motives that govern all other men. The want of confidence and the bitter hatred always existing between the two races have been engendered by the warfare that has lasted for centuries, and by the stories of bad faith, cruelty and wrong handed down by tradition from father to son until they have become second nature in both. It is unfair to suppose that one party has invariably acted rightly, and that the other is responsible for every wrong that has been committed. We might recount the treachery of the red man, the atrocity of his crimes, the cruelties of his tortures and the hideousness of many of his savage customs. We might undertake to estimate the number of his victims, and to picture the numberless valleys which he has illumined by the burning homes of hardy frontiersmen, yet at the same time the other side of the picture might appear equally as black with injustice.

One hundred years before the pilgrims landed at Plymouth, the Spanish government issued a decree authorizing the enslavement of the American Indians as in accord with the law of God and man. Later they were transported to France, to San Domingo and other Spanish colonies, were sold into slavery in Massachusetts, Rhode Island, Pennsylvania, Virginia, the Carolinas, Georgia, and Louisiana, and were hunted with dogs in Connecticut and Florida. Practically disfranchised by our original Constitution, and deprived either by war or treaty of nearly every tract of land which to them was desirable and to the white man valuable, they were the prey to the grasping avarice of both Jew and Gentile. Step by step a powerful and enterprising race has driven them back from the Atlantic to the West until at last there was scarcely a spot of ground upon which the Indians had any certainty of maintaining a permanent abode.

It may be well in this connection to remember the fact that in the main the Europeans were kindly treated by the natives when the former first landed on American shores, and when they came to make a permanent settlement were supplied with food, particularly the Plymouth and Portsmouth colonists, which enabled them to endure the severity of the long and cheerless winters. For a time during the early settlement of this country, peace and good will prevailed, only to be followed later by violent and relentless warfare.

Our relations with the Indians have been governed chiefly by treaties and trade, or war and subjugation. By the first we have invariably overreached the natives, and we find the record of broken promises all the way from the Atlantic to the Pacific, while many of the fortunes of New York, Chicago, St. Louis and San Francisco can be traced directly to Indian tradership. By war the natives have been steadily driven toward the setting sun—a subjugated, a doomed race. In council the Indians have produced men of character and intellect, and orators and diplomats of decided ability, while in war they have displayed courage and sagacity of a high order. Education, science, and the resources of the world have enabled us to overcome the savages, and they are now at the mercy of their conquerors. In our treaty relations most extravagant and yet sacred promises have been given by the highest authorities, and these have been frequently disregarded. The intrusions of the white race and the noncompliance with treaty obligations, have been followed by atrocities that could alone satisfy a savage and revengeful spirit. Facts that have been already referred to make it almost impossible for the two conflicting elements to harmonize. No administration could stop the tidal wave of immigration that swept over the land; no political party could restrain or control the enterprise of our people, and no reasonable man could desire to check the march of civilization. Our progress knew no bounds. The thirst for gold and the restless desire to push beyond the horizon have carried our people over every obstacle. We have reclaimed the wilderness and made the barren desert glisten with golden harvest; settlements now cover the hunting ground of the savages; their country has been cut and divided in every conceivable form by the innumerable railroad and telegraph lines and routes of communication and commerce, and the Indians standing in the pathway of American progress and the development of the wonderful resources of this country have become the common enemy and have been driven to the remote places of our territory.

M—20

During the time that this wonderful change was being wrought, it may be asked if the Indians as a body have made any progress toward civilization, and in the light of past history we would be prompted to reply: Why should they have abandoned the modes of life which Nature had given them to adopt the customs of their enemies?

In seeking the evidences of enlightenment the results are not satisfactory. It is presumed that there is not a race of wild men on the face of the globe who worship the Great Spirit more in accordance with that religion taught in the days of the patriarchs than the natives of this country, and yet after many years of contact with the civilized people the footprints of evil were as plentiful and as common as the evidences of Christianity. Again, in early days the Indian tribes were to a considerable extent tillers of the soil, but by constant warfare, in which their fields were devastated and their crops destroyed, they have become the mere remnant of their former strength, or were pushed out on the vast plains of the West where they subsisted upon wild fruits and the flesh of animals. Could we obtain accurate statistics, we would undoubtedly find that there were more acres of ground cultivated by the Indians one hundred years ago than at the present time. The white race had finally obtained such complete control of every quarter of the country, and the means of communication with every section became so ample that the problem resolved itself into one or the other of two modes of solution, viz., to entirely destroy the race by banishment and extermination, or to adopt some humane and practicable method of improving the condition of the Indians, and in the end make them part and parcel of our great population. The first proposition, though it was found to have thousands of advocates in different sections of the country, was and is too abhorrent to every sense of humanity to be considered. The other method was regarded as practicable, but its adoption was considered doubtful.

Looking at the purpose of our government toward the Indians, we find that after subjugating them it has been our policy to collect the different tribes on reservations and support them at the expense of our people. The Indians have in the main abandoned the hope of driving back the invaders of their territory, yet there are still some who cherish the thought, and strange as it may seem it is a fact that the most noted leader among the Indians advanced such a proposition to the writer within the last few years. They long stood, and mostly still stand, in the position of unruly children to indulgent parents for whom they have very little respect, at times wrongly indulged and again unmercifully punished.

CHIRICAHUA APACHE STUDENTS. 1894.

Coming down to our direct or immediate relations with them we find that our policy has been to make them wards of the nation, to be held under close military surveillance, or else to make them pensioners under no other restraint than the influence of one or two individuals. Living under the government, yet without any legitimate government, without any law and without any physical power to control them, what better subjects or more propitious fields could be found for vice and crime?

We have committed our Indian matters to the custody of an Indian bureau which for many years was a part of the military establishment of the government; but for political reasons and to promote party interests, this bureau was transferred to the department of the interior.

Whether or not our system of Indian management has been a success during the past ten, fifty, or one hundred years, is almost answered in the asking. The Indians, the frontiersmen, the army stationed in the West, and the readers of the daily news in all parts of our country can answer that question. There is another question that is frequently asked: Why has our management of Indian affairs been less successful than that of our neighbors across the northern boundary? and it can be answered in a few words. Their system is permanent, decided and just. The tide of immigration in Canada has not been as great as along our frontier. They have been able to allow the Indians to live as Indians, which we have not, and do not attempt to force upon them the customs which to them are distasteful. In our own management it has all the time been the opinion of a very large number of our people that a change for the better would be desirable. We have the singular and remarkable phenomenon presented of the traders, the contractors, the interested officials of the West, and many of the best people of the East, advocating one scheme, while a great majority of frontier settlers, the officers of the army of long experience on the plains, and many competent judges in the East, advocated another. The question has at the same time been one of too grave importance to admit interests of a personal or partisan nature. It is one of credit or discredit to our government, and of vital importance to our people. In order that peace may be permanently secured, the Indians benefited, and protection assured to the extensive settlements scattered over a greater area than the whole of the Atlantic States, it is believed that a plan could be devised which would enlist the hearty approval and support of men of all parties. The object is surely worthy of the effort. No body of people whose language, religion, and customs are so entirely different from ours can be expected to cheerfully and suddenly adopt our own. The change must be gradual, continuous, and in accordance with Nature's laws. The history of nearly every race that has advanced from barbarism to civilization has been through the stages of the hunter, the herdsman, the agriculturist, and has finally reached those of commerce, mechanics and the higher arts.

It is held, first, that we, as a generous people and liberal government, are bound to give to the Indians the same rights that all other men enjoy, and if we deprive them of their ancient privileges we must then give them the best government possible. Without any legitimate government, and in a section of country where the lawless are under very little restraint, it is useless to suppose that thousands of wild savages thoroughly armed and mounted can be controlled by moral suasion. Even if they were in the midst of comfortable and agreeable surroundings, yet when dissatisfaction is increased by partial imprisonment and quickened by the pangs of hunger — a feeling that is not realized by one man in a thousand in civilized life — it requires more patience and forbearance than savage natures are likely to possess to prevent serious outbreaks.

The experiment of making a police force composed entirely of Indians is a dangerous one unless they are under the shadow and control of a superior body of white troops, and, if carried to any great extent, will result in rearming the Indians and work disastrously to the frontier settlements. There would be a something absurd in a government out on the remote frontier composed of a strictly noncombatant as chief, with a *posse comitatus* of red warriors, undertaking to control several thousand wild savages.

The advantage of placing the Indians under some government strong enough to control them and just enough to command their respect is too apparent to admit of argument. The results to be obtained would be:

First. They would be beyond the possibility of doing harm, and the frontier settlements would be freed from their terrifying and devastating presence.

Second. They would be under officials having a knowledge of the Indian country and the Indian character.

Third. Their supplies and annuities would be disbursed through an efficient system of regulations.

Fourth. Besides being amenable to the civil laws, these officers would be under strict military law, subject to trial and punishment for any act that would be "unbecoming a gentleman, or prejudicial to good order."

It is therefore suggested and earnestly recommended that a system which has heretofore proved to be eminently practicable should in the next emergency receive at least a fair trial. As the government has in its employ men who by long and faithful service have established reputations for integrity, character and ability which cannot be disputed ; men who have commanded armies, reconstructed States, controlled hundreds of millions of public property, and who during years of experience on the frontier have opened the way for civilization and Christianity, it is believed that the services of these officials, in efforts to prevent war and elevate the Indian race, would be quite as judicious as their employment when inexperience and mismanagement have culminated in hostilities. Allowing the civilized and semi-civilized Indians to remain under the same supervision as at present, the President of the United States should have power to place at any time the wild and nomadic tribes under the control of the War Department. Officers of known character, integrity and experience, who would govern them and be interested in improving their condition, should be placed in charge of the different tribes. One difficulty has been that they have been managed by officials too far away, and who knew nothing of the men they were dealing with. The Indians, as far as possible, should be, as they now mostly are, localized on the public domain, in sections of country to which they are by nature adapted.

The forcing of strong, hardy, mountain Indians from the extreme North to the warmer malarial districts of the South was cruel, and the experiment should never be repeated.

Every effort should be made to locate the Indians by families, for the ties of relationship among them are much stronger than is generally supposed. By this means the Indians will become independent of their tribal relations, and will not be found congregated in the large and unsightly camps that are now usually met with about their agencies.

All supplies, annuities and disbursements of money should be made under the same system of accountability that now regulates army disbursements. The officers in charge should have sufficient force to preserve order, patrol reservations, prevent intrusions, recover stolen property, arrest the lawless and those who take refuge in Indian camps to shield themselves from punishment for crime or with the object of enabling them to live without labor, and to keep the Indians upon their reservations and within the limits of their treaties. The officer in charge would be enabled to control or prevent the sale of ammunition, as well as to suppress the sale of intoxicating liquors among the Indians. Many thousands of the

Indian ponies, useful only for the war or the chase, should be sold and the proceeds used in the purchase of domestic stock. A large percentage of the annual appropriations should be employed in the purchase of cattle and other domestic animals ; the Indians desire them, and their reservations even now support many thousands of them. They have already replaced the buffalo, and must finally replace the elk, the deer and the antelope. From a nomadic pastoral people the Indians should be induced to become agriculturists and taught the use of machinery as a means of obtaining food. The step from the first grade to the second would be easily accomplished, provided the Indians were directed by a firm hand. As they accumulate property and learn industry there have already been shown strong incentives to their remaining at peace, namely : occupation, the fear of confiscation of property, and the loss of the comforts of life.

Two more important measures of improvement are also needed, and should be authorized by Congress.

In all communities there will be found disturbing elements, and to meet this difficulty, courts of justice should be instituted. Frequently outbreaks and depredations are prompted by a few mischievous characters, which could easily be checked by a proper government. This is one secret of success with the Canadian system; where disturbances occur, the guilty suffer, and not whole tribes, including innocent women and children.

As a remark from Sitting Bull has been quoted, we will now repeat the words of Joseph, who said that "the greatest want of the Indian is a system of law by which controversies between Indians and white men can be settled without appealing to physical force." He says also that "the want of law is the great source of disorder among Indians. They understand the operation of laws, and, if there were any statutes, the Indians would be perfectly content to place themselves in the hands of a proper tribunal, and would not take the righting of their wrongs into their own hands, or retaliate, as they do now, without the law."

Do we need a savage to inform us of the necessity that has existed for a century? As these people become a part of our population, they should have some tribunal where they could obtain protection in their rights of person and property. A dispute as to the rights of property between an Indian and a white man before a white jury might not be decided in exact accordance with justice in some localities. Fortunately our Constitution provides that "the judicial power of the United States shall be vested in one Supreme Court, and such inferior courts as Congress may from time to

FACES OF NOTED INDIANS.

1. Spotted Tail, Sioux Chief, Rosebud Agency, Dakota.
2. Iron Wing, Sioux Chief, Rosebud Agency, Dakota.
3. American Horse, Sioux Chief, Pine Ridge Agency, Dakota.
4. Red Shirt, Sioux Chief, Pine Ridge Agency, Dakota.
5. White Eagle, Ponca Chief, Indian Territory.
6. Standing Buffalo, Ponca Chief, Indian Territory.
7. Poor Wolf, Mandan Chief, Fort Berthold, Dakota.
8. Son-of-the-Star, Arickaree Chief, Fort Berthold, Dakota.

9. White Man, Apache Chief, Indian Territory.
10. Stumbling Bear, Kiowa Chief, Indian Territory.
11. Tso-de-ar-ko, Wichita Chief, Indian Territory.
12. Big Horse, Cheyenne Chief, Indian Territory.
13. Bob Tail, Cheyenne Chief, Indian Territory.
14. Man-on-the-Cloud, Cheyenne Chief, Indian Territory.
15. Mad Wolf, Cheyenne Chief, Indian Territory.
16. Little Raven, Arapahoe Chief, Indian Territory.
17. Yellow Bear, Arapahoe Chief, Indian Territory.
18. Left Hand, Arapahoe Chief, Indian Territory,

time ordain and establish;" and it is believed that Congress has power, at least in the Territories, to give such jurisdiction either to the military courts, or the Territorial courts, or both, as will secure justice to the Indians in all disputes arising between the Indians and the white men.

That warriors may be made to care for their flocks and herds has been demonstrated, and the industry of the Indians that is now wasted may be still further diverted to peaceful and useful pursuits; yet the great work of reformation must be mainly through the youth of the different tribes. The hope of every race is in the rising generation. This important work seems now to have enlisted the sympathy and support of all philanthropic and Christian people. As we are under obligation to support the tribes until they become self-sustaining, it is undoubtedly advisable to support as many as possible of the children of the Indians at places where they would be the least expensive to the government, and where they would be under the best influence. The children must not be exposed to the degrading influence of camp life, and the constant moving of the tribes destroys the best efforts of instructors. The children that are taught the English language, habits of industry, the benefits of civilization, the power of the white race, after a few years, return to their people with some education, with more intelligence, and with their ideas of life entirely changed for the better. They naturally in turn become the educators of their own people, and their influence for good cannot be estimated. Finally, the Indians, as they become civilized and educated, as they acquire property and pay taxes toward the support of the government, should have the same rights of citizenship that all other men enjoy.

The President of the United States should have power to transfer from the War Department to the Interior Department any tribe that shall become so far civilized and peaceable in its disposition as to render it unnecessary to keep its members longer under the control of the military power.

Whenever an emergency arises which has not been foreseen and provided for by Congress, such as failure or destruction of their crops, the President should have power, on the recommendation of the officer in charge or the governors of the different Territories in which the Indians are living, to order the necessary supplies, as has been done in several instances to white people, in order to prevent great suffering or a serious disturbance of the peace; such supplies to be limited to the smallest necessity, and only until such time as Congress could take action on the matter.

A race of savages cannot by any human ingenuity be civilized and Christianized within a few years of time, neither will 250,000 people with their descendants be entirely exterminated in the next fifty years. The white man and the Indian should be taught to live side by side, each respecting the rights of the other, and both living under wholesome laws, enforced by ample authority and with exact justice. Such a government would be most gratifying and beneficial to the Indians, while those men who have invested their capital, and with wonderful enterprise are developing the unparalleled and inexhaustible wealth that for ages has lain dormant in the western mountains; those people who have left the overcrowded centers of the East, and whose humble homes are now dotting the plains and valleys of the far West, as well as those men who are annually called upon to endure greater exposure and suffering than is required by the troops of any other nation on the globe, would hail with great satisfaction any system that would secure a substantial and lasting peace.

CHAPTER XXVII.

JOURNEY WESTWARD.

PROMOTION FROM COLONEL TO BRIGADIER-GENERAL—BEGINNING OF JOURNEY WEST-
WARD—ORIGIN OF DENVER—THE GOLD SEEKERS FROM GEORGIA—FROM LAWRENCE
AND LEAVENWORTH—THE RECORD ON THE ROCKS—THE TOWN OF MON-
TANA—THE KANSAS COMMISSIONERS—ARAPAHOE COUNTY—OVERLAND
COMMUNICATION—VICE IN THE EARLY TIMES—A HISTORIC
TREE—THE FIRST RAILROAD—THE DENVER OF TO-DAY.

AVING been summoned to Washington to receive my promotion to the rank of brigadier-general in November, 1880, I took leave of the Fifth United States Infantry by the following order:

FORT KEOGH, MONTANA, November 20, 1880.

GENERAL ORDERS.

In relinquishing command of the Fifth U. S. Infantry the regimental commander desires to manifest his gratitude to the officers and soldiers of this command for the zeal and loyalty with which every duty has been performed, however difficult and hazardous. He desires also to express his appreciation and acknowledgements of the most valuable services of this command and the gallantry displayed in moments of great danger.

For twenty-five years the Fifth Infantry has served continually west of the Mississippi River and rendered most important service in the campaigns against the Utes and Apaches of Utah and Wyoming, the Navajos of New Mexico, the Comanches, Kiowas and Cheyennes of Texas, Indian Territory, Colorado and Kansas, and the Sioux, Nez Percés and Bannocks of the Northwest.

During the past eleven years the undersigned has been in command of this regiment, and in that time, by long and intimate association, there has been engendered a feeling of the strongest attachment and highest regard.

For the success that has attended our efforts the Commanding Officer desires to render to the officers and soldiers of this command their full share of credit.

In taking leave of a command in which he has always felt a just pride, it occasions deep regret that, in the exigencies of the service and the various changes incident thereto, we are separated in distant fields of duty.

[Signed.]
NELSON A. MILES,
Colonel and Brevet Major-General.

I reported in Washington, where I remained on duty during the winter of 1880–81, and was then assigned to the Department of the Columbia.

On my way to my new post of duty, I passed through the cities of Chicago, St. Louis, Kansas City, Denver, Salt Lake and San Francisco, stopping a few days in each.

In this journey it was my good fortune to pass through an interesting zone of our country, and to see the progress that was being rapidly made at that time in the civilization of the great West. It would be impossible to describe the moral, intellectual and industrial progress that had then, and has since, been developed. I would be very glad to describe some of the principal towns and cities that were then and are now in course of rapid development, but the want of time and space renders it impossible.

I will mention, however, St. Paul and Minneapolis, those twin cities of marvelous enterprise, of great industrial resources, the center of a vast productive region, located near the magnificent Falls of Saint Anthony on the upper Mississippi. These two great cities were for years rivals, but are gradually growing together to form one great commercial and industrial center, and embracing within their borders the beautiful Falls of Minnehaha, which Longfellow has described in classic verse. I would also love to describe other cities, like Helena and Butte, Montana, made rich by the mines of marvelous wealth found stored in the mountains in the vicinity of these two cities.

Omaha is another city of wonderful growth, of wealth, progress and development, and the center of one of the richest agricultural districts of the United States. The same can be said of Kansas City. Colorado City is noted for its healthful climate, wonderful springs and beautiful scenery, and Trinidad for its iron and coal mines and steel works; while Los Angeles, California, is the center of commerce and communication of Southern California.

Portland, Oregon; Spokane, Washington; Greely, Colorado; and Salt Lake City, Utah, are all interesting and fair types of our western towns and cities, and have grown up practically within the last thirty years.

I will pause in this journey west, however, long enough to give some description of Denver, Colorado, which is a fair type of many of our modern, typical American western cities.

Denver is the chief city of one of the largest states in the Union, and the center of the Rocky Mountain country. On the 7th of February, 1858, eight men left their homes in Dawson County, Georgia, bound for the wild Rocky Mountain region in search of gold. These daring explorers — who might have suggested Whittier's beautiful lines:

"I hear the tread of pioneers
Of nations yet to be,
The first low wash of waves where soon
Shall roll a human sea."—

were the *avant-couriers* of the grand army that presently followed to participate in gleaning the precious deposits they had been the first to discover. They arrived in Kansas early in May, where their party was increased by the addition of ten other men.

These gold-seekers left Leavenworth about the middle of May, and crossed the Kansas River at Fort Riley, striking out from that point across the country to the old Santa Fé trail, arriving at the mouth of Cherry Creek, Colorado, on the 23d of June, 1858. On the Pawnee Fork, Kansas, a party of Cherokee Indians were overtaken, who traveled to Cherry Creek in company with them. Unsettled as to future proceeding, the Indians remained at Cherry Creek, while the others hastened to Ralston Creek, where they hoped to find the treasure of which they were in pursuit. Three days of anxious search, however, brought no better reward than a very meagre quantity of gold particles, the shadows, so to speak, of the substance they were seeking; but still to them an evidence that gold was somewhere in that region, and with what courage they could summon they resolved to prospect thoroughly.

Ralston Creek lies about eight miles distant from the mouth of Cherry Creek, their first halting place, and the Cherokees being still there the company decided to return and make that point their base of operations. To do this they recrossed the Platte River, but found upon joining them that the Indians had determined to return to their own nation, and accordingly they started on the following day, leaving the explorers with the whole range of mountains, the various creeks and their tributaries, the cañons beyond, and the plains stretching out in the distance, from which to choose a beginning for their investigations.

Possessed of marked constancy to a purpose once formed, the leader of the company, upon observing signs of discontent among some of his companions, declared firmly his purpose to prospect the country even if he did it alone, and to that end he proceeded to work with untiring patience, closely examining the soil in every direction. Meanwhile Lawrence, Kansas, was being excited by whispers of golden sands to be found in the water around Pike's Peak. Two Delaware Indians, Fall Leaf and Little Beaver, brought the story that gold in paying quantities was to be found in those streams, and very secretly a company was organized at the old

Commercial Hotel in that city to cross the desert on a tour of discovery. Fall Leaf claimed the distinction of having been a guide to Fremont on one of his exploring expeditions, and as in Fremont's report mention is made of two Delaware Indians, "a fine looking old man and his son," engaged to accompany that expedition as hunters, Fall Leaf and Little Beaver may have been the Indians with Fremont, although they were not so designated by name in his journal. Fall Leaf contracted to guide the party formed at the Commercial Hotel to a locality where gold could be found near Pike's Peak. He was to receive five dollars per day for such service until satisfactorily performed; but pending the deliberations of the party he was to lead, a fall from his horse while in a state of intoxication disabled him, upon which they resolved to proceed notwithstanding and prosecute their investigation without a guide. On May 22, 1858, close upon the departure of the company from Leavenworth, this Lawrence party, numbering forty-four, two of whom were women accompanying their husbands, started from Kansas to cross the plains with eleven wagons and provisions for six months. From their course over the Santa Fé trail the travelers approached Pueblo, and having joined some members of the Leavenworth party were with them on the 6th of July, 1858, encamped upon the same ground in the Garden of the Gods, where Long's expedition had rested thirty-eight years before. There is not a trace of the Long explorers left there, while the pioneers of 1858 have graven upon the rocks a record of their presence, an interesting testimonial now plainly visible. Inside one of the gateways on the great sentinel stones appear the names of several of the party with the year "1858" cut beneath them.

Members of both companies had prospected in various directions for the treasure sought without success, until it was told them one day that those who had remained behind were washing from the sands of the Platte River about three dollars a day to the man. This news reached them in September, after three months' fruitless quest, and they hastened to the locality where fortune smiled, and found that not only were the other members from the Leavenworth company washing gold from the sands, but that also a man named John Rooker, together with his son, had come in from Salt Lake to enjoy a like prosperity. The staying qualities of the leader of the Leavenworth company served him well. Here, within a radius of ten miles from the point where he first stopped, he had by dint of sheer perseverance found in the sands golden returns so valuable as to induce the whole party to become settlers on the ground and hold it under the title of squatter sovereignty, and to found a town which they named Montana.

On the 4th of September, 1858, there were assembled at this point on the Platte River, some five miles from the mouth of Cherry Creek, portions of the Leavenworth company and of the Lawrence company, and the Mormon family consisting of four persons—a colony numbering a little over fifty. Illustrative of the American character it has been said that if a dozen were gathered anywhere, even at the most distant portion of the globe, they would be found at the earliest possible moment framing a con-

AN EARLY FINDING IN COLORADO.

stitution and making laws for self-government. True to the instinct of the race this little band of pioneers far beyond the outposts of civilization were making this their first care. Montana, on the Platte River, burst abruptly into existence governed by a code of laws framed by its founders early in that memorable month of September, 1858, although it was not until February 5, 1859, that a charter for the new town was obtained from the legislature of Kansas.

On September 7, 1858, William McGaa, who subsequently became a local celebrity under the alias of "Jack Jones," arrived at the town of

Montana in company with fourteen men. Curiously enough, within twenty days from its actual settlement this infant town was found too small to contain its ambitious inhabitants, and part of them removed to the east side of Cherry Creek and laid out St. Charles on the identical site of what is now Denver, radiant in her beauty and prosperity. Thirty-seven days after the establishment of the town of St. Charles another town now known as West Denver was located on the left bank of Cherry Creek, the names of one hundred men being appended to its articles of incorporation. A human tide may be said to have set in this direction, and in the latter days of October two merchants arrived with general stocks of goods and were soon followed by a number of others.

Presently the advent of commissioners from Kansas, delegated by the then governor of that Territory, James W. Denver, to locate the tract under the title "Arapahoe County, Kansas," attracted attention. These functionaries arrived on the 12th of November, 1858, and on the 16th they, together with others whom they associated with themselves, took formal possession of St. Charles and called it Denver, in honor of the Governor of Kansas,* and without loss of time proceeded to arrange blocks and streets in the incipient "Queen City of the Plains."

In May, 1859, gold was found in large quantities, and from that time men thronged into that vicinity by the thousand. On the banks of the Platte River, outside of Denver, there were lines of wagons daily waiting ferriage, and along the trail to the gold district eager crowds jostled each other by the way ; a motley concourse of travelers, either on foot or going by any conveyance capable of being pressed into service. Within six months, and a few days after Kansas bestowed her first official notice upon this section of the country, so important did it become that a line of coaches was established, involving an expenditure of $800 daily, and spanning the plains from Leavenworth to Denver. In June, 1859, Horace Greeley crossed the plains in one of these new coaches, and upon his arrival at Denver became a guest at its only hotel—the Denver House—a log structure, canvas-roofed and earthen-floored.

As Denver increased in size and importance she also increased in depravity. The gilded saloon of vice, dissipation, crime and iniquity welcomed its votaries and victims with open doors, and every store in town

---

*The man who has his memorial in this beautiful city occupies hardly a page in the history of Kansas. Denver was born in Virginia in 1818. He emigrated to California in 1850, and was a member of Congress in 1854. During the Kansas troubles in 1857 Denver was Commissioner of Indian Affairs, and in that year was making a visit to the Indian tribes in Kansas. The then Governor Stanton took some official action not approved of by President Buchanan, and Denver was suddenly made Secretary and Acting Governor in Stanton's place. He was commissioned a brigadier-general of the Union forces in 1861.

carried on more business on Sunday than upon any other day of the week. On this day the miners left their claims and gathered in the town; to all it was a gala day. Drunkenness, brawls and street fights became the standard amusement, and murder lifted its arm and smote the peace and order of the community. Finally civilization brought thither a better element, and sobriety, peace, order and prosperity gradually arose from chaos and bloodshed. Refinement appeared with the wives and daughters of the pioneers, and they came like angels bringing the blessings of home

PLACER MINING IN 1858.

to cover the debris and ashes of vice and crime. The schoolhouse, the courthouse, the chimes and the workshop displaced the revelry of the dancehouse and the gambling saloon. Of course there was still a broad line between the law-abiding community and the turmoil of vice, drunkenness and wanton lawlessness. The violence of the bad was checked by the violence of the good. The long outspreading limb of the historic cottonwood that grew by the side of the stream beneath the shadow of the sentinel peaks of the snowy range, had much to do as a civilizing agent with the peace and order of the community, and the perturbed spirits of many outlaws who dangled from the bough still haunt the superstitious who dwell hard by. Such was Denver in the early days of the pioneer and hard-working and hard-drinking miner, and such she became when civilization had uprooted the gnarled and twisted growth whose roots had first struck into the virgin soil.

The Denver of to-day is a familiar figure. Steam has annihilated space and it lies at our doors. It is a beautiful inland city of trade and commerce, the commercial and political center of the rich State of Colorado. It is situated about one mile above sea level, and covers an area of nearly ten miles north and south and six miles east and west. On the east the plains descend gradually to the Missouri River, a distance of near six hundred miles. The foot-hills, which run nearly north and south through the State, begin to rise about fifteen miles west of the city and gradually grow more abrupt until blended into the snowy range fifty miles distant. Over two hundred miles of this mountain range and foot-hills can be seen from Denver, forming a grand panoramic view. Probably the residents of no other city in the world enjoy such a continual feast of ever-changing shade and color; rocks, trees, plains and mountains of perpetual snow. The Platte River runs through the center of the city from south to north, toward which on either side the surface gradually declines, affording a most perfect system of both surface and sanitary drainage. Following the banks of the river on either side are the railroad tracks, affording ample trackage for large manufactories, stockyards, packing houses, storehouses and depots. To the east of these the wholesale houses are chiefly located. Bordering on these are the principal retail houses, and to the east and west the residences. The more pretentious and expensive residences are located on what is known as Capitol Hill. The Highlands on the west of the river are by many considered a very healthy and attractive part of the city; while South Denver, a level plateau lying about one hundred feet above the river, contains a large number of fine residences.

Probably no city in the Union is so thoroughly cosmopolitan. This may be attributed to the fact that it is a new city, in which live but few people who were born and who have grown to manhood within her limits. Every nation upon the globe has contributed to her population. Every country has been drawn upon for desirable improvements and customs. The soil upon which the city is built is a sandy loam, therefore dry and healthy, affording most perfect natural streets except in the center of the city, where they are paved with asphalt or block stone. It is preëminently a city of homes. The laborer, the artisan, the manufacturer, the princely

M—21

merchant, the ranch-owner and the bonanza-miner all usually own their homes. A condition which has largely contributed to this end, especially among the middle classes, is the many strong and well-conducted building associations. Owing to the fire limits extending well out into the suburbs, all houses are built of fireproof material, either brick or stone, both of which are furnished in a great variety of color and combination. The variety of architecture and its pleasing effect is a notable feature. Surrounding most residences are spacious and beautifully-kept lawns. It is said that no city of its size in the United States has such magnificent and attractive public buildings. The capitol, costing $2,000,000, was built entirely of Colorado materials by Colorado workmen.

It has been shown that the summer climate is equal to that of the northern lakes and of Maine on the Eastern coast. Denver has more sunshine, less wind, a dryer air and a temperature allowing more constant outdoor life than any other city in the country approaching it in size. In a period of thirteen years there were but thirty-two days in which the sun was not visible. The population of Denver has so far doubled every five years, and as the number of people within her limits in 1895 is 160,000, it is predicted that at the beginning of the next century the population will be 320,000.

The first railroad to reach Denver was the Kansas Pacific, now a branch of the Union Pacific, in 1870, at which time the city had a population of less than 5,000. To-day Denver is the terminal of eight trunk lines, which carry freight to and fro over 28,000 miles of track, passing through a country but partially settled, but each year adding to its population and to the variety and volume of its tonnage. The city is regarded by railroad men as the strategic point which will eventually regulate a vast interior business, as it is a geographical as well as a commercial and manufacturing center.

It is claimed that the street car service here is the most perfect in the world. The system embraces one hundred and eighty-one miles, one hundred and twenty-five of which are electric. Transfers are given from line to line so that one can ride from any part of the city to his destination for five cents. The system of the Denver Union Water Company supplies the city and adjacent suburbs, all being furnished from the same source. It has about four hundred and fifty miles of mains and conduits, varying in size from six to forty-four inches in diameter. Attached to the mains are twenty thousand service pipes supplying water for domestic purposes.

Denver's school buildings and school system are the pride and boast of her people. Distinguished educators from the east are filled with surprise and admiration for both. There are three high school buildings, one of which is valued at three-fourths of a million dollars. There are fifty graded school buildings and twenty-one miscellaneous private and sectarian schools. There are also eleven academies and colleges. There are nine public and private libraries, and four daily and seventy weekly, monthly or quarterly papers. There are also one hundred and thirty-three organized churches.

The city has six national banks, whose total resources January 1, 1895, were nearly \$25,000,000. The deposits aggregate over \$17,000,000. They have a total surplus of \$720,000, and the capital stock paid in is \$4,100,000. Real estate transactions in 1894 were fairly satisfactory and show a healthful increase over those of 1893, and were far in advance of those of any other city of her class. The aggregate transfers for the year rank sixth in volume of the cities of the United States. The statistics showing the commercial and manufacturing industries are equally remarkable.

CHAPTER XXVIII.

SALT LAKE CITY AND THE MORMONS.

JOSEPH SMITH — THE MORMONS IN NEW YORK, OHIO, MISSOURI AND ILLINOIS — THE EXODUS
ACROSS THE WILDERNESS — SALT LAKE — BRIGHAM YOUNG, HIS CHAR-
ACTER AND WORK — SALT LAKE CITY NOW.

ALT LAKE CITY was founded by the Mormons under Brigham Young in 1847, and in this brief statement is embodied one of the strangest stories in the annals of American civilization. The Mormons, or, as they call themselves, the "Church of Jesus Christ of Latter-Day Saints," form a religious sect founded by one Joseph Smith, whose story is so well known as to make it unnecessary to more than barely outline it here. Smith was born in Vermont, but while a child removed with his parents to the State of New York. He claimed that an angel appeared to him and informed him that he was the instrument chosen to inaugurate a new gospel. He accepted the mission and soon collected quite a number of followers. These, on account of the prejudice against them were obliged to move to Ohio. Later a colony was established in Missouri which grew rapidly. About this time a body of "apostles" was instituted within the church, and among the number of these was Brigham Young, who had become a convert to the new faith in 1832, and had already shown himself a man of wonderful sagacity and force of character.

In 1838 the whole body of the so-called "saints," some fifteen thousand in number, moved to Illinois. Here their welcome was no more cordial than it had been in other parts of the country, and before long Smith and his brother found themselves in jail. Fearing that the prisoners might be allowed to escape, a band of excited men broke into the jail and killed both of them. Brigham Young was then elected as Smith's successor, and as the hostility against them did not abate, the Mormons, under his guidance, all started for the West. They stopped for a year in Iowa, and then under the strictest discipline marched across the wilderness to the Great Salt Lake.

The first reference to this lake is found in a book of American travels in 1689; but it was first explored and described by John C. Fremont in 1842. It lies in a great valley of the Rocky Mountains and measures nearly one hundred miles in length by a little less than fifty in breadth, and its waters are very shallow. Near its center lie a group of islands, upon some of which are found springs of pure, fresh water, although the waters of the lake are of so saline a character that from seven quarts boiled down there can be extracted one quart of pure salt. Yet into this lake rivers of fresh water are pouring continually; from the south the fresh waters of Utah Lake find their way into it through the channel of the Jordan, while from the north it receives the water of the Bear River, a swift mountain stream. There is no visible outlet, and its superfluity of water is supposed to be evaporated, but there are many who believe in the existence of a subterranean passageway having an outlet at some undiscovered point.

BRIGHAM YOUNG.

Geologists declare that at a remote period a vast sheet of water filled a far greater area than that now occupied by the Great Salt Lake. In the mighty intervals of time, as indefinite as the geological periods, certain changes in the rainfall caused the waters to evaporate to the present size of the existing lake. This theory is confirmed by the various terraces running in long parallel lines on the sides of the surrounding Wasatch Mountains. These terraces mark off the various intervals at which the waters remained stationary for a while in their gradual lessening of volume. Another remarkable property of the

water is its density. It is next to impossible to sink to the bottom, for
one can float upon the surface with the greatest ease.

The so-called "Prophet," Brigham Young, declared that the site of the
forthcoming city was indicated to him in a vision by an angel who, standing on a conical hill, pointed out to him the locality where the new temple
must be built.   Upon the entry of the Mormon pioneers into the Salt Lake
Basin he beheld the identical mountain he had seen in the vision, with a
stream of fresh water flowing at its base.   The Prophet immediately commanded his followers to halt and pitch their permanent tents, as they had
finally arrived at the site of the
city of the New Jerusalem. He
immediately named the mountain Ensign Peak a n d
the stream at its base
City Creek.
A n o t h e r
l a r g e r
stream of
fresh water
he n a m e d
after the old historical stream
of the Jews, the Jordan.
Here the people were com-
manded to "wash" as of old.

When the Mormons ar-
rived in the valley in July,

THE MORMON EXODUS.

1847, the Territory belonged to Mexico, but the next year it became,
together with New Mexico, Arizona and the whole of upper California, a
portion of the domain of the United States.   This was a severe blow to
the designs of the Prophet.

With the Mexican government Brigham Young could, in his remote
fastnesses, negotiate his own terms and secure for himself and his followers
all the concessions necessary for their temporal as well as their peculiar
spiritual welfare.   Here they could revel in polygamy and indulge in all
the doctrines declared to be a part of their faith.   But suddenly the war
with Mexico closed, and, as if to overthrow their schemes in this remote
section, the territory on which they had already begun the erection of

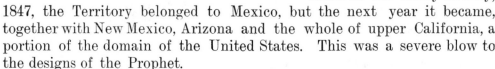

their temple became the property of the federal government. Still, not to be defeated in his original enterprise, the Prophet laid claim to everything. Under a system of law enacted by themselves, and in the absence of federal legislation and the persons and powers to enforce it, all this basin and nearly every arable acre of soil in the Territory was seized and apportioned to their own uses. Sparse and distant settlements were created for the sole purpose of maintaining their hold upon the lands they had taken possession of, and the authority of the church, through its great high priest, was extended in all directions. Not an acre of land should ever be in such condition as to be converted to the use or benefit of the Gentile element. All that in the way of business would tend to attract them thither should be avoided. Under the operations of this rule mining for the precious metals was prohibited under penalty of the "anger of God." Young declared publicly that none of the vast mineral wealth of the Territory should be disclosed until the Lord, through him as His vicar, should so order. While great mineral wealth lay at their doors and a mighty industry might have been established, they were not permitted to turn a spadeful of earth save in the way of cultivating the soil. These mines of gold and silver were to be kept a secret from the outer world so as to prevent an accretion of Gentile population. The peculiar people were sealed within themselves in their mountain walls, and the Gentile was almost an absolute stranger within their gates until the advent of Johnston's army in 1857. Along with that came the mail and express, and the telegraph soon followed. But not until General Conner came with his California regiment of miners and mountain prospectors was Utah's vast mineral wealth made known to the world. Then followed a greater influx of the Gentile element. But Brigham Young, as the high priest of the church, still maintained his absolute sway over his people, controlling and directing every movement of their lives in all their social, religious and business relations. The government of the Mormons was thus a pure pseudo-theocracy, controlled by the will of one man.

Few men of the present century have attracted more notice from writers of all creeds, both at home and abroad, than Brigham Young. He was born of humble parentage in Vermont in 1801. His education in the schools was limited, according to his own statement, to eleven and a half days. He learned in early life the trade of a painter and glazier. He joined the Mormon church in 1832, and journeyed with them to Ohio, Missouri and Illinois. By simple force of character and intellect he reached the highest pinnacle of power in the Mormon Church and State.

He was not only a man of great force of character, but was also possessed of great executive ability. To his clear judgment, firmness of decision, inflexible will, unceasing industry, power of government and ability to control men, directness of purpose and a self-sustaining individuality that overpowered all opposition, the Mormon Church owes much of the prosperity that attended its lodgment in the then sterile valleys of these mountains. Had it not been for him and his ability to command, the multitude of his followers would have fled before the disasters and threatened starvation that assailed them in the early days of their entry into the valley.

While he directed their spiritual faith and by pretended "visions" and "dreams" pointed out "the will of the Lord," he superintended all the great labor of laying out and building the city of Zion. All plans were submitted first to his inspection before a stake was driven. As time went on and privations ceased, and the city had grown great and prosperous, and Mormon immigrants began pouring in from all parts of the world, personally he superintended their movements and established the various settlements throughout the Territory. When the lines of telegraph were laid it was by Young's contract with the company, sublet to others. When the roads were built for the mail and express companies it was by his order, and it was through him that the great trans-continental railroad entered his domain.

A late writer, an apostate from the Mormon faith, speaking of the absolute power of Young over the lives and property of his people, says: "No one to-day, even in Utah, can form any idea of the thorough control that Young exercised over the people. Nothing was ever undertaken without his permission. He knew of everything. No person could enter into business without consulting him, nor would any one ever think of leaving the city to reside in any other part of the country without having his approval. Merchants who went east or west to purchase goods had to present themselves at his office and report their intention of going to the States at such a time, if he had no contrary orders to give them. He claimed that no Saint should do anything without his knowledge and approval."

He claimed the power of performing miracles, foretelling events and doing other strange and wonderful things. It is said that he rarely made a prophecy or prediction that it did not come true. By the exercise of most adroit cunning he usually succeeded in making his predictions and prophecies seem inspired. He was very intelligent and with intelligent people he would make a prediction something like this: "You will have a successful journey. You will enjoy your trip and will all return to your homes in good health." When asked if he intended this as a prophecy he would reply: "You can call it whatever you please. I make the prediction." With his own people it was quite different, for he knew they would believe whatever he told them. Near the close of a very severe winter that had caused much suffering he happened to be down in the lower part of the Territory. While there he noticed a warm breeze and the appearance of birds whose coming usually preceded the opening of spring. Making as rapid a journey as possible, he hurried back to Salt Lake, went into the Tabernacle and proclaimed that the Lord was about to put an end to the terrible winter. He told them there would be an early spring, the sun would shine, the snow would disappear; the face of the Lord was again turned toward his chosen people, and that he would breathe upon them the blessings of life. All this would happen very soon. Naturally this prophecy came true.

Another story is told of him illustrative of his shrewdness. One of his followers had been unfortunate enough to lose a leg and was obliged to go about on a wooden one. This man came to him one day and told him that he knew he was a prophet of the Lord; that he could perform miracles and foretell events, and that he wanted him to perform a miracle for him by giving him back his lost leg. He stated that with only one leg he could not support his families, and that he had a strong desire to make himself useful. After thinking over the matter a few moments, Young assumed a very solemn and wise attitude and expression and said: "What you say is true. I am a prophet of the Lord; I can perform miracles and foretell events and do many other wondrous things; but it is possible that you have not thought this thing out as seriously as you ought to have done. You know it is told us that what is lost to us in this world will be restored to us in the next. If you continue in the faith in the other world your lost leg will be given back to you, and if I give you another now you will have to go through eternity on three legs." This was a view that had not occurred to the man before, and he concluded that he would not insist on having the miracle performed. He went away a more fervent believer in Brigham than ever.

When Brigham Young died, in 1877, John Taylor was elected to succeed him, but his real power descended to George Q. Cannon, entitled "First Counselor" to the president, and who was also a delegate to Congress.

Salt Lake City at the present time covers about nine thousand acres of ground, some of which is unoccupied, but the city is handsomely laid out. The streets are one hundred and twenty-eight feet in width, crossing at right angles. They are thickly shaded, and through many of them flow streams of pure water from the distant mountains, enabling the people to irrigate their gardens. Nearly every ward contains a public square. The houses are mostly built of adobe, but there are many handsome buildings. The Mormon tabernacle is the largest structure. It seats twelve thousand persons and has an immense organ. It is elliptical in shape and its interior space is sufficient to permit the drilling of a regiment of men. It was designed by a young German architect, and its acoustic properties

MORMON TEMPLE.

are remarkable; unexcelled, I presume, by those of any building in the world. The new temple, built at a cost of $5,000,000, is in the same enclosure. It is a magnificent building intended to endure for ages. Its foundations are sixteen feet deep and composed of hard gray granite. There is still another very interesting building in the same enclosure known as the Endowment House. Here for many years converts to the Mormon religion have been received into the bosom of the church with mysterious forms and ceremonies. It is built of adobe and contains but four windows, one of which is blocked up.

On a high bench of land commanding a magnificent view of the city and surrounding country stands the imposing residence formerly occupied by the Prophet with many of his wives and children. At the west end of Brigham's Block, as it is called, lies the Tithing House. This is a large building with numerous cellars, storerooms, receiving rooms, payrooms and offices. Here are collected and stored all the vast tithes of the products of Mormon industry in each and every department of skill and labor—

the resultant of that system of tithing which compels each individual member of the church to devote to its support one-tenth of all the products of his or her labor. These possessions of the church always found a ready sale, and its revenues were thus easily converted into cash. Brigham Young as its prophet ruled the church with an iron hand, and not even the most poverty-stricken member ever failed to contribute his share to the general fund. In many cases these tithings may have been a voluntary offering, but there was a large class who could ill afford to part with the smallest portion of the product of their labor. As trustee in trust for the church Brigham Young was the sole beneficiary of this vast fund. In other words, he held absolute control of these tithings, and while doubtless a considerable portion of the fund was used for ecclesiastical objects, such as the erection of the Temple, the repairs of the Tabernacle and the assistance of the needy immigrants, yet the greater portion was securely retained by the chief of this religious sect, who is said to have been a very large depositor in the bank of England.

There are now three hospitals in the city, many Gentile churches, a prison and a penitentiary. There are also several collegiate institutions, more than twenty public schools and nine periodicals. From 1880 to 1890 the population more than doubled, being at the latter date more than forty-four thousand. In 1894 it was estimated at seventy thousand.

The Mormons have sent out colonies into Idaho, Wyoming, Colorado, Nevada, Arizona, New Mexico, California and Mexico, and they are

DISTANT VIEW OF SALT LAKE CITY.

increasing very rapidly. Many of their men and women have been educated at our eastern colleges. A number of the boys have been sent to West Point and Annapolis and brought in contact with other boys, but have adhered to their principles and theories, still believing that Joseph Smith was a true prophet, and that Brigham Young was a great prophet and statesman.

Universal industry, great economy and simplicity of life, with rigid temperance, were the main sources and pillars of their prosperity and wealth. They have been a very prosperous people. They lived under a system of perfect discipline. They are a healthy people and great care has been taken that their immigrants should bring no disease with them. They for a long time allowed no intruders in the country. Anyone who was very troublesome disappeared very promptly, and the Mountain Meadow massacre will forever be a blot upon the history of the Mormons. When finally the railways were established, giving employment to a large number of men, the result was a rapid increase of wealth. The number of buildings erected grew steadily larger, and the luxuries usually found in wealthy communities were gradually adopted, until now Salt Lake City is one of the picturesque and prosperous cities of the West. They point to their success, the productive resources of the territory and the growth and beauty of Salt Lake City as the direct evidences that they were the chosen people of the Lord and the especial recipients of His blessing. Yet they forget in this argument the great prosperity of St. Paul, Minneapolis, Los Angeles, San Francisco, Portland, Tacoma, Seattle, Denver, Omaha, Kansas City and hundreds of other American cities and towns that have prospered and been made beautiful during the same period.

CHAPTER XXIX.

ACROSS UTAH AND NEVADA.

FROM SALT LAKE TO SAN FRANCISCO — ON THE PACIFIC — THE COLUMBIA RIVER — MOUNT
HOOD — MOUNT SHASTA — A MOUNTAIN LAKE — CITY OF PORTLAND — OREGON —
WASHINGTON — CLIMATE OF THE NORTHWEST — WILLAMETTE VALLEY — THE
FORESTS — GOLD — CATTLE RAISING — SPOKANE AND TACOMA — IDAHO.

ROM Salt Lake City I journeyed across the arid plains of southern Utah and western Nevada to San Francisco by way of the Central Pacific, which was a continuation of the Union Pacific, at that time the only trans-continental line. I remained in San Francisco several days, but as I shall have occasion later to speak more fully of this city I will not at this time attempt to describe it.

At that time there was no way of reaching Portland, Oregon, except by water, unless one went by stage and the mountainous route through the interior, the latter being a long, tedious and most undesirable journey. I took passage on board the "Columbia," and passing out of the beautiful San Francisco harbor found myself on the billows of the broad Pacific. The trip along the coast was a most delightful one until we were overtaken by a severe storm, when the water became so rough that even those who were most accustomed to ocean voyages were obliged to succumb to seasickness. Even those who had crossed the Atlantic many times without any unpleasant effects were forced to acknowledge the power of the Pacific when once roused from its usually placid condition.

At the mouth of the Columbia River at that time there was a bar which, if the wind was fresh, was covered by a dashing surf, while in a storm this surf appeared like a great white wall. There were several breaks in this bar, allowing ships to enter, but it was at all times a dangerous passageway, many steamers having been wrecked there and many valuable lives lost. During the last few years the government has constructed extensive and costly jetties that have greatly improved the navigation at the entrance of this great river. It is to the Columbia, which once bore the name of Oregon, that Bryant refers in his poem "Thanatopsis" when he says:

> " Or lose thyself in the continuous woods
> Where rolls the Oregon, and hears no sound
> Save its own dashings — yet the dead are there."

After passing the bar and entering the river one is reminded of the lower

SCENE ON THE COLUMBIA RIVER.

Mississippi by the dark, sombre trees growing down to the water's edge. This most majestic river has been styled the "Hudson of the West," but it far surpasses the Hudson in the volume of water it sends to the sea and in the magnificence of its scenery. At that time it was five miles wide at its mouth, but for some distance as one ascended toward its source it rapidly widened, being about fifteen miles across a few miles from where it entered the ocean. Together with its tributaries it drains a territory of 395,000 square miles, and penetrates in every direction through twelve degrees of latitude and thirteen degrees of longitude. Although navigation upon it is not continuous, it has seven hundred and twenty-five miles of navigable waters. These are broken by the cascades, The Dalles, and other obstructions. The distance across the country between its navigable waters and those of the Missouri is only four hundred and fifty miles, which gives it great value as a means of transportation. On the Snake River, one of its branches, steamers can go as far as Lewiston, Idaho, a distance of four hundred miles east of Portland, Oregon.

The most interesting part of the river is that known as the Gorge of the Columbia. From above The Dalles for fifty miles or more the river flows through the solid mountain range of the Cascades, and the farther it penetrates these mountains the more majestic and awe-inspiring grows the scenery. As we ascend, fantastic forms of rock attract the attention on every hand, and from lofty ledges silvery water from mountain rivulets descends hundreds of feet to the Columbia below. The narrow channel of the river, the high over-hanging cliffs which confine the wind as if in a funnel, and the changes of temperature to which mountain localities are subject, make this a stormy passage at some seasons of the year. As the rapids are approached the heights recede and enclose a strip of level rock on which stands a solitary pyramid know as Castle Rock. Above the

MOUNT HOOD.

cascades the scenery is so grand as to almost defy description.

The most interesting part of this Gorge of the Columbia is The Dalles. Here the river flows for fifteen miles through such a narrow channel in the solid rock that one accustomed only to the lower part can hardly believe that this great, dashing, rushing, foaming torrent of water is the Columbia. So narrow and so deep, indeed, does it appear at this place that it has been aptly likened to "a great river set on edge."

As I stood on the deck of the steamer on the occasion of my first ascending the Columbia I noticed what appeared to me to be a triangular white cloud above a deep bank of darker ones. Some one quietly remarked, "Mount Hood!" "Where?" I inquired; and great was my surprise when he pointed out my beautiful three-cornered cloud as the snow-capped peak of the famous mountain. At first I was incredulous, but as we drew nearer and it gradually unfolded its graceful and symmetrical form, seeming to reach into the very heavens, I was forced to acknowledge that he was right. Most mountain ranges stand on a plateau so that we do not get the full effect of their height. Pike's Peak, for instance, reaches an altitude of 13,500 feet above the sea level, but the country around it rises so gradually that the actual mountain is only about half that height above the surrounding country. Mount Hood, however, stands forth in all its majestic proportions, as one sees it from the sea level 12,500 feet from foot to summit, and loses nothing of its grandeur by reason of any surrounding table land. According to a tradition of the Indians, Mount Hood was an active volcano at a comparatively recent period. As we move on up the Columbia the remainder of the cluster of mountains of which Mount Hood forms one become visible against the sky; Mount Adams, Mount Jefferson, Mount St. Helens, and further to the west Mount Rainier or Tacoma, as the Indians called the great mountain towering up two thousand feet higher than even Mount Hood, and all contributing to form a grand picture that I have never seen surpassed. One of Oregon's native poets speaks of

>   . . . . "clouded Hood,
> St. Helens in her sea of wood —
>   Where sweeps the Oregon, and where
> White storms are in the feathered fir,
> And snowy sea-birds wheel and whir."

Mount Shasta is one of the grandest of this great mountain range. It towers above the surrounding country, symmetrical in form, impressively majestic in proportions, rising 14,440 feet in height.

The grandest of all these mountains at one time must have been what is now known as Crater Lake in southeast Oregon, ninety miles east of the Oregon and California Railway. It is one of the most wonderful features of nature that I have ever seen. As you approach it you pass over what is known as the Lava Beds, a large district of country that must have been covered by the lava from a great eruption. You gradually ascend for four or five miles what looks like a mountain range. As you approach and finally reach the summit you are suddenly appalled by finding your-self upon the verge of a precipice looking down two thousand feet upon a body of water six miles long and five wide, encircled by an almost per-pendicular wall, with only one or two places where it is possible for a man to descend to its margin. The area of this lake is about thirty square miles and its depth over two thousand feet. There is no apparent outlet, but some twelve or fifteen miles away there rolls out from the earth a large stream of water as cold as ice, which seemingly comes through some sub-terranean channel from the great lake above. Near the center of this lake is a cone of what was once a volcanic mountain. The indications point to a volcano that must have been in action for a long time. Part of the cone is covered with grass and trees. Evidently by some tremendous con-vulsion the top of the mountain was blown up, its sides were thrown out-ward, and the cone falling stands surrounded by this great shell or crater; one of the most interesting and awe-inspiring natural wonders in exist-ence. One is well repaid for a long and tedious journey in beholding it. Everything indicates that before the eruption it must have been equal if not superior in height and grandeur to anyone of the great mountain peaks south of Alaska.

On the Willamette River, twelve miles from where it enters the Colum-bia, stands the city of Portland in a situation of wonderful natural beauty. Although it is one hundred and twenty miles from the ocean, yet its posi-tion near the head of navigation on the Willamette makes it virtually a seaport. A rather amusing account is given of the way in which Portland received its name. The site of the present city was purchased in 1844 by two men from New England, one being a native of the chief city of the state of Maine, while the other came from Boston. In 1848 the number of people in their new settlement had so increased as to seem to warrant the dignity of a name, and naturally each of the owners was desirous of hon-oring his own city with a namesake in the far West. After long discussion, no agreement being reached, a penny was tossed up, and the man from Maine winning, the town was called Portland. Afterward he bought out his partner, but eventually sold the whole property for $5,000, taking his pay in leather.

When I visited the city in 1881 the population numbered 20,000, but since then it has increased rapidly, and after it was consolidated with East Portland and Albina in 1891 the population was estimated at 72,000.

M—22

Portland is a thriving city and Oregon a prosperous State because of the vast natural resources of the surrounding country. Its waters are alive with the most delicious trout and salmon. Its forests are of great value. Its agricultural resources are unsurpassed. Its mines, manufactures and commerce and the enterprise of its people all contribute to its wealth and prosperity. Many have grown rich as a result of the wonderful discoveries of mines in California, Idaho and Oregon. These mines increased the population and brought in many additional industries. Portland is now a handsome city, lighted by gas and electricity, with many miles of street railway, and containing numerous massive buildings. Naturally its commerce is of great importance.

The discovery and exploration of Oregon and Washington is credited to the Spanish navigators early in the sixteenth century. In 1592 Juan de Fuca, a Greek pilot sailing in the service of the Viceroy of New Spain, entered into "a broad opening between forty-seven and forty-eight degrees, and sailed eastward for one hundred miles, when he saw men clad in the skins of beasts and emerged into the Atlantic." Considering his duty done, he sailed back through his strait and down to Acapulco. Afterward he was sent to Spain to report this marvel to the king. Then began that series of voyages in search of the "Straits of Aman," which resulted in the telling of such wonderful stories. These fabled straits were supposed to lead through to the Atlantic, and their rediscovery and exploration was the ambition of the greatest navigators of two centuries. The first who claimed to have explored them was a Portugese, who was supposed to have sailed through them from the Labrador coast into the Indian Ocean in 1500.

The Strait of Juan de Fuca is a magnificent highway eighty-three miles in length and in places not more than twelve miles in width, the great gateway to one of the grandest of all our inland seas, Puget Sound. The latter, with its arms and inlets, covers a surface of two thousand square miles. Its waters are of very great depth, and its harbors are capable of accommodating the largest vessels. For safety of navigation it is unequaled.

In 1792 Captain Gray of Boston in his ship "Columbia" sailed up the great river which now bears the name of his vessel, and it was upon his discoveries and explorations that the United States based her claim to that vast region comprising Washington, Oregon and a part of Idaho, and which contains thirty-two times as many square miles as Massachusetts, the native State of Captain Gray. The overland expedition under Lewis

CASCADES OF THE COLUMBIA. INDIAN DIPPING FOR SALMON.

and Clark crossed the Rocky Mountains and followed the Columbia River from its source to its mouth in 1805. The wonderful resources of this part of the country were first made known to the world through that expedition.

The first attempt at settlement was made by Captain Winship with fifty men in 1810, but the hardy pioneers who were afraid of neither man nor beast were forced to own themselves vanquished by another adversary when the summer freshet swept down from the mountains, carrying away their gardens, flooding their houses and forcing them to abandon their enterprise. Captain Winship returned to San Francisco and began making plans for planting another colony on the Columbia, but before they were completed he heard of the establishment of Astoria, named in honor of its founder, John Jacob Astor, at the mouth of the river. He then abandoned his enterprise. The Hudson Bay Company subsequently obtained this property and ruled supremely in the valleys of the Columbia and the Willamette until 1848, excepting for a few years when its sway was disputed by the Northwest Fur Company. In 1824 the first fruit trees were planted in Oregon, and seven years later some servants of the Hudson Bay Company abandoned hunting and trapping and attempted wheat-growing in the Willamette Valley.

The sad story of the Nez Percé Indians who took the long journey from the far West to St. Louis in search of "the Book" is well known in that country. In the end their journey did not prove a fruitless one, for their pathetic story became known, and when in 1835 two exploring delegates of the American board of missions met the Nez Percés on Green River, Dr. Whitman, one of these agents, concluded that he had discovered his life work. When he returned to the east to make his report and arrange his plans he took with him two of the Nez Percé boys as specimens of the people among whom he wished to be allowed to labor. As soon as his plans were completed he returned to the West and founded a small colony in Walla Walla Valley. Afterward it was largely due to his patriotic efforts and sacrifices that the whole of this vast region did not become a part of the British possessions, as will be shown in a future chapter.

In 1841 Captain Wilkes of the United States Navy, at the head of an expedition, surveyed the coasts, bays, harbors and rivers of this territory, and two years later Lieutenant Fremont of the army arrived at Vancouver on the Columbia River, thus connecting his reconnoissance with the eastern terminus of Captain Wilkes's explorations.

In the course of time this territory became the occasion of numerous disputes between the United States and the British government. These were not finally settled until 1872, when the German Emperor acted as arbitrator between the two governments. During the years when the owner-ship of the territory was unsettled it was held by the people of both countries; but no form of civil government existed until 1848, when Oregon Territory was organized by Congress. The country was really settled by the Ameri-cans, for while the British hunter and trapper came in search of game only, the American farmer brought his wife and family and remained in the country permanently.

A "donation law" was passed by Congress in 1850, which enabled early settlers to secure titles to their holdings. In 1859 Oregon was admitted as a State. For several years thereafter her progress was slow, but the coming of the railroads overcame the most serious obsta-cles to her advancement and assisted her to the present substantial prosperity.

The history of Washington was closely connected with that of Oregon until 1853, when Congress endowed the former with a separate territorial government. It was admitted as a State in 1889.

For many years there was a very mistaken opinion regarding the cli-mate of the northern Pacific Coast, it being supposed that the winters were very cold and severe, while in reality the reverse is true. The mean tem-perature in January ranges from ten to twenty degrees higher on the Pacif-ic than it does on the eastern side of the mountain chain which divides the continent. The difference in the temperature is caused by the Kuro Siwo or Japan Current, which modifies the climate of the North Pacific Coast just as the Gulf Stream tempers the climate of the British Isles. West of the Cascade Mountains in Washington and Oregon the winters consist of the long rainy season, but the weather is not cold. Snow sometimes falls, but rarely in great quantities. Thunder storms seldom if ever occur, and hurricanes and cyclones are almost unknown. The rainfall at Portland, Oregon, averages fifty-one inches.

In western Oregon and Washington whenever the temperature falls a few degrees below the freezing point the weather is generally bright and pleasant, with heavy frosts at night. When frosts occur during spring or early summer, which in other lands would be sufficiently severe to injure fruit and the growing crops, they are commonly followed here by heavy fogs which roll in from the ocean and spread themselves throughout the country. These fogs are so very dense that their humidity dissolves the frost before the heat of the sun can strike the vegetation and cause the subsequent injury.

In eastern Oregon and Washington the temperature is much lower in winter and higher in summer than it is west of the mountains. Although the days are often very hot in the summer, the nights are always cool and refreshing. As there are four or five months of what is known as the dry season, between May and October, it gives the farmers an opportunity to harvest their crops at leisure.

Wheat forms the staple agricultural product of both Washington and Oregon. In Washington much of the land devoted to the raising of wheat is from 1,500 to 3,000 feet above the sea level. Hundreds of miles of irrigating canals are in operation, and the annual product averages 15,000,000 bushels. Oats also yields heavily and fruits and vegetables are extensively raised in both States. In Oregon the Willamette Valley is the chief region of agricultural wealth, and is famed alike for its beauty and fertility.

This charming valley, which has sometimes been called the "Eden of Oregon," is one hundred and twenty-five miles in length, and its breadth for the entire distance averages over forty miles. Its area is five times that of Delaware, or nearly equal to the entire State of Maryland. The valley presents most delightful alternations of scenery, from lofty mountains to rich meadows, wooded hills and pastoral dales. It is the most populous portion of the State and embraces within its limits nearly all the important towns and cities. At the time that I was in that part of the country the valley was being rapidly settled, and in the loneliest parts might be noticed new houses; so new in fact, that the sawdust sometimes still clung to their boards. The prairies of the Willamette Valley are not an uninterrupted level like those of Illinois. Ranges of hills and isolated buttes occur frequently enough to save the landscape from monotony.

It would hardly be possible to exaggerate the value of the forests throughout Washington and Oregon, especially in the former State. The principal growths are fir, pine, spruce, cedar, larch and hemlock, though other varieties are found in considerable quantities. Trees attain an unusual development, both in regard to height and symmetry of form. They are so tall and straight and gently tapering that they are peculiarly adapted for making the masts and spars of ships, and for this purpose large quantities one hundred and fifty feet in length are shipped from the forests of Douglas County to all parts of the world.

Gold was first discovered in Jackson County in Oregon in 1852, and mining is still carried on there for the same precious metal, though it has since been discovered at many other places. In Washington gold is found on the Yakima River and in various other localities. Rich deposits of silver and iron, as well as many other minerals, abound in both States. Washington has been called the Pennsylvania of the Pacific on account of its vast coal region lying in or near the Puget Sound Basin.

Stock-raising is also a great industry, and the country is well adapted for it in both of these States. The waters in this region abound with fish, the most important of which is the salmon. Such large quantities of these are canned every year as to make it one of the most important industries. An extensive commerce is carried on, especially with China and Japan. Port Townsend is the port of entry in Washington, and the number of American vessels engaged in the foreign trade here is exceeded at two ports only in the United States — New York and San Francisco.

Washington, with her rich and varied resources, undoubtedly has a great future before her. In the terse language of the West, her people state that if you should build a Chinese wall around Washington her inhabitants could supply themselves with everything they absolutely required without going outside, and the statement is practically true. In 1853 the population was less than 4,000 for the entire territory; in 1890 it had increased to 349,000, and in 1894 it was estimated at 410,000. Oregon in 1842 had only two hundred and forty white people within her borders, while in 1890 the census gave the number of inhabitants at nearly 314,000.

The chief city of western Washington is Seattle, with a population of over 40,000. When we consider that its progress has been made against railroad opposition instead of by the aid of this powerful influence, its size and business importance seem almost incredible, and its public-spirited men can hardly lay claim to too much credit. From the harbor it makes an impressive appearance because it is built in a manner peculiar to itself, though the result is that its streets are exceedingly steep. After some of the best engineers and most prominent officers of the army had for years recommended without success the construction by the government of a short canal to unite the waters of Puget Sound with the fresh water basin of Lake Washington, the citizens of Seattle, with commendable enterprise and public spirit, have undertaken the great work themselves. The canal will be completed within a few years, and when finished will have cost about $7,000,000.

Tacoma, an hour and a half distant from Seattle by water, is also a substantial city, and especially remarkable for the beautiful homes that adorn its streets. It is the center of a large circle of cultivated people and, though it is not as large as Seattle, it has exhibited great enterprise.

Spokane is the principal city of eastern Washington. It is a very active place, with electric cars, electric lights, cable cars, elevators, etc., though it is not at all peculiar in these respects, as nearly all progressive western towns have the same, and their hotels rank with the finest in the leading cities of the world. The Spokane River and Falls are of great beauty and utility.

Idaho is essentially different from the States we have been considering in many important particulars. It has formed successively a part of Ore-

SHOSHONE FALLS.

gon, Washington, Utah and Nebraska. Although explored by Lewis and Clark on their famous expedition, but little was known of it until 1852, when gold was discovered near the northern boundary. On July 3, 1890, Idaho entered the Union, being the forty-third State in the order of admission. The name Idaho is said to mean "Light of the Mountains."

Its mountain system is peculiar. The Salmon River range in the central part of the State is one of the most picturesque in America and of itself covers an area as large as New Jersey. Streams radiate to nearly every point from their sources in this great central range, yet they all flow into the Snake River and thence into the Columbia. The crests and summits of many of these mountains rise from 10,000 to 13,000 feet above the level of the sea.

One of the most remarkable features of Idaho is the vast lava bed which covers a large area of that part of the State on the east and south along the course of the Snake River. This is the principal river, and drains all the State except the most northern and the southeastern portions. The Shoshone Falls of this river are second only to those of Niagara, the Yellowstone and the Yosemite. The stream here is six hundred feet wide, and above the falls it is divided by five islands into six parts. Then, after flowing four hundred yards further, it passes in one unbroken sheet over a precipice, making a descent of two hundred and twenty-five feet.

Forests abound in the north. There is but little rainfall in the southern part of the State, but toward the center there is a heavy snowfall for several months in the year. The climate is dependent upon the elevation, and varies from a dry area of almost torrid heat along the Snake River and the foot-hills to the cold of the mountain peaks where the snow lies frequently through the summer, and ice forms nearly every night. Even in winter the ice and snow are often rapidly melted by the Chinook winds blowing from the Pacific Coast.

The country is not well adapted to agriculture, yet on both sides of the Snake River irrigation has produced the same results that it has in Utah. In the aggregate the grazing lands form a considerable tract, but these lands are widely scattered. There are many rich mines in the State, but as yet they have not been fully developed. The Mormon Church is strong in Idaho, but as polygamy is prohibited by law, about 3,000 Mormons are practically disfranchised. The largest town is Boisé City, which in 1890 contained about 3,300 people.

CHAPTER XXX.

A Chapter Out of Early History.

Ideas of American Statesmen Fifty Years Ago — Discovery of the Columbia — Claims of the United States to the Northwest Territory — The Early Missions — Dr. Whitman and Mr. Spalding — The First Overland Journey — The Old Wagon — General Lovejoy — Result in Washington of the Teaching of the Hudson Bay Company — The Pending Treaty — The Return Journey of Whitman and Lovejoy — A Change of View in Washington — The Lesson of the Old Wagon — Work and Death of Dr. Whitman.

IN our day, when the great northwestern part of our country with its vast resources is so well known and so thoroughly appreciated, it seems almost incredible that only fifty years ago so little was known of that region that a man like Daniel Webster was willing to believe it a "sandy desert." That this great country which now comprises the States of Washington, Oregon and Idaho is not to-day part of the British possessions is largely due to the unselfish exertions of Dr. Marcus Whitman, a missionary sent out to that part of the United States by the American Board of Missions in 1836.

That this country, which was then known as Oregon, belonged rightfully to the United States there can be no shadow of doubt. Captain Robert Gray of Boston discovered the Columbia River in 1792 and gave the name of his good ship to that beautiful and majestic Hudson of the West. The English navigator, Vancouver, was informed of its existence by Captain Gray before he ever entered its waters. The second claim of the United States was based on the Louisiana purchase. This territory had been ceded by France to Spain in 1762, re-ceded to France in 1800, and sold by the latter country to the United States in 1803 "with all its rights and appurtenances as fully and in the same manner as they were acquired by the French republic." Although there was some doubt whether France could rightfully claim the territory along the Pacific Coast as far north as the parallel of forty-nine degrees, it was Spain who disputed her claim, and not England.

A third claim of the United States was based on the explorations of Lewis and Clark, who were sent out by Jefferson in 1803, and who followed the Columbia from its headwaters to its mouth. A fourth claim was based on the actual settlement made at Astoria in 1811. A fifth was the treaty of the United States with Spain in 1818, when Spain relinquished any and all claims to the territory in dispute to the United States. The sixth and last claim was the treaty with Mexico in 1828, by which the United States acquired all interests in the territory in question that had been claimed by Mexico.

DR. MARCUS WHITMAN.

When the appeal of the Flat Head Indians of the Northwest was made known to the people in the eastern part of the United States, it touched a responsive chord and stirred the church to unusual activity. The Methodists sent out the Lees in 1834, and the American Board tried to get the right men to send with them, but were unable to do so until 1835, when they sent out Dr. Marcus Whitman and the Rev. Samuel Parker upon a trip of discovery. On reaching Green River, Dr. Whitman and Mr. Parker met large bodies of Indians, who endeavored to induce them to remain, and it was decided that Dr. Whitman should return to the East, and, after making the necessary arrangements, snould return the following year.

After hearing Dr. Whitman's report the American Board at once decided to occupy the field. He had for a long time been engaged to marry Miss Narcissa Prentice of Prattsburgh, New York, who was as enthusiastic with respect to work among the Indians as Dr. Whitman himself. The Board did not consider it expedient to send the young couple alone, so the day of the wedding was deferred while search was being made for suitable persons to accompany them. The Rev. H. H. Spalding and his wife, who had been recently married, were at length induced to go. Then, all other necessary arrangements having been made, Dr. Whitman and Miss Prentice were married, and the four young people started on one of the most formidable wedding journeys ever undertaken. The company was composed of Dr. and Mrs. Whitman, Mr. and Mrs. Spalding, H. H. Gray, two teamsters and two Indian boys who had accompanied Dr. Whitman on his return from the West.

The American Fur Company was sending out a large expedition to Oregon which Dr. Whitman expected to join at Council Bluffs, and great was the consternation of himself and his companions on arriving at that place to find the company already gone, its members not caring to wait, as they feared ladies might prove a very troublesome burden on such a rough journey. Nothing daunted, Dr. Whitman decided to follow them as rapidly as possible, and here the Indian boys proved to be of great service. The little party traveled for nearly a month before they overtook the fur company's caravan. Their route was now in an almost unknown part of the country, and led them across rivers and over deserts and mountains. While they were passing through the buffalo country, food was easy to obtain, but afterward game was much more difficult to secure, and at times they were reduced to a diet of dried buffalo meat and tea.

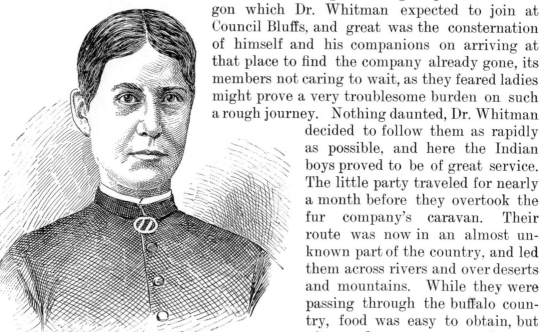

MRS. NARCISSA PRENTICE WHITMAN.

In spite of all drawbacks and efforts to persuade him to leave it behind, Dr. Whitman persisted in hauling along the wagon which afterward had so much influence on the destiny of that country. It was always getting stuck in the creeks and rivers and being upset on the steep mountain sides, and made it necessary for him to walk over all the most difficult portions of the way. Even his wife did not sympathize with him in this effort, but with undaunted courage he persisted, realizing the importance of getting it through.

On reaching the Green River they were met by the Cayuse and Nez Percé Indians, who were awaiting the return of Dr. Whitman and the boys who had left them the year before. The Indians were delighted to see

them and paid them the most delicate attentions.   After the little missionary band reached Walla Walla, before deciding on a permanent location,
they decided to consult the ruling powers of Oregon, the officials of the
Hudson Bay Company, at Vancouver.   Dr. McLoughlin, chief factor of this
company, received them cordially and decided that Dr. Whitman had better
begin his work in the Walla Walla country three hundred miles away, and
Mr. Spalding a hundred and twenty-five miles further on.

Dr. Whitman built his little house on a peninsula formed by the
branches of the Walla River, in what is now
one of the most fertile and beautiful portions
of Washington.   The Indians called it
Wai-i-lat-pui, meaning "the
place of rye grass."   One of the
first efforts of Dr. Whitman
was to induce his Indians
to raise their own grain, fruits
and vegetables.

All the missionaries in that
part of the country believed
that under the existing treaty
between the United States
and Great Britain, the nation
which first settled and organized the territory would
hold it.   The glowing accounts
given of the soil, climate, great forests and indications of mineral
wealth had induced a small number
of Americans to immigrate, and in the
vicinity of each mission was quite a population of farmers and traders.   In 1840–41
many of them met and discussed the subject

THE OLD WAGON.

of organizing a government under the American flag, but were unable to do
so, being outnumbered by the English.   In the fall of 1842 Elijah White, an
Indian agent for the government, brought a party of Americans, men, women
and children, numbering one hundred and twenty, to Waiilatpui.   Among
this party was a most intelligent gentleman, General Amos L. Lovejoy,
who was thoroughly informed in national affairs, and told Dr. Whitman of
the treaty then pending between England and the United States regarding

the boundary line between the United States and the British possessions in North America.

The statesmen of this period were ignorant on the question of the great value of the territory in dispute, and the "interminable desert," "arid plains" and "impassable mountains" were constantly quoted as impediments in the way to a country, most of which was "as irreclaimable and barren a waste as the Desert of Sahara." All this ignorance was the

WHITMAN PLEADING FOR OREGON BEFORE DANIEL WEBSTER AND PRESIDENT TAYLOR.

result of the teachings of the Hudson Bay Company, which, wishing to secure a monopoly of the country, constantly decried it and endeavored to persuade all outsiders of its worthlessness. In this they succeeded so well that, although our statesmen were thoroughly persuaded of the justice of the claims of the United States, they regarded the country as being of so little value that they were very little concerned when, in the Ashburton Treaty of 1843, Oregon was again ignored, the mind of Daniel Webster, the then Secretary of State, having been concentrated during the negotiations on the question of a few thousand acres, more or less, in Maine.

When General Lovejoy left for Oregon this treaty was still under consideration, and when through him Dr. Whitman learned of the state of affairs at Washington, he determined to go there and explain to the authorities the true value of the country they were about to allow to slip from their grasp. He consulted with his brother missionaries and received their hearty concurrence, but they were not willing to allow him to undertake such a journey alone. When a volunteer was called for, General Lovejoy, who had just finished his tedious five months' journey to Oregon, promptly offered to retrace his way to assist Dr. Whitman in his great endeavor.

Before leaving, Dr. Whitman made a visit to Fort Walla Walla to procure the necessaries for his journey, and while there an express messenger of the Hudson Bay Company arrived from Fort Colville, three hundred and fifty miles up the Columbia, with the announcement that a colony of one hundred and forty Englishmen and Canadians were on their way. Great was the joy among the Englishmen present, and a young priest expressed the sentiments of most of the people present when he threw his cap into the air and shouted, "Hurrah for Oregon—America is too late; we have got the country!" Naturally Dr. Whitman did not share in the general pleasure, but carefully avoided all mention of his purpose in going to Washington, and on his return to his home hastened his preparations for departure. On the third day of October, 1842, he bade his young wife a reluctant good-bye, and with General Lovejoy and one guide set out on a journey whose success or failure meant so much to our whole country.

He reached Fort Hall, in the southeastern part of Idaho, at the end of eleven days, and thus far the journey was comparatively easy, as each member of the party was familiar with the road. Captain Grant, the commanding officer at Fort Hall, had for years done all in his power to discourage immigration to that part of the country, and, with the single exception of Dr. Whitman, he had been uniformly successful in persuading settlers that they would be unable to move their wagons, and consequently the greater part of their goods, across the mountains, thus compelling them to go on horseback or on foot for the remainder of the way. He now suspected that the missionary had some important business on hand, and tried in every possible way to thwart it. He dwelt on the hopelessness of crossing the Rocky Mountains, already covered with snow in some places twenty feet deep, and on the almost certain death of anyone who might encounter the Pawnee or Sioux Indians who were then at war with each other.

Dr. Whitman fully realized the difficulties and dangers attending his enterprise, but he refused to return and Captain Grant had no authority to stop him, as he carried with him a permit signed "Lewis Cass, Secretary of War." Instead of turning back he set out in a southeasterly direction over a route to the States, untrodden, as far as he knew, by the foot of a white man. The course he pursued took him past the vicinity of the present Salt Lake City, Fort Uintah in the northeastern part of Utah, Fort Uncompahgre in the western part of Colorado, and from there down into New Mexico to Santa Fé, thence back into Colorado to Bent's Fort, from which point his way lay in a generally easterly direction through the States of Kansas and Missouri to St. Louis.

The weather the little party encountered was terribly severe, and they were obliged to change guides several times. On their way to Taos, New Mexico, they met with a terrible snowstorm which compelled them to seek shelter in a defile of the mountains, where in spite of all efforts to get away they were detained for ten days. At the end of that time they contrived to make a fresh start, but soon encountered a snowstorm so severe that it almost blinded them and made the mules unmanageable. At last the guide stopped and acknowledged that he could show them the way no further, and on attempting to retrace their steps, they found that all traces had been completely covered by the fast falling snow. They knew not which way to turn, and after coming so far, it seemed that they must perish in the snow with their errand still unaccomplished.

In this extremity General Lovejoy tells us that "Dr. Whitman dismounted, and, upon his knees in the snow, commended himself, his distant wife, his missionary companions and work, and his Oregon, to the Infinite One for guidance and protection.

"The lead mule, left to himself by the guide, turning his long ears this way and that, finally started, plunging through the snowdrifts, his Mexican guide and all the party following instead of guiding, the old guide remarking: 'This mule will find the camp if he can live long enough to reach it.' And he did."

On returning to the camp the guide refused to go any further with them, which was a terrible blow to Dr. Whitman as they had already lost much valuable time. He told General Lovejoy to remain in the camp and rest while he returned to Fort Uncompahgre for another guide, whom he brought back at the end of a week. The Grand River at the point they encountered it, was about six hundred feet wide ; for two hundred feet on either shore the water was frozen solid, and a terrible torrent two hundred feet wide rushed between. The guide declared that it was impossible to cross, but Dr. Whitman plunged boldly in, and his horse with great difficulty succeeded in swimming to the other shore, and then the rest followed. Owing to the many delays, they had consumed all their provisions, and were obliged to subsist upon a dog and a mule they had killed, but on reaching Santa Fé they were again abundantly supplied with provisions.

When near Bent's Fort, Colorado, Dr. Whitman pushed ahead to try to meet a party of men who he had heard were on their way to St. Louis. But he lost his way, and when he finally reached the fort, some time after his companions arrived there, he was exhausted and almost discouraged. Still, he delayed only a single night, and hurried on to overtake the party which had already started, while General Lovejoy remained at the fort until he had recovered from his exertions.

The trail to St. Louis was a most dangerous one, being infested with wild beasts and savages, but he reached that town in safety and learned that the Ashburton treaty had been signed August 9, 1842, nearly two months before he left Oregon. But this treaty only related to the Maine boundary, so there was still hope that he would be in time to save Oregon for the Union.

When he reached the capital he was worn and exhausted, and his hands, feet and ears had all been frozen; but he cared little for this if the President and Secretary of State would only grant him an interview to enable him to explain to them the great mistake they would make if they permitted Oregon to slip from their grasp, and this he had no difficulty whatever in securing.

Long before Dr. Whitman reached Washington there was an understanding that the settlement of the boundary question between Oregon and the British possessions had been delayed because there were negotiations pending looking to the exchange of the American interests in Oregon for the fisheries of Newfoundland. When he heard of this, Dr. Whitman assured Mr. Webster that it would be better to barter all New England for Newfoundland rather than part with Oregon. He told President Tyler and Mr. Webster of the fertile soil, of the healthful climate, of the great forests, of the indications of mineral wealth, only to be met with the supposed unanswerable objection that all this could not matter since Oregon was shut off by impassable mountains, and a great desert which made a wagon road impossible. It was then that the heroic missionary had his reward for all his toil and trouble in hauling his old wagon across the country, for he could now reply: " Mr. Secretary, that is the grand mistake

M—23

that has been made by listening to the enemies of American interests in Oregon. Six years ago I was told that there was no wagon road to Oregon, and that it was impossible to take a wagon there, and yet in despite of pleadings and almost threats, I took a wagon over the road, and have it now." This plain statement had an effect which any amount of argument and oratory could not have produced.

It was a new experience to these experienced politicians to meet a man who could plead so eloquently for the cause of his country, and still have no selfish interests of his own to serve, and when he asked that they would not barter away Oregon until they had given him an opportunity to lead a band of stalwart American settlers across the plains, they could not well refuse. After receiving this promise he hurried to Boston to report to the missionary board, who in turn severely censured him for leaving his station.

Meanwhile General Lovejoy had published far and wide that Dr. Whitman and himself would lead a party of emigrants across the country to Oregon early in the spring, and a rendezvous was appointed not far from the spot where Kansas City now stands. The grass that year was late and the band of emigrants did not start until the first week in June. The journey was long and dangerous, but was safely accomplished, and when in September one thousand immigrants with their wagons and stock entered the long disputed territory, the hearts of Dr. Whitman and all other patriotic Americans with him thrilled with joy as they realized that at last Oregon was saved to the Union.

That Dr. Whitman was the means of saving Oregon to the United States there can be no doubt. A Senate document, the forty-first Congress February 9, 1871, reads: "There is no doubt but that the arrival of Dr. Whitman, in 1843, was opportune. The delay incident to a transfer of negotiations to London was fortunate, for there is reason to believe that if former negotiations had been renewed in Washington, and that if for the sake of a settlement of the protracted controversy and the only remaining unadjudicated cause of difference between the two governments, the offer had been renewed of the 49th parallel to the Columbia and thence down the river to the Pacific Ocean, it would have been accepted. The visit of Whitman committed the President against any such action." Before Dr. Whitman left Washington a message was on its way to Mr. Everett, our minister to England telling him that "the United States will consent to give nothing below the latitude of forty-nine degrees."

After Dr. Whitman's return to Waiilatpui he resumed his labors among the Indians, and for a number of years devoted himself entirely to their

CHIRICHUA APACHES AS THEY ARRIVED AT CARLISLE FROM FORT MARION. FLORIDA, NOVEMBER 4, 1885.

THE SAME CHILDREN FOUR MONTHS AFTER ARRIVING AT CARLISLE.— SEE PAGE 350.

interests, healing the sick, teaching the ignorant, and counting no labor too great if it resulted in their benefit. Yet the Indians seemed changed. When the Whitmans first began to work among them they were willing to comply with all requests, but now for some years a feeling of dissatisfaction had been slowly creeping in. The missionaries insisted on their cultivating the ground and supporting themselves by their own labor, and of this mode of life the Indians soon grew weary. They were also instigated to deeds of violence by various enemies of the missionaries. Although Dr. Whitman was aware of the existence of this hostile spirit, it seemed impossible to believe in the existence of any real danger in the face of his loving service among them for eleven years, when on the 28th of November, 1847, an Indian named Istikus, who was the firm friend of Dr. Whitman, told him of threats against his life and also that he had better "go away until my people have better hearts." Knowing Istikus as he did, the brave missionary for the first time became seriously alarmed, and began to think of removing his family to some place of safety, but still went about his work as usual.

The next morning the doctor assisted in burying an Indian, and having returned to his house, was reading. Several Indians were in the house; one sat down by him to attract his attention by asking for medicine, while another came behind him with a tomahawk concealed beneath his blanket, and with two blows brought him to the floor senseless; still he was not dead when another Indian, who was a candidate for admission to the church and on whom Dr. Whitman had bestowed numberless benefits, came in and cut his throat and mutilated his face, but even then the murdered man lingered until nearly night. This was only the beginning of a most sickening massacre in which fourteen people, including Mrs. Whitman, lost their lives.

It was believed by those familiar with the facts that this foul massacre was instigated by the enemies of the people murdered and of the cause in which they were engaged.

Despite his cruel and bloody death, the missionary work of Marcus Whitman was far from fruitless. Though the work of the American Board ended so suddenly and disastrously, years afterward it was found that many of the Indians were still faithful to the religion taught them by Dr. and Mrs. Whitman. Neither will his name be forgotten so long as the walls of Whitman College stand as a monument to the memory of a man who was glad to suffer untold privations for the good of his country and his fellow men, and at last perished through his devotion to his duty.

If Dr. Whitman could to-day make the long journey from the Columbia to the national capital on the banks of the Potomac, and could the institutions of learning and church spires now standing in the districts, villages, towns and cities through which he would pass be placed in line at convenient distances, he would never for a moment be out of sight of these objects most pleasing to him in life.

CHAPTER XXXI.

DEPARTMENT OF THE COLUMBIA.

THE INDIAN SIGN LANGUAGE — THE CHINOOK LANGUAGE — VANCOUVER BARRACKS — TROOPS IN
THE DEPARTMENT — WORK ACCOMPLISHED — UNEXPLORED REGIONS — EXPEDITION OF
LIEUTENANT SYMONS — OF LIEUTENANT PIERCE — OTHER SURVEYS — VISIT OF
GENERAL SHERMAN — EFFECT OF RAILROAD BUILDING — NEW COAST
BATTERIES — RESERVATIONS AND NUMBER OF INDIANS.

N assuming command of the Department of the Columbia, August 2, 1881, I found the headquarters located at Vancouver Barracks, on the right bank of the Columbia River, in what was then Washington Territory. This post is six miles north of Portland, Oregon, and was formerly an old Hudson Bay trading station, having been located there during the early days when the principal commerce of the territory was in the form of barter with the Indians for the furs which were the chief articles of merchandise at that time.

In order to communicate with the different tribes scattered over that vast territory it had become necessary to invent or create a common language. For, unlike the Indians east of the Rocky Mountains, the tribes on the Pacific seaboard spoke tribal languages, and had no common means of communication. The various tribes of Plains Indians communicated with each other by means of what is known as the sign language. Motions, and positions of the fingers and hands, conveyed their ideas and constituted a language almost identical with that used by the deaf and dumb of the present day in the asylums and schools established for their benefit.* In the absence of any such method of communication, the Hudson Bay fur traders were obliged to create one, and this eventually came to be known as the Chinook language, consisting of a few words whose meaning was agreed upon to express the ideas most used in ordinary conversation. This was adopted by nearly all the tribes

---

The difference being that the deaf mutes use our common alphabet, each sign meaning a letter, and that words are in their way spelled out by them in talking. To the Plains Indians an alphabet was unknown, and with them a sign might express an animal, an occurrence, a day, an entire fact of any kind.

on the Pacific Coast, and is still understood by some of the tribes now in Alaska.

Vancouver Barracks was located near the town of Vancouver, on the Columbia, and upon a mesa a few hundred feet above the level of that river, on a command-ing position overlook-ing the beautiful valley, and within sight of the picturesque Cascade range, which embraces a cluster of the grandest mountains on the con-tinent. The post was at that time commanded by Colonel Henry H. Morrow, Twenty-First In-fantry, a

THE SIGN LANGUAGE.

most accomplished and gallant soldier and a man of great learning. He was a fine lawyer, having been a judge on the bench in Michigan during a period of ten years at a very early age. He afterward won high dis-tinction in the Civil War, reaching the rank of general, and being, in addition, breveted for extraordinary gallantry.

I found in the Department of the Columbia a force of over fifteen hundred troops, located at the various military stations which were scat-tered over a territory (not including Alaska) about two hundred and fifty thousand square miles in extent. This vast region was then occupied only by scattered settlements, ranches, mining camps, and isolated homes. It was also the home of bands of nomadic Indians. The interests and welfare of the two races were constantly clashing, and there was danger of serious hostilities at any moment. The white settlers looked to the army for defence, and the Indians in turn applied to the military for the protection of their rights and privileges.

In order to make the best use of troops, measures were taken to facilitate communication between these scattered posts, to aid in the concentration of the available forces, and at the same time to promote their general efficiency. In addition to their ordinary duties the troops were put to work in the construction of military roads and the establishment of military telegraph lines. These not only added to the efficiency of the military force, but also greatly benefited the citizens. Measures were also taken at all the military posts to improve the physical condition of the troops by a thorough system of athletic drills and exercises. Colonel Morrow was one of the first to establish what has since been so beneficial to the army, the Canteen Exchange. This is really a post club for the benefit of the soldiers. One of the first, largest, and best of the military gymnasiums was established at Vancouver.

During this year facilities were afforded the soldiers with families to provide homes for themselves at the expiration of their term of service, and to secure suitable employment. All the troops in the department were thoroughly equipped for immediate field service; each company, troop, and battery was made a unit of organization and demonstration. Each had its allowance of field equipment, including tents, field supplies, transportation, cooking utensils, extra clothing, hospital supplies, and everything required for immediate and continuous service in the field, and enough to last for several months.

In the department were several sections of country that had not been fully explored, and other sections of whose topography there was no knowledge whatever. With a view of obtaining the knowledge which would be indispensable in case the country had to be occupied by the military, and that would also be valuable to citizens seeking a knowledge of those districts, I organized several exploring expeditions. In fact, during the four years in which I was in command of that department, there was constantly some expedition in the field obtaining information about those interesting and to a great extent unknown portions of our country.

In January, 1882, Lieutenant Thomas W. Symons made an exploration and examination of the Columbia River from the line of British Columbia to the mouth of the Snake River, and obtained much valuable information concerning that extensive district.

In July of the same year an expedition was organized to explore the region between the upper Columbia and Puget Sound, then but little known. It was a small expedition, and was placed under the command of Lieutenant Henry H. Pierce of the Twenty-first United States Infantry, who performed the duty in a most efficient manner.

After making the necessary preparations at Fort Colville, the above mentioned expedition left that place on the first of August, and the next day crossed the Columbia by ferry and encamped on the western side. From there the Columbia was skirted along a good trail for a distance of six miles; thence the expedition moved westward past lofty mountains, dashing torrents and beautiful lakes, fording numerous creeks and rivers, and at the end of ten days reached the Okinakane, a swift, deep river that flows into the Columbia from the north.

From one of his camps on this river, Lieutenant Pierce desired to send back a telegram and letters to Fort Colville, and engaged an old Indian to carry them. Before giving the Indian his compensation, Lieutenant Pierce asked him if he was an honest man; not that he doubted him, but he wished to hear his answer. With great dignity, and with something of an injured look, the old man replied, " Me honest Indian. Me afraid to do wrong for fear some one there," pointing upwards, "see me and be angry." Then shaking hands, he mounted his pony and rode slowly away.

Leaving the Okinakane, they passed over to the Methow. The latter is a beautiful stream, so clear that the granite boulders beneath its surface may be plainly seen as it winds along its tortuous course, fringed on either side with poplars, balms and evergreens, and draining an extremely fertile country. Then, still moving toward the west, they journeyed on between lofty mountains and over dizzy paths where a downward glance was enough to make the firmest head to reel; fording turbulent rivers, pushing through almost impenetrable underbrush, crossing swampy areas, they went on until at last they gained the passage of the main cascades. Here they were beset by so many obstacles that it was almost impossible for them to proceed further, but their courage and perseverance finally overcame every difficulty and they reached the other side of the mountains in safety. From here they followed the course of the Cascade River, crossing it several times, down to the point where it empties into the Skagit. For their passage down that river they were fortunate enough to obtain canoes from the Indians, and on September 5, landed at Mount Vernon to await the coming of the steamer.

This reconnoissance of two hundred and ninety-five miles was through a country never before, so far as known, visited by white men, and was the first contribution to its geography.

Other surveys and reconnoissances were made of which the following were the more important; reconnoissance from Fort Townsend, Washington, to the Dungeness River; reconnoissance through Bruneau and Duck Valleys, Idaho; reconnoissance of the country bordering on the Sprague River, Oregon; surveying route for telegraph line between Forts Klamath, Oregon, and Bidwell, California, and from Fort Spokane to Spokane Falls; surveying route for road from Fort Colville to Fort Spokane, Washington; march of instruction from Fort Lapwai to the Lolo Trail, Idaho.

DIZZY HEIGHTS.

At this time the condition of the various Indian tribes in the territory was satisfactory, and they were in better condition to receive the full benefits of protection and share the responsibilities of civil government than was generally supposed.

In August, 1882, General Sherman visited the northern posts in the Department of the Columbia, on his last official tour of inspection, and was received with every token of respect and affection. He expressed himself as much pleased with the military bearing and discipline of the troops.

The construction of the Northern Pacific Railway and other routes of travel made a great change in the means of communication with that northwest country, making it possible to move troops in a single day as great a distance as would previously have occupied several weeks. As far as possible, I discontinued the small and ineffective posts and concentrated the troops in larger garrisons where they would have better advantages in the way of instruction and discipline, and could be maintained at less expense. Fort Canby at the mouth of the Columbia River, Forts Walla Walla, Spokane, Cœur d'Alène, and Sherman, were made the principal posts of the department, with troops stationed for immediate use in the sections of country most liable to Indian hostility, while Vancouver Barracks served as a station for a strong reserve force for the entire department. This last-named post was particularly adapted to the purpose mentioned, owing to its near proximity to Portland, Oregon, which, from its railroad connection and river and ocean service, was accessible from all sections of the country.

In 1884, in spite of its great commercial importance, and the large number of thriving towns that had grown up on its shores, Puget Sound was still in a defenseless condition. The government had reserved important sites for batteries and defensive works at the entrance of the sound, and during the year mentioned I ordered a board of experienced artillery officers to report as to their relative importance, and the proper armament, garrison, and work necessary to place them in proper condition for use.

Having occasion to mount one battery of artillery, I secured several Hotchkiss revolving cannon, invented by an American and manufactured in Paris, France, and the result of the practice with these was most satisfactory. Although the fact of a cannon being fired from the shoulder of an artillerist seemed somewhat novel, yet experience proved these guns to be the most destructive that had up to that time been used in the United States army. It is singular that many American inventors have to go to Europe to have their inventions adopted. Here was a case of an American officer on the Pacific Coast making application for a certain class of artillery guns; they were manufactured in Paris, bought by our government, shipped across the Atlantic, then across the continent and placed in service on the Columbia River.

Instruction in signaling and the familiarizing the troops with the use of the latest modern appliances received attention at all the posts in the department, and experiments were made with the heliostat with most gratifying results. From Vancouver Barracks to the summit of Mount Hood, fifty miles in an air line, these flashes of the heliostat could be distinctly seen with the naked eye.

Owing to the rapid settlement of the country the lower Columbia Indians were in many cases unjustly deprived of their cultivated grounds, their salmon fisheries, and other means of support, and I had great difficulty in preventing active hostilities between them and the settlers. The Indians were finally pacified, however, and numbers of them were assisted by the military in locating their claims to homesteads under the laws of Congress.

In the Territory of Washington there were in 1884 fifteen Indian reservations, inhabited by over ten thousand six hundred Indians. The total amount of land comprised within these reservations was over six hundred thousand acres, and consisted largely of the best agricultural, grazing, timber and mineral lands in the Territory. In many places the Indians were engaged in cultivating the soil with good results, the system of allotting a suitable quantity of land to them in severalty having a most excellent effect.

CHAPTER XXXII.

CHIEF MOSES AND HIS TRIBE.

THE BEGINNING OF TROUBLE — CHIEF MOSES AND THE MOSES RESERVATION — CAUSES OF DISSATIS-
FACTION — ACTION OF COLONEL MERRIAM — INVESTIGATION BY CAPTAIN BALDWIN —
MEETING AND COUNCIL AT VANCOUVER — A NEW TREATY AND A NEW
RESERVATION — THE RESULTS — LOOPLOOP'S STATEMENT OF THE
SITUATION — REVIEW OF THE NEZ PERCÉ SITUA-
TION ON THEIR FINAL RETURN FROM
THE INDIAN TERRITORY.

ONTROVERSIES arose in 1878 between the Indians of the upper Columbia and the white people of Yakima County and vicinity. These troubles eventually resulted in the arrest of Chief Moses, who was a prominent character, although many of the Indians did not recognize him as having any authority over them. Chief Moses was kept in prison for some time, but this did not allay the restlessness of his followers, and additional troops were sent to the Yakima Valley.

In 1879 Moses, with a number of other Indians, was sent to Washington, where he made a treaty with the Secretary of the Interior by which a tract of land was set apart for the use of himself and his people. This reservation was bounded on the east by the Okinakane River, on the south by the Columbia and Lake Chelan, on the west by the forty-fourth parallel, and extended to the Canadian boundary on the north. The country in question embraced approximately four thousand two hundred square miles, known as the Moses reservation, and was worth many millions of dollars. Certain white men afterward declared that they had discovered mines and occupied ranches on this reservation long before it was transferred to the Indians. This region was rich in agricultural, pastoral and mineral resources and contained rich deposits of gold and silver.

The benefits intended to be secured by this treaty did not last very long, as Moses and the other Indians soon complained that its various provisions were not carried out by the government, while, on the other hand, citizens who had made their homes in the reservation before it became such, remonstrated strongly against a treaty by which they were deprived of their property and rights. These settlers had discovered, had claimed according to law, and had actually worked valuable mines located in Stevens County. There had even been voting precincts established, and elections had been held within its boundaries. In spite of these facts, when the Moses reservation was set apart by executive order all these people were peremptorily told that they must leave that part of the country, although some of them had lived there for many years. They, however, did not all obey the order. The Indians grew more and more dissatisfied, and Moses demanded that if the white people would not leave, they should at least acknowledge their holdings to be on an Indian reservation and ask his permission to work their mines.

An executive order restoring a strip of land fifteen miles wide south of the Canadian boundary was also much resented by the Indians.

At last there were rumors that a general war council of the Indians had been called, whereupon Colonel Merriam, a very intelligent and judicious officer of the Second United States Infantry, the commander at Fort Spokane, was assigned the duty of adjusting the causes of dispute. This he endeavored to do by rigidly excluding white settlers from any part of the Moses reservation south of the fifteen-mile limit of the strip above mentioned, that had been restored

WATCHING THE COMING OF THE WHITE MAN

to the public domain by executive order. Indians who had farms on this strip were recognized by him as having the same rights on unreserved public land as the white people had.

In May, 1883, Captain Baldwin, one of the most judicious and competent officers I had in that department, was ordered to proceed to the Moses and Colville reservations, and investigate the reported dissatisfaction of the Indians located there. On the Colville reservation he succeeded in meeting Tonasket, head chief of the Okinagans, and found him an intelligent, industrious Indian, much respected by all his people as well as by the white settlers. He said that neither he nor his band desired to have trouble with the white people, but on the contrary wished to live in peace with them if possible. He complained that their agent had not visited them for several years. These Indians greatly desired a gristmill, as they were obliged to take their grain thirty miles into British Columbia in order to have it ground, and even then the miller claimed one-half of it for toll. They were also anxious for a sawmill and other appliances used by civilized people.

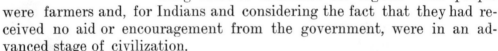

After Captain Baldwin's conversation with Tonasket, Sarsopkin, a chief of the Okinagans on the Moses reservation, came to him to have a talk. This Indian and his followers were the ones who really had to suffer from the restoration of the fifteen-mile strip, as they had lived within its boundaries and cultivated the farms there for many years. Sarsopkin expressed a strong desire to remain in the place which had been his home for generations, but disclaimed all idea of using force to maintain his rights. His people

CAPTAIN BALDWIN.

were farmers and, for Indians and considering the fact that they had received no aid or encouragement from the government, were in an advanced stage of civilization.

All the Indians who were approached on the subject, united in expressing the same views; and all complained very bitterly because Moses was recognized by the government as their chief. Both Tonasket and Sarsopkin asked: " Why does the government place over us, who make our living by farming, a man who never works, but gambles, drinks and races horses with the money he collects from the white men who graze cattle on our reservation? We want a chief who works, and sets a good example for our young men." Nearly all the Indians expressed a desire to have the white people come among them and work the mines, but emphatically expressed their determination not to allow them to usurp the farming and pasture lands. They reasoned in this way: " When the white men come and get the money out of the rocks they will give it to us for what we can grow from the ground, and for our cattle and horses, and in this way we will get rich like the white men."

Regardless of these friendly protestations on the part of many Indians, the hostile feeling between the two races increased until it became so violent that a serious Indian war was threatened. The white people seemed determined to exterminate the Indians, and the Indians to annihilate the white settlers or drive them out of the country. Realizing the difficulties, expenses and sacrifices, as well as the cruelties of Indian warfare, I thought it better if possible to endeavor to secure justice for the Indians, and, at the same time, protection for the white settlers. I therefore sent out officers to find Chief Moses and other prominent men, and summon them to my headquarters at Vancouver, for counsel. When they came I listened to all their grievances and their statements of what they believed to be their rights; what they expected the government to guarantee to do for them, and also to their recital of the aggressions of the white people. I also heard the accounts of the depredations of the Indians and their trespasses upon the property of the white settlers. With a view of settling the whole difficulty without proceeding to hostilities, I obtained permission to send a delegation of the Indians, accompanied by Captain Baldwin, to Washington, that they might have an opportunity to negotiate a treaty that would be satisfactory to both Indians and settlers, and at the same time be creditable to the general government.

On the 7th of July, 1883, they made an agreement with the Secretary of the Interior, whereby they engaged to give up all claim to the Columbia or Moses reservation, and remove to the Colville reservation. In consideration of this concession, Moses and Tonasket were to receive an annuity of $1,000 each as long as they lived. Moses was also to receive a house costing $1,000. For the benefit of the whole number of Indians, two schoolhouses were to be built and two sawmills and gristmills. There were to be provided, three teachers, two sawyers, two millers, and one doctor, for the use of each of whom a house was to be erected. Four hundred and sixty cows were to be furnished, as well as a large number of wagons and agricultural implements. The Indians already located on the Moses reservation who wished to remain were to be allowed to take up land there in severalty under existing laws.

On the 31st of August an order was issued, directing Captain Baldwin to visit the Indians concerned in this agreement and explain to them all its terms and effects. First Lieutenant James Ulio, Second Lieutenant John S. Mallory, and Topographical Assistant Alfred Downing were detailed to assist him in carrying out these instructions.

All necessary preparations having been concluded at old Fort Colville, on September 10, Captain Baldwin directed Lieutenant Ulio to proceed to the southern portion of the Moses reservation, explain the agreement to the Indians, and should any of them desire it, locate and carefully survey for each head of a family or male adult, a tract of land containing not more than six hundred and forty acres.

Topographical Assistant Downing was detached under orders to proceed to, and carefully examine the falls of Bonaparte Creek and the Nespilene, where it was proposed to locate the promised sawmills and gristmills. Lieutenant Mallory remained with the main party until the 13th, when he was sent to that part of the Columbia reservation lying north of the region to be examined by Lieutenant Ulio.

The result of his own investigations satisfied Captain Baldwin that great good had been effected by the visit of the three chiefs to Washington. They had all carefully explained the agreement to their people, who seemed disposed to look upon it favorably. Sarsopkin and his following, without an exception, were willing to move to the Colville reservation, many of them having even gone so far as to select the location of their future homes. On the 18th Captain Baldwin dispatched a messenger to Moses to notify him that he desired to see him, and the chief arrived on the evening of the 20th, having ridden eighty miles that day. He said that all his people had made up their minds to go with him to the Colville reservation, and would be ready as soon as the fishing season was over. This band was made up of what were known as "wild" Indians; they had always depended upon fish (salmon) and game

CHERUBS, INDIAN BABIES IN THEIR CRADLES.

for food, and knew absolutely nothing about farming.

Tonasket, the principal chief of the Colville Indians, was a man of great force of character. Although he had received little or no help from the government, he exhibited a deep interest in the fortunes of his people, urging them to work and take up lands, but his greatest desire was to see a suitable school provided for them. He and his people not only consented that all the Indians on the Columbia should establish themselves on the Colville reservation, but that all others who wished to settle down and become industrious farmers should enjoy its benefits. Captain Baldwin was much pleased with the members of Tonasket's band, considering them further advanced in civilization than any Indians he had seen west of the Mississippi.

Lieutenant Ulio visited a number of families, five of whom consented to allow him to locate farms for them. He also had a conversation with Chelan Jim, who had become the recognized chief of a small band of Indians. At first this man refused to either locate any land or to move on the Colville reservation, but afterward he consented to consider the matter.

Lieutenant Mallory, after leaving Captain Baldwin's camp near the junction of Curlew Creek with Kettle River, continued over the Little Mountain trail to the mouth of the creek just mentioned, and from there over a magnificent belt of country to the lake where the creek takes it source. This lake proved to be a beautiful body of water about eight and a half miles in length. Soon afterward he came to another lake, much smaller than the first and oval in shape, which proved to be the source of the San Polle River. He had never seen a map on which either of these lakes was noted. Having crossed the Okinakane and marched along its farther bank for some distance, he came upon several ranches owned by Indians. One of them named Looploop was a man about fifty years of age, with a thoughtful, intelligent face. In a long talk with Lieutenant Mallory this Indian expressed his opinion very freely, both concerning the pretensions of Moses and the general situation of affairs, and as he voiced the sentiments of a great many others his words are worth repeating. He said: "There are four things above all others which you white men tell us we should avoid; lying, thieving, drunkenness and murder. Moses is a liar; Moses is a thief; Moses is a drunkard, and Moses is a murderer. Yet, he is the man you have set as chief over us, and he is the man you send to Washington to represent us. He has traded away our rights, he has sold our lands, and there is no help for us. He will have a fine house built for him and will get one thousand dollars every year, and he and his people will be given wagons and harnesses and many cows. Looploop is not a beggar; he has never asked nor received any help from the government, nor does he ask it now. He is able to take care of himself; and all that he asks is to be let alone. When Moses came back from Washington the first time, there was a great council between the whites and the Indians. General Howard stood up in the midst and said: ' The Indians have for many years been wanderers from place to place and there has been no rest for any of them, but now they are to have a reservation — Moses — which will be a home for them forever. While the mountains stand and the rivers run the land is to be theirs, their children's and their children's children's forever.'

M—24

INDIAN WEAPONS.

1. Comanche Tomahawk.
2. Ute Tomahawk Pipe.
3. Bow Case and Quiver of the Bannock Indians.
4-5. Sioux War Clubs.
6-7-8. Sioux Bows and Arrows.

9. Comanche War Shield.
10-11. Sioux War Clubs.
12. Comanche Tomahawk Pipe.
13. Tomahawk Pipe which once belonged to Little Bear, a prominent chief of the Northern Apaches

" The Indians heard ; they believed and were satisfied. Scarcely four years have passed by and we are told that we must leave this reservation, this land which was to be our home forever. How do we know that if we move to the Colville reservation we will be left in peace? Why should we not be driven from there in a few years, and then what can we do? There is no other place left. But you tell us that we who do not recognize Moses or any other chief, are not obliged to leave our home; that you will mark out for each of us a square mile and will set stakes so that no white man can take the land away from us; and you wish to know whether we will go or stay. There are but few of us here, and our blood is the same, but our minds are different. As for me, why should I go? Here I have a house, and fields that raise oats and hay and all kinds of vegetables. When white men pass through here they need these things and pay me for them. Did you not, yesterday, give me $25 for one thousand pounds of oats? With money in my pocket, I feel that I am a man, and respect myself. Why should I give up all this, and move on the Colville reservation, to become a wild Indian again? But I am getting an old man now. My daughter is married and has children. I love them, and like to be with them ; but my son-in-law thinks he will go on the Colville reservation. My only son has two sons; sometimes he thinks he will go, and again he thinks he will stay. Our hearts are sad, and we know not what to do. You must give us time to think and talk among ourselves, and we will then tell you whether we will go or stay. But we cannot tell you to-day, or to-morrow, or for many days to come. Leave us now, and return after we have had time to think ; we will then know our minds, and what we say we will do."

Eventually, though only after much indecision, the Indians concerned in the matter all yielded, and the treaty went into full effect. But a long period elapsed before the government completely fulfilled its part of the agreement. Nevertheless, there was a marked improvement almost immediately. In 1885, when Captain Baldwin once more visited the valley of the Okinakane, where, in 1883, he had found only half a dozen farms, there were hundreds of acres fenced and under cultivation, almost every available spot on the river and its tributaries was occupied, and large herds of domestic stock belonging to the Indians were grazing on the hills.

In 1885 I at last succeeded in having the remnant of Chief Joseph's band of Nez Percé Indians brought back from the Indian Territory to the vicinity of their old home, as stated in a preceding chapter. Popular feeling in Idaho Territory was decidedly against them. Several Nez Percé warriors were under indictment for murders perpetrated in 1877, and as there had been rumors of threats of violence on the part of some of the white people, every precaution was taken to prevent collision between them and the Nez Percés while the latter were on their way back to the Northwest. The Nez Percés entered the Department of the Columbia in June by way of the Union Pacific and Oregon Short Line Railways, and were met at Pocatello by Captain Frank Baldwin, who was then acting judge advocate of that department.

After their arrival they were divided into two parties, one proceeding under military escort to the Lapwai agency in Idaho, and the other, including Chief Joseph, to the Colville reservation opposite Fort Spokane. The Indians who were taken to the Lapwai agency numbered one hundred and sixteen persons, who soon disappeared among their relatives and friends. Upon their arrival thirty days rations were supplied them, but after that they were self supporting with the exception of a few of the aged. Some of them afterward showed a desire to visit their old haunts in the Wallowa Valley, but readily acquiesced when told that it was not advisable for them to do so. Altogether, their conduct was most peaceful and satisfactory.

That portion of the band immediately under Chief Joseph, numbering one hundred and fifty persons, was in a most destitute condition, and many of them must have starved if the military had not come to their assistance. They were poorly clad, and were obliged to live in thin cotton tents. They had no cattle, tools or implements of any kind, those left behind in the Indian Territory not having been replaced. Both Chief Joseph and those under him showed every disposition to make homes for themselves, to settle down and live like white people, and to conform to every requirement of the government.

The tribe of Nez Percés was originally a confederacy of numerous bands, each with its own chief. Primarily the tribe occupied a large extent of territory west of the Bitter Root Mountains in Washington, Idaho and Oregon, their title running back to a time before the memory of man. In June, 1855, a treaty, which I have alluded to in a previous chapter, was concluded between the United States and the Nez Percés, by the terms of which a large part of their country was ceded to the United States, the Wallowa Valley being embraced within the land reserved. Several chiefs protested against this treaty, and Looking Glass and the father of Joseph signed it much against their will. In this, as in many other cases where an Indian

MAJOR-GENERAL GEORGE CROOK.

MAJOR-GENERAL ALFRED H. TERRY.—See Page 196.

(413)

treaty is concerned, its terms were not kept on the part of the United States.   In 1863, another treaty was negotiated which greatly reduced the reservation established by the treaty of 1855, and among the lands yielded in this case the Wallowa Valley was included.   A number of the chiefs refused to sign this treaty, and would never afterward recognize it as binding, but always repudiated it, refusing to accept any of its benefits.

These bitter feelings finally culminated in the Nez Percé war, by which a tribe of Indians that had always made the proud boast that no white man was ever slain by the hand of a Nez Percé, were driven to open hostilities, resulting in a serious war between the Nez Percés and the troops of General Howard in Idaho, a series of engagements between the Nez Percés and troops under General Gibbon in western Montana, and the pursuit and capture of the Nez Percés by troops under my command as related in a preceding chapter of this volume, and their final return, eight years later, reduced in numbers and in a wretched condition, to their country where they have since peacefully remained.

CHAPTER XXXIII.

Our Alaskan Possessions.

Discovery of Alaska by Behring — The Fur Hunters — The Russian Companies and Their
Successor — Sale of the Country to the United States — The Transfer — Vast Size
of Alaska — Climate — Mountains — Mount St. Elias — Glaciers — Muir
Glacier — Expedition of Lieutenant Schwatka — Character of the
Natives — Their Boats — Expedition of Lieutenant Aber-
crombie — The Copper River Country — Seals and
Their Rookeries — Salmon, and the Canning
Industry — British Strength in the
Northwest Territory.

EHRING'S famous voyage and the discovery of Alaska is the history of a series of privations and disasters. He set sail from Okhotsk in 1740, in a vessel called the "St Paul." He sighted and named the magnificent mountain St. Elias. Behring was finally wrecked on an island which now bears his name, and died there December 8, 1741, without ever attaining any benefit from his valuable discoveries. The vessel was little more than a wreck, but out of its ruins the crew managed to build a little shallop in which they set sail on the 16th of August, 1742. They finally reached civilization bearing with them a large number of valuable peltries, which stimulated the prompt fitting out of many new expeditions for Alaska.

These fur hunters ventured out from their headquarters at Kamchatka and by 1769 a large area of Russian America was well known to them. Prior to the establishment of the control of the Russian American Company over the whole of Alaska, more than sixty distinct Russian trade companies had been organized and had plied their vocation in these waters. In 1799 this last named company received a charter which conferred upon it very great privileges, but also burdened it with many obligations. It was obliged to maintain at its own expense the new government of the country, a church establishment, a military force, and at many points in the country magazines of provisions and stores to be used by the Imperial government for its naval vessels.

As time wore on it was found that Russian America did not prove as profitable to the home government as it ought, and in 1844 the Emperor Nicholas offered to sell the whole country to the United States for the mere cost of transfer if President Pierce would maintain the United States line at 54° 40' and shut England out from any frontage on the Pacific. In 1854 it was again offered to the United States, and yet·again in 1859, but with no result. But in 1867 Secretary Seward effected the purchase of the whole vast territory at the rate of about half a cent an acre. Figures show that from the very beginning Alaska has been to us a paying investment. The first lease of the two seal islands returned into the treasury a sum equal to the purchase money ($7,200,000). The gold mines have since added an equal sum to the wealth of the world, while the salmon fisheries in the six years from 1884 to 1890 yielded $7,500,000.

As soon as the treaty was ratified, immediate military possession was decided upon. The commissioners on behalf of both the United States and Russia, met at Sitka in October, 1869. Three men-of-war and two hundred and fifty troops were present on the afternoon when the Russians joined the United States officers at the foot of the government flagstaff. Double national salutes were fired by the men-of-war and a land battery as the Russian national flag was lowered and the American flag was raised. As soon as the United States took possession of Alaska all the Russian inhabitants who were able to travel left the country, their government giving them free transportation.

In 1877 the last garrison in Alaska was vacated, and a few months later the Indians had destroyed all government property outside the stockades, and threatened a massacre. Hearing of the desperate plight of the Americans the captain of an English ship which happened to be at Esquimault at the time, hastened to their assistance, and remained until a United States revenue cutter and a man-of-war arrived.

Alaska is nine times the size of New England, twice the size of Texas, and three times as large as California. It stretches for more than a thousand miles from north to south, and the Aleutian Islands encroach upon the eastern hemisphere, placing the geographical center of the United States on the point midway between the eastern and western extremities a little to the west of San Francisco. The island of Attu is two thousand miles west of Sitka, and it is as far from Cape Fox to Point Barrow as from the north of Maine to the southern extremity of Florida. The coast line has a length of more than 18,000 miles; greater than that of all the States bordering on the Atlantic, the Pacific and the Gulf of Mexico combined.

The climate and physical features of southeastern Alaska very much resemble those of southern Norway. While St. Johns, Newfoundland, is surrounded by icebergs in summer and its harbor is frozen solid in winter, Sitka, ten degrees farther north, has always an open roadstead. The thermometer rarely registers in winter as low as ten degrees below zero. It is the isothermal equal of the District of Columbia and Kentucky, skating being a rare sport for Sitkans. When William H. Seward was making his trip around the world he wrote from Berlin: "We have seen enough of Germany to know that its climate is neither so genial, nor its soil so fertile, nor its resources in forests and mines so rich as those of southern Alaska." The lofty mountain ranges and the Japan Current give southeastern Alaska a greater rainfall than that of Norway, the annual rainfall in Sitka averaging eighty-one inches. There have been wet seasons there in which there were respectively two hundred and eighty-five and three hundred and forty rainy days ; but all this moisture favors a luxuriant vegetation and keeps the foliage fresh during the greater part of the year.

Thunder storms are almost unknown, and there are beautiful auroral illuminations during the long winter nights. There have been only two great hurricanes since the transfer of the country, one occurring immediately after that event and the other in 1880. Fine grass springs naturally on any clearing ; coarser grasses grow three or four feet high, and clover thrives unheeded. Hay has been cured there since as early as 1805, and some varieties of vegetables have been raised. In summer there is usually about a fortnight of really very warm weather, and the days at that time of year are eighteen hours long.

The greater part of Alaska is exceedingly mountainous. The most celebrated of all her lofty summits is Mount St. Elias, the central peak of a crescent-shaped range of mountains on the southern coast of Alaska. This mountain lifts its glittering white head more than 19,000 feet above the level of the sea. The whole of this great peak is not often seen at one time, as a perfectly clear atmosphere is very rare in that region. The vapor from the warm ocean current is condensed into clouds as it strikes the frozen sides of the mountain, keeping it perpetually cloud-capped. Its summit is a bold pyramid placed on a rugged mountain mass, and surrounded by foot-hills each one of which is of sufficient size to be widely noted were it in any country where colossal peaks are not so common. The mountain can be distinctly seen one hundred and fifty miles at sea, and at that distance it appears to tower up with all the grandeur and beauty that ordinary mountains have when viewed from a short distance.

Some of the most magnificent glaciers to be found on the globe fill the gorges of the Alaskan mountain ranges. The Malaspine Glacier is one of the largest known. It is one vast, slowly-moving prairie of ice, and from the mountain spurs projecting into it one may look down upon it from a height of two or three thousand feet without being able to discover its southern limits. The outer border is covered with earth and supports a dense growth of vegetation, and in some places thick forests of spruce trees. These evergreen forests, with undergrowths of ferns and flowers, growing on living glaciers hundreds of feet thick, are among the most interesting features of Alaska. The entire region is remarkable for the glaciers which abound in the valleys and along the coasts. The Muir Glacier at Glacier Bay is one of the best known, its face being a solid wall of ice, two miles wide. Another glacier situated on the Stickine River is forty miles long and five miles wide. The Miles Glacier, so named by Lieutenant Abercrombie, who discovered it during his exploration of the Copper River country, is one of the largest and most interesting of these wonders of nature.

Some idea may be formed of these colossal glaciers by imagining a valley between two ranges of mountains packed solidly with ice, formed from the packed and semi-liquid snow of mountains from forty to fifty miles back from the rivers or bays into which the glaciers empty. Although actually in constant motion, the movement is so slow that it is imperceptible except from final results. The continual fall at the end of the glacier of masses of ice from the size of a man's hand to that of a block acres in extent, produces a noise like the constant roar of thunder, and is frequently heard eight or ten miles away. The glaciers that empty into bays and navigable rivers produce icebergs that are usually four or five times as deep below the surface of the water as they are above. These masses of ice are forced back against the faces of the glaciers when the tide is coming in, and are held there firmly until it goes out, when they again go rolling on their course to the sea. As the huge masses fall from the face of the glacier they produce a motion of the water which is sometimes dangerous to vessels in the immediate vicinity, and when the ice floe is moving out with the tide it sometimes becomes necessary for steamers to seek shelter behind some promontory.

The beauty and grandeur of these scenes is equal to anything that I ever witnessed. There is only one feature of nature that compares with it in grandeur, although of an entirely different character, and that is the geysers in the Yellowstone Valley. During our visit to Alaska it required twenty-four days going and returning, the distance being a thousand miles each way. Now the journey can be made in fourteen days, and even this time will be lessened as better facilities for travel are afforded.

In the year 1883 there were frequent reports of disturbances of the peace between the whites and Indians in Alaska which seemed to indicate that there might be serious hostilities between the two elements in the near future. Although the Territory was included within the geographical limits of the Department of Columbia, its area of nearly six hundred thousand square miles was practically an unexplored and unknown country, but little acquaintance having been made with its topographical features, the number and character of its inhabitants, its resources or climate. Deeming further information in these respects to be exceedingly desirable, in April, 1883, I sent one of my aides-de-camp, Lieutenant Frederick Schwatka, Third United States Cavalry, a distinguished explorer, together with Assistant-Surgeon Wilson and Topographical Assistant Homan and three soldiers, to Alaska to obtain intelligence of the country that might be of use to us in the case of any serious disturbance.

ALASKAN TOTEM.

Frederick Schwatka was born at Galena, Illinois, in September, 1849. He was appointed to the Military Academy from Oregon and graduated at West Point in 1871, after which he studied law, being admitted to the bar in 1875. He then took up the study of medicine, receiving his degree in New York in 1876. He was in command of the Franklin expedition which sailed for the Arctic regions in 1878, and which succeeded in finding many relics and evidences of the fate of Sir John Franklin's party, during its two years' absence. He afterward led various other exploring expeditions and has written many interesting books and articles concerning his travels. His death, which occurred a few years ago, was a severe loss to the scientific world.

Lieutenant Schwatka and his party left Portland, Oregon, on May 22, 1883, arriving at Pyramid Harbor in Chilcat Inlet early in June. The instructions of Lieutenant Schwatka were to " endeavor to complete all information in each section of country before proceeding to another, in order that if time should not permit the full completion of the work, it may be taken up the following season," and he accordingly selected the valley of the Yukon River as the district most important in the Territory. This great river rises in British Columbia at a point about two hundred miles northeast of Sitka, and forming the arc of a huge circle over two thousand miles in length, enters Behring Sea through an extensive delta. The volume of water which it pours into the sea is so great as to freshen the ocean ten miles from its mouth.

The difficulties that had been experienced by others in exploring the Yukon from its mouth, led Lieutenant Schwatka to believe that it might be easier to descend than to ascend, and he made his preparations with this end in view. He finally decided to make the attempt to reach its headwaters by way of the Chilcoot trail which leads up the inlet of the same name, to a branch called the Dayay, then through this to the mouth of the Dayay River, thence to its head, and thence across the mountains to Lake Lindeman. Here they stopped for the purpose of building a raft on which to descend the river. After the completion of this, they passed through several other lakes and their connecting streams, reaching Lake Marsh on the 29th of June. This is a body of water nearly thirty miles long, but filled with mud banks from one end to the other, making it extremely difficult to navigate even on a raft. From Lake Marsh they entered the Yukon River and on July 1, found themselves approaching the grand cañon of the Yukon. This is the only large cañon in the entire length of the great river, and was named by Schwatka after the department commander. The river, which before reaching this point is about three hundred and fifty yards in width here begins to grow narrower, until it is hardly more than thirty-five yards wide. The walls of the cañon are of perpendicular basalt nearly a mile in height, being widened in the center into a huge basin about double the usual width of the stream in the cañon, and this basin is full of whirlpools and eddies in which nothing but a fish could live. Through this cañon the wild waters rush in a perfect mass of foam, with a reverberation that can be heard a considerable distance away. Overhanging the cañon are huge spruce trees standing in gloomy rows. At the northern end the water spreads rapidly to its former width although not losing any of its swiftness, and falls in a wide, shallow sheet over reefs of boulders and drifts of huge timber. About four miles further down, the river grows narrower than ever, and the volume of water is so great that it ascends the sloping banks to a considerable height and then falls back into the narrow bed below.   The shooting of the cañon and rapids was an exciting adventure, and I will give Lieutenant Schwatka's experience in his own words.

"Everything being in readiness, our inspection made and our resolution formed, in the forenoon of the 2d of July, we prepared to shoot the raft through the rapids of the grand cañon, and at 11:25 the bow and stern lines were cast loose, and after a few minutes' hard work at shoving the craft out of the little eddy where she lay, the poor vessel resisting as if she knew all that was ahead of her and was loath to go, she finally swung clear of the point, and like a racer at the start, made almost a leap forward, and the die was cast.   A moment's hesitation at the cañon's brink, and quick as a flash the whirling craft plunged into the foam, and before twenty yards were made had collided with the western wall of the columnar rock with a shock as loud as a blast, tearing off the inner side log and throwing the outer one far into the stream.   The raft swung around this as upon a hinge, just as if it had been a straw in a gale of wind, and again resumed its rapid career.   In the whirlpool basin of the cañon, the craft, for a brief second or two, seemed actually buried out of sight in the foam.   Had there been a dozen giants on board they could have had no more influence in directing her course than as many spiders.   It was a very simple matter to trust the rude vessel entirely to fate, to work out its own salvation.   I was most afraid of the four miles of shallow rapids below the cañon, but she only received a dozen or a score of smart bumps that started a log here and there, but tore none from the structure, and nothing remained ahead of her but the cascades.   These reached, in a few minutes the craft was caught at the bow by the first high wave in the funnel-like chute and lifted into the air until it stood almost at an angle of thirty degrees, when it went through the cascades like a charge of fixed bayonets, and almost as swiftly as a flash of light, burying its nose in the foam beyond as it subsided.   Those on board the raft now got hold of a line from their friends on shore, and after breaking it several times they finally brought the craft alongside the bank and commenced repairing the damage with light hearts, for our greatest obstacle was now at our backs."

At various intervals below the cañon a number of large rivers flow into the Yukon, greatly increasing its width.   On the 12th of July they shot the Rink Rapids, the last rapids of importance on the river, and the next day reached the site of old Fort Selkirk, a trading post of the Hudson Bay Company which was burned in 1851 by a party of Indians because it interfered with their trade with other tribes. This was an important point on the Yukon, as above it the river had never before been explored.

From Fort Selkirk they went on down the river, passing a number of Indian villages and old Fort Yukon, which had been abandoned several years before, and on August 10, drifted by the spot known as "the rapids of the Yukon" which they had been dreading for some time, and which they feared might prove disastrous to their rough means of navigation. It was not until they had passed them that they observed the rapids at all, as they consisted of nothing but a bar of white boulders around which the water flowed as placidly as around any bar in the river. Some distance below these rapids they met a small steamer, one of the three that then comprised the entire steam fleet on the river. Not long afterward they were overtaken by another steamer, the "Yukon," which took them in tow as far as St. Michaels, where they arrived on the 30th of August. During this reconnoissance much valuable information was obtained regarding the inhabitants of the country, the whole number belonging to the various tribes observed by the expedition aggregating over eleven thousand.

Lieutenant Schwatka's exploration was one of exceeding interest and value, adding a very important chapter of information about that remote country. The territory he passed over, however, had not been entirely untraversed by prospectors and miners, as a few of those adventurous spirits had previously penetrated that country in search of gold and other minerals. Schwatka describes the country as of little value except for its fisheries and minerals. The summers along the Yukon Valley are of very short duration, and the country is so infested with mosquitoes as to make life there almost intolerable during

GROUP OF ESKIMO GIRLS.

that season, while the severity of its winters—the thermometer often registering sixty degrees below zero—makes it an equally undesirable country for occupation at that time of year.

Schwatka expresses the opinion that all other desirable parts of the United States will be occupied before that country is settled. Nevertheless, he describes the natives as a hardy, brave people, and most expert boat-builders. Their way of making these boats is very rude ; burning and hewing out great trees, which are then fashioned into well-drawn lines, making excellent boats capable of carrying thirty or forty people and pro-pelled by paddles or sails. With these rude crafts they do not hesitate to go out into the open sea of the Pacific, or to take journeys of three hundred miles along the coast outside the inland passage.

In their small canoes built of skins, in which one or two oarsmen are lashed, covered with water-tight, thin skin garments, they go out into the open sea to attack the sea otter, which is the most valuable fur-bearing animal in that country. The prows of these boats are built of such light material that it is impossible to keep them under water, and the water-proof garments of the oarsmen are fast-ened in such a way that not a drop can penetrate the interior of the boat, even though it should be entirely submerged

NATIVE KAYAKS.

or turned over by the surf. This being the case, when the canoe is capsized, as occasionally happens in passing through the surf, the light prow immediately rights itself and brings, with the aid of the skillful oarsman, both canoe and passengers right side up again, and without damage to either.

Schwatka found these native races among the hardiest and strongest on the continent. All his baggage had to be carried over the mountains on the backs of men hired for that purpose, and he reports that they could take a box of ammunition or supplies weighing a hundred pounds and go up the side of a mountain as rapidly as an ordinary man could go without any burden. One of their races that I witnessed, near Juno, in which five of their largest boats, with twelve to fifteen men in each, took part, was as good a display of muscular strength and activity as I have ever seen.

Desiring to gain more information regarding a country which up to that time had been wholly unknown, I organized a similar expedition, in charge of Lieutenant W. F. Abercrombie, in the summer of 1884, to explore the

Copper River region, and, if possible, the Aleutian range of mountains and the valley of the Tanana. A party of Russians, under Seribriekob from the Russian War Department had, in 1848 compelled the natives to drag their sledges up this river. At a preconcerted signal the rebellious Indians suddenly attacked and massacred the entire party. From that time no successful expedition had been made up the Copper River, and the natives had been very much opposed to civilized men entering their country. But Lieutenant Abercrombie found them inoffensive, and employed them to drag his boats up the river. The currents, however, were so strong, and he experienced so much difficulty in making the ascent, beside the drawback of a number of his party being sick, that he found it impossible to go as far as he intended. He did, however, accomplish a very good reconnoissance and exploration, and made some important discoveries as to the character of the country, obtaining much information of interest and value.

Returning to the mouth of the river in December, he was relieved by Lieutenant Allen, whom I had ordered to that duty. Lieutenant Allen left Portland, Oregon, January 29, accompanied by Sergeant Robinson and Private Pickett, of the signal corps. The Secretary of the Navy, Mr. Chandler, at my request, had very kindly sent them on one of the United States gunboats from Sitka to the mouth of Copper River.

After a long but unavoidable delay at Sitka, the party was conveyed by the "Pinta" to Nuchek. Although the "Pinta" was only a fourth rate man-of-war with a very small armament, she made a great impression upon the natives. One of them, in describing her proportions, estimated her length as equal to the distance between two designated islands, which were really about half a mile apart. On the morning of the 20th of March the party left Nuchek for the mouth of the Copper River, but experienced great difficulty in reaching that point on account of grounding so often in the mud in their canoes, and being continually exposed to a driving storm of sleet and rain.

Lieutenant Allen here took up his exploration late in the winter, starting in January, 1885, thus having the advantage of passing up on the ice, the difficult portion of the Copper River, where Lieutenant Abercrombie had found such difficulty in dragging his boats against the rapid current. He employed the natives to drag his sledges in his further ascent of the river and his passage over the Alaskan mountains.

During the whole expedition they experienced great difficulty in obtaining natives for transportation purposes. At Alaganik, a point on the Copper River, they could find only six men available for that purpose.

These men would promise faithfully to go at one moment and at the next refuse to have anything to do with the expedition. At last, in order to make them believe that it was a great favor to them to be allowed to go at all, Lieutenant Allen decided to take only five, and made them draw lots to determine who should be unfortunate enough to remain behind. This had the desired effect, though he would have been glad to hire ten men instead of five.

The ascent of the river soon became extremely difficult, as the channel in a short time grew so shallow that they could not use their canoes, thus making a portage necessary. Taral, of which they had heard much on their way up the river, they found to consist of but two houses, one of which was unoccupied. Here all the natives but one either deserted or were sent back, and here the explorers left the Copper River to explore one of its important branches called the Chittyna. As they went on, their food supply became so low that on Lieutenant Allen's birthday they could celebrate in no better way than by making a banquet of some moose meat that had been left by the natives and their dogs as unfit to eat. Afterward matters grew so much worse that they would have been glad to obtain even that delicacy.

They completed their exploration of the Chittyna, and on May 4, once more reached Taral. They then continued their way up the Copper River by " cordelling." That is, two men remain in the boat, one to steer and the other in the bow with a long pole; the remainder of the party pull on the rope as they walk along the shore. From Liebigstag's, a settlement on the river, could be seen a magnificent series of grand peaks, the highest, Mount Wrangell, rising more than seventeen thousand feet above the sea level.

On the 5th of June they commenced to ascend the mountains on their way to the Tanana, whose head waters lie very near those of the Copper, although the two rivers are marked by such entirely different characteristics. After a wearisome journey, as they climed to the top of a high divide four thousand five hundred feet above the level of the sea, they suddenly found themselves in full view of their promised land. In front of them lay the Tanana Valley with its numerous lakes and low, unbroken ranges of mountains; a scene which no white man had ever looked upon before. As they went on, vegetation began to be rank, and they suffered from the heat instead of from the cold. The Tanana is a muddy river full of quicksands and boilings, but with no rocks, and the spruce trees grow down to its very edge. It was decided to descend the river in a boat made of skins, and in this manner the voyage was made in spite of the many rapids which greatly increased the dangers of the descent. After suffering much from hunger and weakness, the party reached the Yukon, into which the Tanana empties fifteen hundred miles from its source. They then explored the Koyukuk, another tributary of the Yukon, for some distance, after which they made their way down the latter river as rapidly as the means at their disposal would permit, reaching St. Michael's on August 29, and thus concluding a most successful exploration, though made at the cost of much privation and suffering. Most of the people they met on the upper Copper and Tanana Rivers had never seen white men before, and much interesting information was obtained concerning them.

SEAL "ROOKERY."

The principal industries of Alaska at present are the fur trade, mining, and the curing and canning of fish. The value of the Seal Islands was not appreciated at the time of their transfer to this country. In 1870, the Alaska Commercial Company of San Francisco obtained a twenty years' lease of the islands of St. Paul and St. George, and are believed to have divided from $900,000 to $1,000,000 profits annually between twelve original stockholders. In 1890 another twenty years' lease was awarded the North American Commercial Company of San Francisco for an annual rental of $100,000.

At the rookeries the seal families herd in little groups on the rocks, the patriarch staying at home with the cubs, while the mother seal swims sometimes as far as two hundred miles daily in search of their food. These cubs are very timid, and rush into the water on hearing any strange noise. The toughness of the cubs is somewhat amusing. If anything happens to frighten them a patriarch weighing several hundred pounds will often flop and tumble over a whole mass of them apparently without injuring one. Only the male seals from two to four years of age are killed. These "bachelors" herd alone, and the aleuts, running between them and the water in the early morning, drive them slowly to the killing grounds, where they dispatch them by a blow on the head.

Salmon is the most important fish, but halibut and herring are cured in great quantities. At Loring a fine opportunity is presented of watching the canning of salmon, which continues from June to September. The outdoor work is done by a few white men, with sometimes a few Indians employed under them. Although naturally industrious the Tlingit cannot be depended on, as he is very apt to leave without warning to attend to some business of his own right in the height of the salmon season. But neither the white man nor the Indian can compete with the Chinese in the skillful manipulation of the machines. As he works by the piece, the Chinaman takes no note of time but will keep the machinery going as long as there are any fish left. The canneries are of no actual benefit to the country, as they drain it of its natural wealth and in return result in no improvements or permanent settlements.

The inhabitants of this country are classed as Oranians and Indians, the Esquimaux belonging to the former, but there are besides numerous and complicated subdivisions. The Greek church was early established in Alaska, and there are now also many important mission stations belonging to the Protestant church. Public schools have been in operation since 1886 and the attendance of children living within a certain limit is compulsory.

Who can foretell the future of this country when the similarity between its people and the ancient Britons, according to the descriptions handed down to us is remembered? In fact, the similarity in construction of their boats and of those described by the companions of Cæsar is remarkable. Their waters are filled with an abundance of fish, the brain-producing food. In the works of their construction — their implements, their means of transportation, and their most interesting carving in wood, copper and slate — they have given us evidence not only of their enterprise, but of their industry and great ingenuity. Should the country be occupied by civilized races who have the advantages of all the wonderful modern inventions and implements, Alaska may yet play an important part in the great future, and the development of the resources of its mines, waters and forests may one day contribute largely to the welfare of the human family.

Coming down from that far remote region we passed through the great zone of British territory which that government has so tenaciously held, and the ownership of which was for so long a time the subject of dispute between Great Britain and the United States. If we had maintained our position, our territory would be now increased by a domain of great value not only in material wealth but in political importance, and our Pacific Coast line would have been uninterrupted from California to Alaska. But the British statesmen have with consummate diplomacy, astute management, tact and sagacity utilized this territory to their own advantage. Their possessions stretching across the continent, divide our territory into two widely separated parts. The country is not thickly populated, and will not be, probably, for many generations. It is very sparsely settled indeed, yet the vast wealth comprised in its magnificent forests, rich agricultural country and great mineral resources, makes it a valuable and important territory.

The British have subsidized and constructed a great avenue of commerce between eastern Canada and the Pacific Coast, known as the Canadian Pacific Railroad. The energy, enterprise and skill of their engineers, contractors and managers in that great work are most commendable to the men concerned. They claim with reason, to have the short route to the Asiatic trade. It is estimated that the distance between Hongkong and Liverpool by that route is nineteen hundred miles shorter than it would be by way of San Francisco and New York.

Esquimault is one of the best and most sheltered harbors in the world. The British have there established a great naval station and have constructed a navy yard, with extensive dry docks, costing many millions of dollars. They have laid out their lines of fortifications so as to make it one of the strongholds of the British empire. It is the headquarters of the British Pacific squadron, usually under the command of a British admiral. It is not unusual to see there a fleet of British war ships that are equal to, if not larger than any of our beautiful white squadron, of which we are so proud, and so confident when we speak of its prowess; and it is far from uncommon to see a stronger fleet of more formidable battle ships under the flag of the cross of St. George at anchor in this harbor near Victoria than we now possess.

The morning and the evening gun fired at the navy yard near Victoria is heard distinctly at Port Townsend and along Puget Sound and the

Straits of Fuca, yet the United States has not a single battery of modern guns in position to protect the interests and commercial wealth of that great northwest territory. The question of suitable navy yards, dry docks, depots of construction, coast defences, and other matters in which the United States should be interested, has been to a great extent overlooked, and should be a matter of serious consideration in the near future.

Before bidding adieu to that great empire of the Northwest I can only consider further the changes that occurred under my observation between the years 1881 and 1885. Four years is certainly a brief period, yet in that short time the Northwest passed through a complete transformation. As I have said in the early chapters on this subject, we came up the coast from San Francisco. During the four years, I saw the Northern Pacific, that great avenue of commercial communication, constructed from the East to the West with all its various branches and connecting systems. Next to that was constructed what was known as the Oregon Short Line, a branch of the Union Pacific, diverging to the northwest from Ogden, Utah, and developing a great territory through Idaho to Oregon and the Columbia River. Then was constructed the Coast Line south from Portland, Oregon, along the old stage route to San Francisco by which the Central Pacific and Southern Pacific were connected with that great northern country. Next in importance was the great international line, the Canadian Pacific, built under the auspices of the Canadian government and supported by the British empire, with its branch line down to Puget Sound and the Columbia, thus giving us an additional line of communication to the east. Then with marvelous enterprise, commencing in a small bankrupt line of road out from St. Paul, that enterprising railroad builder, Mr. Hill, continued on and on, constructing his roads at little expense until he crossed the Rocky Mountains, and finally found a terminus on the Pacific Coast, thus giving us that vast system now known as the Great Northern.

ALASKAN TOTEM.

These five great systems of railway communication that were constructed principally, though not entirely, within this period of four years, opened to the world the vast resources of a country capable of contributing so largely to the welfare of the people of the United States; for in that country are natural resources capable of producing all that is required by mankind. There are its immense forests of gigantic trees affording wealth and employment to thousands; its soil of unsurpassed fertility, capable of producing a wonderful variety of products, and making possible unbounded fields of waving grain and prolific orchards of delicious fruits; its mines of gold and silver, and its rich deposits of coal and iron so essential to any country desirous of excelling in manufactures; its great commercial advantages; its wondrous scenery, varying from picturesque and rugged mountain peaks to smiling, fertile valleys; and to crown all other blessings, its delightful climate, mild in winter, free from tempests in summer, and so amazingly invigorating to both mind and body. With all these, and countless other natural advantages there seems almost no limit to the future possibilities of this extraordinary country.

CHAPTER XXXIV.

FROM INDIAN TERRITORY TO ARIZONA.

SITUATION IN THE INDIAN TERRITORY IN 1885 — THE UTES IN NEW MEXICO AND COLORADO — VISIT
TO THE CHEYENNES AND ARAPAHOES — BEGINNINGS OF NEW APACHE TROUBLES IN
ARIZONA — EARLY ARIZONA, AND EARLIEST EXPLORATIONS — ANCIENT RUINS
— CHARACTER OF THE COUNTRY — MINES — POPULATION.

IN this chapter it will be necessary to revert to occurrences following my transfer from the command of the Department of the Columbia to that of the Missouri, and thence to that of Arizona.

In 1885, and for some time previous to that year there had been clashing between the interests of the Indians in the Indian Territory and the owners of the immense herds of cattle that roamed over their reservations. This, in the summer of 1885, seemed ready to ripen into open hostilities. A large part of the Territory had been leased, under authority of the government, fenced in, and to some extent stocked with cattle.

On account of this authorized occupation of the Territory by white men connected with the cattle interest, a large number were either permanently located there or moving back and forth through the country to attend to their affairs. It also gave opportunity for a large number of lawless men to travel about the Territory, the result being that many disorderly acts were committed against the persons and property of the Indians. This created a feeling of discontent, disaffection and hostility on the part of the Indians toward the white people.

As a result of these disturbances, in July, 1885, I was assigned by the President to the command of the Department of the Missouri, of which department the Indian Territory formed a part, and one-fourth of the army was placed at my disposal. Under telegraphic orders I proceeded from Vancouver, Washington, to General Sheridan's headquarters, Chicago, and thence to the Indian Territory.

Upon investigation I found that, as usual, the Indians were not entirely in the wrong. The disaffected Utes in northern New Mexico and Colorado were in a most desperate state, and only withheld from actual outbreak by the presence of troops in their midst. Six of their number had been murdered by lawless white men, their reservation had been overrun and their game destroyed. They were nearly starving, their daily ration having been reduced to one-half a pound of beef and one-quarter of a pound of flour for each Indian. Happily this last cause of discontent was remedied by the prompt action of the Secretary of the Interior, who immediately increased the food allowance. The hostile Apaches were at the same time threatening the frontier of southern New Mexico, and it was necessary to keep troops in that part of the country to guard against their incursions. The extensive settlements in southern Kansas also made it necessary for a large body of troops to remain in that vicinity for their protection. Bad as was the state

of affairs in the Territories adjacent to the Indian Territory, the conditions there threatened immediate and serious hostility between the Indian tribes and the white people living in that Territory and in the States

ARIZONA VEGETATION, (GIANT CACTUS).

of Texas, Kansas and Colorado. In company with Lieutenant-General Sheridan I visited the Cheyenne and Arapahoe reservations and found them in a most desperate condition. The Indians were huddled together in disagreeble camps, and were entirely beyond the control of the agent and his Indian police. Two of their prominent men had been murdered, and they were turbulent, disaffected, and on the verge of open hostilities.   As is usually the case when any disturbance occurs, there was a large number of white men with no visible means of support hovering about, and endeavoring to turn the turbulent condition of affairs to their own advantage.

While Lieutenant-General Sheridan listened to the complaints of the Indians, investigated the relationship between the Indians and the white people, and the effect produced by leasing the lands to white men, I devoted much of my attention to the condition of the troops and their proper equipment, organization, supplies, means of transportation and everything that was required to put them in proper condition for active campaigning in case United States troops were required.   Fortunately I had known many of the principal Indians as a result of the campaign of 1874-5 in the southwest; also a number of the prominent Cheyenne Indians had surrendered to me in Montana in 1877 and had since been moved down to the Indian Territory.   These were sent for and counseled with, and I was enabled to give them good advice which they heeded.   General Sheridan had also met many prominent warriors in 1869 and subsequently.

The threatening condition of affairs was soon changed.   The President revoked the cattle leases, and the Indians were soon brought under control.   A very efficient officer, Captain Lee, was placed in charge of the agency.   Under his able administration their condition rapidly improved. One hundred and thirty of the most active and restless of the young men were enlisted as soldiers, and performed good service under the command of competent officers.   In addition to their military duties they were required to cultivate ground enough to raise all the vegetables they would require during the year.   The reservation was summarily cleared of the lawless white men who infested it and peace and confidence were once more restored.   The military garrisons were increased, and affairs speedily became so quiet, that the large bodies of troops which it had been necessary to call from other departments were returned to their proper stations.

As the tide of white settlers rolled westward, driving the Indians before it, the idea of setting apart the huge block of country known as the Indian Territory, where the scattered tribes of Indians could be congregated, was at the time a good one, and wise and judicious in every respect.   But in 1885 the Territory had outlived its usefulness, and served merely as an impediment in the pathway of progress.   Without courts of justice or public institutions, without roads or bridges or railways, it was nothing more than a dark blot in the midst of a great and progressive country.   It had naturally become the refuge of outlaws and the indolent of all races and classes, and the vices introduced in this way were rapidly destroying the Indians. Although it contained land sufficient to maintain millions of enlightened people, it was actually costing the government hundreds of thousands of dollars yearly to maintain nearly seventy-five thousand Indians who made it their home.

Being firmly convinced that such was the case, I could do no less than recommend that measures should be taken to bring about a decided change, as I believed, for the better. The recommendation contained in my annual report of 1885 was substantially as follows :

That Congress should authorize the President to appoint a commission of three experienced, competent men, empowered to treat with the different tribes ; to consider all legal or just claims to titles ; to grant to the Indian occupants of the territory such quantity of land in severalty as might be required for their support, but not transferable for twenty years ; that their title to the remainder be so far extinguished as that it might be held in trust or sold by the government, and that a sufficient amount of the proceeds should be granted them to indemnify them for any interest they might possess in the land ; that enough of said proceeds be provided to enable the Indians in the Territory to become self sustaining. The land not required for Indian occupation to be thrown open for settlement under the same laws and rules as have been applied to the public domain.

This was the same course that I had recommended before in the northwest, while in command of the Department of the Columbia, and, having demonstrated its success by actual experiment, I knew that the plan was practical, just and humane. If there have been failures in attempting to carry it out, it was because the officials appointed to treat with the Indians were inexperienced and did not understand the Indian's method of reasoning, his tastes or his ambitions; or because they were theorists, instead of being practical men, capable of inspiring confidence. I also favored the employment of a number of Indians in the army, as scouts, guides and trailers knowing from personal experience that they were endowed with many of the qualities that would make them useful. I had commanded Indians in various parts of the West for years, and, besides having found them of great value in numerous ways, never in the whole course of my acquaintance with them did I know one of them to be unfaithful to a trust.

Everything pertaining to the Department of the Missouri now being quiet, I was looking forward to a peaceful sojourn at Fort Leavenworth, which had formerly been my headquarters for several years while colonel of the Fifth Infantry ; but the wily Apaches were busily at work in a way to completely frustrate any such designs on my part. Within nine months from the time I took command of the Department of the Missouri I was assigned to the Department of Arizona, where the Apaches were devastating the country.

For many years there had been serious troubles with these Indians. They would allow themselves to be placed on reservations, and after remaining there as long as their own convenience dictated, would suddenly escape to the mountains, and from there send out raiding parties in all directions to burn, plunder and terrorize the inhabitants of the country. While the Indians still remaining at the agencies did not take active part in these hostilities they aided and abetted the actual offenders in many ways, thus enabling them to resist the troops sent against them much longer than would otherwise have been possible.

In Arizona the state of affairs was altogether different from that which had prevailed in my campaigns against the Sioux. In the north the terrible cold was the chief obstacle to success, while in Arizona the heat and want of water were equally formidable. The Apaches had for generations been accustomed to the heat, the rugged mountains, and the scarcity of water, against which the troops found it so difficult to contend, and had moved from one place to another so quickly and stealthily that the settlers could never for a moment feel sure of the safety of their lives and property. The Apaches devoted themselves with great impartiality to Arizona, New Mexico, and Northern Mexico; and the citizens of these parts of the country had become so paralyzed with terror, as to cause in many instances the abandonment of the ordinary avocations of life.

Before entering upon the history of the campaign against the Apaches, it may be interesting to glance briefly at the peculiar history and still more peculiar geographical features of the vast region the Apache so long dominated.

In prehistoric times, Arizona was probably inhabited by a very superior race, judging by the ruins of their cities, aqueducts, fortifications, etc. But the known history of the territory extends back only to the time of Narvaez's ill-starred expedition to Florida, after the failure of which Cabeza de Vaca, the treasurer of the expedition, who probably little realized the extent of his undertaking, with three companions started to walk across the continent as the only possible chance of being able to join the Spaniards in Mexico. The wanderings and adventures of these men during their tremendous pedestrian tour read like a romance. They waded the swamps and bayous of Florida, passed through what is now Georgia, Alabama and Mississippi, discovered the Father of Waters nearly ten years before the eyes of De Soto rested upon it, followed along the course of a great river supposed to have been the Arkansas, entered New Mexico, and finally reached a Pima settlement on the Gila River in Arizona. These Indians treated them with marked deference, and having heard of the coming of the Spaniards to the south, were able to direct the wanderers to Mexico, where they finally arrived, bronzed, dirty, and so wild in their appearance that their fellow-countrymen could hardly believe that they were gazing upon white men and Spaniards.

The stories told by these men of the wonders encoun-

CLIFF DWELLINGS ON BEAVER CREEK, ARIZONA, THREE MILES FROM FORT VERDI, SOMETIMES CALLED MONTEZUMA'S PALACE.

tered by them during their journeying, aroused the spirit of adventure and cupidity in the Spaniards, who were never very loath to undertake any enterprise that promised either gold or glory. The priests also listened to the wonderful tales and one of them, Padre Marco de Niza, organized an expedition that pushed north to the valleys of central Arizona, and thence northeast to beyond the Little Colorado, where they beheld the first of the Seven Cities described by Cabeza de Vaca. The return of this party wrought the Spaniards up to such a pitch of excitement that the expedition of Coronado, in 1540, was the result. This expedition was a strong one, numbering nearly a thousand men, all of whom expected to find and conquer another people as rich in the precious metals as they had found the Aztecs to be. Only a few poor and insignificant villages rewarded their search, however, and disappointed in his dreams of conquest in that direction the Spanish leader turned to what is now New Mexico, where he met with no better success. From New Mexico he traveled to the north and east and explored the country as far as the site of the present city of Denver, and probably even reached the Missouri, after which, at the end of the two years of profitless wanderings, he and his men returned to Mexico.

Both Cabeza de Vaca and Coronado observed the numerous traces of a prehistoric race scattered throughout this region. First in importance among these ruins was the famous Casa Grande, which is still standing, though naturally not in so good a state of preservation as it showed three hundred and fifty years ago. In 1540, when visited by Coronado, this ruin was described as being four stories high with walls six feet in thickness. Around it were many other ruins which proved that a city of considerable size had once existed there. Like the Egyptians who now dwell beneath the shadow of the pyramids and know nothing of their origin, the Pima Indians who were living in its immediate vicinity knew nothing of its origin or history, and it had been a ruin farther

OLDEST HOUSE IN THE UNITED STATES, SANTA FÉ, N. M.

back than the earliest date mentioned in any of their traditions.

After Coronado's visit forty years elapsed before another attempt was made to explore Arizona, but in 1582 Espejo led an expedition far toward the north and discovered rich silver ore at a spot which is now supposed to have been in what we have named the Black Hills, in Dakota. So far as we know this was the first finding, in that vast region, of the precious metals which have since given that country its chief importance in the world.

As the Spanish cavaliers undertook these expeditions merely for the sake of gaining sudden wealth such as had been acquired by the conquerors of Mexico and Peru, they never troubled themselves to plant colonies, so that the history of most of the old Spanish towns in America dates back no further than to the missions established there by the priests.

The first mission within the present limits of Arizona was founded at a place then called Grevavi, in 1687, by Fray Eusebio Francisco Kino and Padre Juan Maria Salvatierra, and by 1720 there had been nine such missions established. After the great Indian revolt which occurred in 1751, in which the Spaniards were driven entirely out of the country, the presidios of Tucson and Tubec were founded and maintained with small garrisons of soldiers for the protection of the missions. Besides these there were a number of small but flourishing settlements possessing large flocks of sheep and herds of cattle; mining was also vigorously prosecuted.

As a result of the Mexican war, by the treaty of Guadalupe in 1847, all that portion of the territory north of the Gila River was ceded

PETRIFIED FOREST, ARIZONA.

to the United States. At that time there was not a single white inhabitant in all that vast region which stretched from the Gila River north to the present Utah boundary, and from the Colorado River to the present line of New Mexico. In 1854 that portion of the territory lying south of the Gila was acquired from Mexico by the treaty negotiated by James Gadsden, then minister to Mexico, and at a cost of $10,000,000. On the last day of December, 1854, a memorial to Congress was introduced in the legislature of New Mexico praying for the organization of the western portion of that territory into a separate political division. Pimeria was the first name given to the territory thus cut off from New Mexico, but it was soon changed to Arizona. The origin of the latter name is not positively known; some claiming that it means "little creek" in the Pima language, while others hold that it is derived from two Pima words "ari" a maiden, and "zon" a valley or country, having reference to a traditionary maiden queen who once ruled the whole Pima nation. The name can also be traced to the meaning of two Spanish words combined into one, and signifying a dry belt—an "arid zone."

This attempt to secure a Territorial government was unsuccessful, but still the country slowly prospered. A stage route was organized, the mines were worked, and despite the continual ravages of the Indians the country seemed on the high road to prosperity up to the time of the breaking out of the Civil War. The troops were then ordered out of the country for service elsewhere, and every American who could do so fled to California or to Sonora, Mexico. Then, as there was absolutely no one to control them, the Apaches swept down from their mountain heights and indulged in a perfect saturnalia of slaughter among the settlers who had been so unfortunate as to remain behind. In February, 1862, the Confederates took possession of a portion of the country, but retreated in May on the coming of a column of volunteers from California. The presence of these inspired confidence, and settlers again ventured into the Territory. Gold was discovered on the Colorado, and business once more began to revive.

THE PAINTED DESERT.

It was not until 1863 that the country gained a political existence separate from New Mexico. During the following ten years its history was a bloody one, the Indians laying waste the country and killing the white settlers whenever they could get an opportunity. But immigration still went on, the rich mines being the lodestone that drew crowds of adventurers in spite of the terror inspired by the Apaches. Settlements gradually took root, and in 1878, when the Southern Pacific Railroad was built through the Territory, a brighter period in Arizona's history begins.

The surface of Arizona may be described as a vast, lofty plateau, in the northern part crossed and recrossed by mountain ranges, deep cañons and narrow valleys. This northern part is from five thousand to seven thous-

and feet above the sea level, but gradually decreases in altitude toward
the south. The highest mountain peak is Mount San Francisco, a huge
extinct volcanic cone, thirteen thousand feet in height, which may be seen
two hundred miles away. During the melting of the winter snows and

after the heavy summer rains,
the deep gorges and ravines
are filled with wild and furious
floods that carry everything
before them.

The most extensive of the
table lands of Arizona is known
as the Colorado plateau. Between the massive mountain
ranges that diversify its surface are extensive grassy plains
and valleys with a fertile soil
and delightful climate. This
great region is drained by many
rivers. The southwestern portion of the territory adjacent
to the gulf is made up of plains
covered with coarse grass and
scanty shrubbery, but almost
devoid of all other vegetation.
The soil is unproductive without irrigation, and in places
water is very scarce. In the
southeast a different order of
things prevails. Here the lofty
mountain ranges are covered
with some verdure and are in-
terspersed with broad valleys

A Cañon a Mile Deep.

affording fair pasturage. Central Arizona contains the richest body of
agricultural land in the Territory, and the valleys of the Gila and the
Salt Rivers rank among the best. In these valleys is a soil on which
anything will grow that can be raised within the temperate and semi-
tropical zones, and the climate is almost unequaled but here also, as
elsewhere, irrigation is required.

North from the junction of the Little and Great Colorado Rivers is a most remarkable region known as the Painted Desert, or as the Indians, who carefully avoid the spot, call it, "the country of departed spirits." It is a perfect picture of desolation, being entirely destitute of water and vegetation, and with its entire surface covered with isolated peaks and

SHINI-MO ALTAR FROM BRINK OF MARBLE CAÑON.

buttes fashioned by the floods of ages into the most fantastic and grotesque shapes. The air is wonderfully clear, and shows marvelous mirages in the form of temples, fountains, fortifications, beautiful landscapes, companies of people, and all painted by the atmosphere in such a way that it seems impossible to doubt their reality.

The Colorado River, which crosses the northwest corner and forms part of the western boundary of Arizona, ranks among the great rivers of the continent. The Grand Cañon of the Colorado is one of the wonders of nature, the duplicate of which can nowhere be found. This tremendous gorge, from one thousand to seven thousand feet in depth, cuts its way through the solid rock for more than four hundred miles, and though its beauty is of a dark and gloomy character, it is superbly grand. Standing beside its rushing waters it gives one a strange sensation to realize that he is over a mile below the crust of the earth. The Colorado is one of the principal tributaries of the Pacific Ocean on the American continent, and down its course there flows a volume of water rivaling that of the Nile, and capable of irrigating a territory several times the extent of Egypt.

The first miners in Arizona were the old Jesuit fathers. Their success encouraged others, and many rich discoveries were made. The largest piece of silver ever found, and which weighed twenty-seven hundred pounds, was taken from an Arizona mine. Philip V. of Spain confiscated this nugget on the ground that it was a curiosity and, therefore, belonged to the crown. The first mining by Americans was undertaken in the Santa Rita Mountains by a company organized in 1855. Naturally, mining was carried on with considerable difficulty, as all supplies had to be brought overland from St. Louis or from the Gulf of California, and the terrible Apaches were ever alert to destroy any white man that came within their power.

At the time of the Civil War, mining, like everything else in Arizona, came to a standstill, but in spite of all drawbacks the Territory soon took rank with the foremost mining localities in its output of silver. The placing of the hostile Apaches on reservations, and the entrance of two of the great railroads into the country, largely contributed to this result. The closing of some of the silver mines caused by the low price of silver in these recent times has resulted in a marked increase of the gold production, and the prospects are that Arizona will soon be prominent among the States and Territories in the production of that metal. The gold output of 1894 was valued at $2,080,250, and the silver at $1,700,800, and, besides this, 48,270,500 pounds of copper were mined. One of the most valuable products of the Territory is copper, and in this, Arizona rivals the great deposits of Lake Superior and western Montana.

In 1890 the census returns gave the population of Arizona as 59,620. Phœnix, the present capital of the Territory, is pleasantly situated in the Salt River Valley. In this region much has been done by irrigation, and large orange groves and fine vineyards are the result. Tucson is the largest city.

While in command of the Department of the Columbia, in the spring of 1882, I visited San Francisco, and there met General W. T. Sherman, commanding the army. He had just passed through the Territories of New Mexico and Arizona. The condition of affairs at that time, especially in Arizona, was not satisfactory, and in fact was very serious. The Apache Indians were on the warpath, and were committing depredations in various sections of the Territory. It had been decided to make a change in the command of that department, and General Sherman suggested that I should be assigned to the command, but said the change would not be made unless it was agreeable to me. I replied that I did not desire to go there; that other officers had had experience in that part of the country and I thought it better to give them an opportunity of restoring peace,

M.—26

subjugating the Indians and eventually bringing them under control; that I had been but recently assigned to the command of the Department of the Columbia and was much interested in the cares and responsibilities of that command and in the development and progress of that great northwest country. This ended the conversation, and the subject of my going to that part of the United States was at that time dismissed.

Still I watched with great interest the reports from that section of country; all that was published regarding the depredations of the Indians, the movements of troops, and the various phases incident to hostilities of that nature were carefully noted. I traced on the best maps that I could obtain of that country the movements of the Indians according to the dates as they were reported, observed where and when hostilities were committed, where and when certain bands of warriors appeared, from whence they came and in what direction they were reported to have gone, comparing one report with another, and thereby tracing as far as practicable the habits and actions of the hostile Indians. I thus became somewhat familiar with the raids of the Indians and the routes of travel they most frequently pursued along certain ranges of mountains the topographical features of which were given on the official maps. I kept trace of these to a certain extent while in command of the Department of the Columbia, and when afterwards transferred to the Department of the Missouri, with headquarters at Leavenworth, Kansas, continued to follow the course of events with more or less interest.

CHAPTER XXXV.

THE APACHE AND THE SOLDIER.

GENERAL CROOK AND HIS EXPERIENCES—CHARACTER OF THESE INDIANS—ILLUSTRATIVE IN-
STANCES—A WILDERNESS CEMETERY—MOUNTAIN FASTNESSES OF ARIZONA—
RESOURCES OF THE APACHE IN WAR—A FORMER CAMPAIGN.

GENERAL CROOK had been trying for years to bring the Apaches to terms, and on several occasions within thirty years they had pretended to surrender and had accepted the terms given them by the government. They would then go back to their agencies with their plunder, stolen stock, and for a fresh supply of the munitions of war, and after remaining quiet for some time would suddenly break out again with renewed ferocity.

There were various bands of Apaches—Yuma, Mohave, White Mountain, Chiricahua and other branches. The Chiricahuas were the worst, wildest and strongest of all. The Apache regarded himself as the first man; the "superior man," as the word Apache indicates. In some respects they really were superior. They excelled in strength, activity, endurance, and also in cruelty. They were cruel to everything that came within their power. If the young Apache could capture a bird or a mouse or any living thing, he took the keenest delight in torturing it, and this species of cruelty did not disappear even when they grew to be stalwart men. They took pleasure in tormenting any living creature from a bird to a horse. Their atrocities are simply too horrible and shocking to write out in words.

There is an Indian by the name of Schimizene still living in that Territory who, for a number of years was in the habit of traveling past a certain white man's dwelling, and on these occasions was always treated kindly, given food, and made comfortable whenever he cared to tarry. One morning after having stayed there long enough to secure a good breakfast, he picked up his rifle and killed his benefactor, and then went away boasting of what a strong heart he had. "Why," he remarked, "a weak man or a coward could kill his enemy or any one who had done him an injury; but it takes a man of a strong heart to kill a friend or one who has always treated him kindly." This is a specimen of Apache reasoning.

At another time during Indian hostilities he captured an unfortunate white man and buried him, all but his head, in close proximity to a large black ant hill such as are found in that country, sometimes two feet high and from one to three feet in diameter. The unhappy victim lived for two days, suffering the most excruciating torture while the ants slowly ate away the flesh from his head.

Apache Cruelty.

Another incident showing the heartlessness of this people was related to me by one personally cognizant of the facts, and of undoubted trustworthiness. A renegade, or outlaw Indian, had committed several murders and was wanted to answer for his numerous crimes, but the official at the agency had found it impossible to arrest him, as he rarely appeared there, and kept himself concealed in some safe mountain retreat. Seeing no other way of securing the criminal the officer in charge called up a dissolute Indian, a cousin of the outlaw, and told him that if he would go out into the mountains and bring in the culprit alive, or if that was impossible, a proof of his death, he would give him a certain horse, which was pointed out to him. One morning not long afterward, the officer was in his quarters seated at the breakfast table, when this Indian appeared before him carrying a sack over his shoulder. He advanced to where the officer was sitting and remarked with much apparent satisfaction that he had come for the horse, at the same time shaking the head of his relative from the sack to the floor at the officer's feet; and the Indian received his fat gray horse.

A short time after this, as the officer was going about the agency, the same Indian motioned to him to come round the corner of the agency building that he might speak to him in private. The officer naturally not having much confidence in the sense of honor of this particular savage, called an interpreter to go with him. He need not have feared, for the Indian merely wished to say that if the officer had another good gray horse, he had another cousin whose head he could bring in at any time.

The instance given conveys but a faint idea of the unique character of the Indian I found myself called upon to subdue. He was, besides, possessed of resources not under the control of the white man.

He required nothing of the white man to support life, and wanted only his weapons for warfare. The deserts and the mountain fastnesses were his allies, and with his knowledge of the entire country, he could find in the rocks tanks of water where a white man would die of thirst. Even in the desert the cactus was used for both food and drink, nature aiding

CLAIMING HIS REWARD.

him where she was fatal to the white man. From the United States these Indians fled to the most inaccessible mountains of Mexico, and not till the treaty made in 1882, did it become possible for our troops to pursue them into that country.

As previously stated, General Crook had been trying for years to bring the Apaches to terms and keep them under control. In 1883 he made an expedition into Mexico which resulted in the return of the Chiricahuas and Warm Springs Indians under Geronimo and Natchez to the Apache reservation.

For nearly two years they remained quiet, when tiring of peaceful pursuits, Geronimo, Natchez, Mangus and many others, in May, 1885, again went on the warpath and fled into Mexico. They were vigorously pursued but succeeded in eluding the troops and commenced again their work of death and destruction from their base in the Sierra Madre Mountains. Captain Wirt Davis, Fourth Cavalry with his troop and one hundred Indian scouts, pursued them and surprised their camp near Nacori, Mexico. Lieutenant Hay, Fourth Cavalry (of the command), with seventy-eight scouts, attacked their camp, surprising them, but only succeeded in capturing their camp outfit and killing two boys and a woman. Captain Crawford, Third Cavalry, with a bat-

HIS ACTIONS WERE CURIOUS.

talion of scouts also proceeded to Mexico in pursuit, and his scouts under Chatto encountered Chihuahua in the Bavispe Mountains and captured fifteen women. An account of this campaign is given by Captain Maus. Captain Dorst also commanded a similar expedition.

Despite constant pursuit these Indians succeeded in crossing back into the United States, murdering people, and destroying property. One band, Josanie with ten men, crossed into the United States, raided the Apache reservation, killed some of the friendly Indians as well as thirty-eight white people, captured about two hundred head of stock, and returned to Mexico. This expedition occupied only four weeks and the Indians traveled a distance of over twelve hundred miles. That such a raid was possible despite the fact that in addition to the commands already mentioned, there was a large force of regular troops in the field (forty-three companies of infantry and forty troops of cavalry), shows the energy and daring of these Indians.

The necessity of following and constantly harassing them being evident, two expeditions were again formed to go in pursuit. One consisted of a battalion of Indian scouts (one hundred and two men) and a troop of cavalry under Captain Wirt Davis, Fourth Cavalry, and the other of a battalion of Indian scouts (one hundred men) under Captain Crawford, Third Cavalry. The first battalion (Davis) was composed of San Carlos and White Mountain Indians, principally, and the second (Crawford) was composed of Chiricahuas, Warm Springs and White Mountain Apaches. The Indians of the battalion were largely a part of the band to be destroyed, and in every respect as savage and as able as they. Captain Davis operated in Chihuahua, while Captain Crawford proceeded with his command into Sonora. Captain Crawford selected the people composing his command on account of the fact that they were mountain Indians and knew the haunts of these to be pursued, being, indeed, a part of their bands. Many doubted the wisdom of taking these men alone with no troops, and predictions of treachery were freely made, but still officers volunteered for the duty. Those selected were Lieutenant Marion P. Maus, First Infantry, and Lieutenant W. E. Shipp, Tenth Cavalry, to command the companies, while Lieutenant S. L. Faison, First Infantry, was the adjutant, quartermaster and commissary officer, and Acting Assistant Surgeon T. B. Davis was the medical officer. The scouts were selected and enlisted, fifty each, by Lieutenants Maus and Shipp, thus forming the battalion of one hundred men.

The history of this expedition into Mexico, its unique formation, the almost unparalleled hardships and dangers it encountered, the tragic death of its commander, Captain Emmet Crawford, and the international phase of the affair, all give it an especial interest, and we will follow its movements in detail from the time the command left Apache till its return and muster out of the service—a period of six months. This account is best given in the narrative of Captain Marion P. Maus, who accompanied Captain Crawford, and is himself one of the most experienced officers in the service. His account illustrates the difficulties to be overcome, as well as the fortitude and courage of our officers and soldiers.

CHAPTER XXXVI.

A Campaign Against the Apaches.   [Captain Maus' Narrative.]

Beginning of the Campaign of 1885 — Crossing Into Mexico — Methods of the Indian Scouts —
Little Mexican Towns and Their People — Mescal and its Use by Indians — First News of
the Hostiles — Beginning of a Mountain March on Foot — Abandoned Camps — The
Devil's Backbone — Finding the Hostiles — The Attack — A Battle with
Mexican Troops That Was Fought by Mistake — Captain Crawford
Mortally Wounded — Later Action of the Mexicans — The Home-
ward March — Messenger from Geronimo — A Conference —
An Indian Trick — Death of Captain Crawford — Bur-
ial at Nacori, Mexico — Unfriendly Disposi-
tion of the Mexicans — Arrival in United
States Territory — Return for
the Hostiles — The Signal —
The Escape and Pursuit
— Results of the
Expedition

THE following sketch graphically illustrates the warfare of times of peace, and the duties and perils of the American regular soldier.   Such narratives, were they all written, would constitute much of the history, almost to date of the southwest.   The narrative has an added value in the fact that it is the story of personal experiences.

The command, fully equipped for field service, left Apache, Arizona, on November 11, 1885, for Fort Bowie.   Here it was inspected by Lieutenant-General Sheridan and Brigadier-General Crook, and with words of encouragement from these officers, the command started south by way of the Dragoon Mountains, endeavoring to find the trail of a band of Indians who were returning to Mexico after a raid into the United States.   Thoroughly scouting these mountains without finding the trail, we went on to the border and crossed into Mexico twenty miles north of the town of Fronteras, with the object of pursuing the renegades to their haunts in southern Sonora.   We believed that if we could trace this band we could find the entire hostile camp under Geronimo and Natchez.   Under instructions from Captain Crawford, I preceded the command to the town of Fronteras to notify the Presidente of the town of our approach, of our object in coming, and to gain information.   It was a small place, composed of the usual adobe buildings, and its people lived in a constant state of alarm about the movements of the hostiles.   The command arriving, we proceeded to Nocarasi, a small mining town in the Madre Mountains.   On account of the roughness of these mountains we found great difficulty in crossing them with the pack-train.   We found one horse which had evidently been abandoned by the hostiles, but no distinct trail.

In marching the command it was interesting to notice the methods adopted by our Indians in scouting the country to gain information and prevent surprise. It illustrated to us very clearly what we must expect from the hostiles, who would employ the same methods.   It was impossible to march these scouts as soldiers, or to control them as such, nor was it deemed advisable to attempt it.   Among them were many who had bloody records; one named Dutchy had killed, in cold blood, a white man near Fort Thomas, and for

CAPTAIN MAUS.

this murder the civil authorities were at this time seeking to arrest him.   Their system of advance guards and flankers was perfect, and as soon as the command went into camp, outposts were at once put out, guarding every approach.   All this was done noiselessly and in secret, and without giving a single order.   As scouts for a command in time of war they would be ideal.   Small of stature, and apparently no match physically for the white man, yet when it came to climbing mountains or making long marches, they were swift and tireless. The little clothing they wore consisted of a soldier's blouse, discarded in time of action, light undergarments and a waist cloth, and on the march the blouse was often turned inside out to show only the gray lining. Nothing escaped their watchful eyes as they marched silently in their moccasined feet. By day small fires were built of dry wood to avoid smoke, and at night they were made in hidden places so as to be invisible. If a high point was in view, you could be sure that a scout had crawled to the summit and, himself unseen, with a glass or his keen eyes had searched the country around. At night only was the watch relaxed, for these savages dread the night with a superstitious fear. It was necessary to allow them their way, and we followed, preserving order as best we could by exercising tact and by a careful study of their habits. Under the influence of mescal, which is a liquor made in all parts of Mexico and easily procured, they often became violent and troublesome and we could not help realizing how perfectly we were in their power. However, no distrust of them was shown. One of my Indians, a sergeant named Rubie, followed me one day while I was hunting. I thought his actions were curious, but they were explained when he suddenly came from the front and told me to go back. He had seen the footprints of hostiles near by. In the action which followed later he came to me and warned me to cover. There was, however, very little evidence of affection or gratitude in them as a class.

Continuing the march, we reached the town of Huasavas in the valley of the Bavispe. Orange and lemon trees were filled with golden fruit, although it was now the 22d of December. This valley, surrounded by high mountains, was fertile though but little cultivated. The only vehicles in use were carts, the wheels of which were sections sawed from logs. The plows were pieces of pointed wood. The people were devoid of all the comforts of life. Corn flour was obtained by pounding the grains on stones. They were a most desolate people, and completely terrorized by the Apaches, who were a constant menace to them, as they were to the inhabitants of all these towns. Here occurred the first serious trouble with the Indian scouts. One of them, who was drunk but unarmed, was shot by a Mexican policeman. At the time I was on my way to the town and met the Indian, who was running down the road toward me, followed by two policemen or guards firing rapidly. One ball passed through his face, coming out through the jaw. The other Indian scouts were much incensed, and at once began to prepare for an attack on the town, giving us much trouble before we were able to stop them. The officers were unable to sleep that night, as many of the Indians had been drinking and continued to be so angry that they fired off their rifles in the camp. The next day I released one of them from prison, and subsequently had to pay a fine of five dollars for him. It was claimed by the Mexicans that the Indians had committed some breach of the peace.

Here we got the first reliable news of the hostiles who were murdering people and killing cattle to the south. Crossing the mountains we passed the towns of Granadas and Bacedahuachi, the latter being the site of one of the fine old missions built by the daring priests who had sought to plant their religion among the natives many years before.

Proceeding on our way over a mountainous country, we finally came to the town of Nacori. This place was in a continual state of alarm, a wall having been built around it as a protection against the Apaches, the very name of whom was a terror. From our camp, sixteen miles south of this town, two of our pack-trains were sent back to Lang's Ranch, New Mexico, for supplies. To our surprise a deputy United States marshal from Tombstone came here to arrest Dutchy. Captain Crawford declined to permit the arrest, and in a letter to the marshal (now on file in the State Department) asked him to " delay the arrest till I may be near the border where protection for myself, officers and white men, with my pack-trains, may be afforded by United States troops other than Indians," offering to return if desired. The scouts were intensely excited, and under the circumstances the marshal did not wish to attempt to arrest Dutchy, and returned without delay.

We had now penetrated over two hundred miles into the mountains of Mexico, and we were sure the hostiles were near. It was decided to move immediately in pursuit of them. In this wild and unknown land even our Indians looked more stolid and serious. One by one they gathered together for a medicine dance. The Medicine Man, Noh-wah-zhe-tah, unrolled the sacred buckskin he had worn since he left Apache. There was something very solemn in all this. The dance, the marching, the kneeling before the sacred buckskin as each pressed his lips to it and the old man blessed him, impressed us too, as we looked on in silence. Afterward, the Indians held a council. They said they meant to do their duty, and would prove that they would fight to those who said they would not, and they seemed very much in earnest. I am satisfied that they desired to get the hostiles to surrender, but do not believe they intended or desired to kill them—their own people. In view of their relations it was little wonder that they felt in this way.

It was decided that all must go on foot, and that officer and scout alike must carry his own blanket, all else being left behind. Leaving a few scouts (the weakest and the sick) to guard the camp, a force of seventy-nine was equipped with twelve days' rations, carried on three or four of the toughest mules best suited for the purpose, and we started forward. We marched to the Haros River, which we forded, and then ascending the high hills beyond, discovered first a small trail, and then a large, well-beaten one, evidently that of the entire band of hostiles. The trail was about six days old, and as we passed over it, here and there, the bodies of dead cattle, only partially used, were found. The hostiles had but a short time previously moved their camp from the junction of the Haros and Yaqui Rivers a few miles to the west, and were going to the east to the fastnesses of some extremely rugged mountains : the *Espinosa del Diablo*, or the Devil's Backbone—a most appropriate name, as the country was broken and rough beyond description. The march was now conducted mostly by night. We suffered much from

CROSSING THE HAROS RIVER.

the cold, and the one blanket to each man used when we slept was scanty covering. Often it was impossible to sleep at all. At times we made our coffee and cooked our food in the daytime, choosing points where the light could not be seen, and using dry wood to avoid smoke. Our moccasins were thin and the rocks were hard on the feet. Shoes had been abandoned, as the noise made by them could be heard a long distance. The advance scouts kept far ahead. Several abandoned camps of the hostiles were found, the selection of which showed their constant care. They were placed on high points, to which the hostiles ascended in such a way that it was impossible for them to be seen; while in descending, any pursuing party would have to appear in full view of the lookout they always kept in the rear. The labor of the Indian women in bringing the water and wood to these points was no apparent objection.

Crossing the Haros River the trail led direct to the Devil's Back-bone, situated between the Haros and Satachi Rivers. The difficulties of marching over a country like this by night, where it was necessary to climb over rocks and to descend into deep and dark cañons, can hardly be imagined. When we halted, which was sometimes not until midnight, we were sore and tired. We could never move until late in the day, as it was necessary to examine the country a long distance ahead before we started. No human being seemed ever to have been here. Deer were plentiful, but we could not shoot them. Once I saw a leopard that bounded away with a shriek. It was spotted and seemed as large as a tiger. At last, after a weary march, at sunset on the 9th of January, 1886, Noche, our Indian sergeant-major and guide, sent word that the hostile camp was located twelve miles away.

The command was halted, and as the hostiles were reported camped on a high point, well protected and apparently showing great caution on their part, it was decided to make a night march and attack them at day-light. A short halt of about twenty minutes was made. We did not kindle a fire, and about the only food we had was some hard bread and some raw bacon. The medical officer, Dr. Davis, was worn out, and the interpreter also unfortunately could go no further. We had already marched continuously for about six hours and were very much worn out and footsore, even the scouts showing the fatigue of the hard service. These night marches, when we followed a trail purposely made over the worst country possible, and crossing and recrossing the turbulent river, which we had to ford, were very trying. But the news of the camp being so close at hand gave us new strength and hope, and we hastened on to cover the ten or twelve miles between us and the hostiles. I cannot easily forget that night's march. All night long we toiled on, feeling our way. It was a dark and moonless night. For much of the distance the way led over solid rock, over mountains, down cañons so dark they seemed bottomless. It was a wonder the scouts could find the trail. Sometimes the descent became so steep that we could not go forward, but would have to wearily climb back and find another way. I marched by poor Captain Crawford, who was badly worn out; often he stopped and leaned heavily on his rifle for support, and again he used it for a cane to assist him. He had, however, an unconquerable will, and kept slowly on. At last, when it was nearly daylight, we could see in the distance the dim outlines of the rocky position occupied by the hostiles. I had a strong feeling of relief, for I certainly was very tired. We had marched continuously eighteen hours over a country so difficult that when we reached their camp Geronimo said he felt that he had no longer a place where the white man would not pursue him.

The command was now quickly disposed for an attack, our first object being to surround the hostile camp. I was sent around to the further side. Noiselessly, scarcely breathing, we crept along. It was still dark. It seemed strange to be going to attack these Indians with a force of their own kindred who but a short time before had been equally as criminal. I had nearly reached the further side, intending to cut off the retreat, when the braying of some burros was heard. These watch dogs of an Indian camp are better than were the geese of Rome. I hurried along. The faint light of the morning was just breaking, and I held my breath for fear the alarm would be given, when all at once the flames bursting from the rifles of some of the hostiles who had gone to investigate the cause of the braying of the burros, and the echoing and reëchoing of the rifle reports through the mountains, told me that the camp was in arms. Dim forms could be seen rapidly descending the mountain sides and disappearing below. A large number came my way within easy range,— less than two hundred yards. We fired many shots but I saw no one fall. One Indian attempted to ride by me on a horse; I fired twice at him, when he abandoned the horse and disappeared; the horse was shot, but I never knew what became of the Indian. We pursued for a time, but as few of our Indian scouts could have gone farther, we had to give up the pursuit. The hostiles, like so many quail, had disappeared among the rocks. One by one our scouts returned. We had captured the entire herd, all the camp effects and what little food they had, consisting of some mescal, some fresh pony meat, a small part of a deer and a little dried meat, which the scouts seized and began to devour. I had no desire for food. Every one was worn out and it was cold and damp. In a little while an Indian woman came in and said that Geronimo and Natchez desired to talk. She begged food, and left us bearing word that Captain

Crawford would see the chiefs next day. The conference was to be held about a mile away on the river below our position, and he desired me to be present. What would have been the result of this conference will never be known on account of the unfortunate attack of the Mexicans next day. It was fortunate that we occupied the strong position of the hostile camp. Our packs as well as the doctor and interpreter had been sent for, but unfortunately they did not arrive that night.

We built fires and tried to obtain a little rest, but I could not sleep on account of the intense cold, and, besides, we had been without food for many hours; in fact, we had not partaken of cooked food for days. With the continual marching day and night no wonder our Indians were tired out and now threw themselves among the rocks to sleep, failing to maintain their usual vigilance. We had no fear of an attack. At daylight the next morning the camp was aroused by loud cries from

ONE INDIAN ATTEMPTED TO RIDE BY ME.

some of our scouts. Lieutenant Shipp and I, with a white man named Horn employed as chief-of-scouts for my companies, ran forward to ascertain the cause of alarm. We thought at first that the disturbance must have been occasioned by the scouts of Captain Wirt Davis. A heavy fog hung over the mountains, making the morning light very faint. But by ascending the rocks we could see the outlines of dusky forms moving in the distance. Then all at once there was a crash of musketry and the flames from many rifles lighted up the scene. In that discharge three of our scouts were wounded, one very badly, and we quickly sought cover. The thought that it was our own friends who were attacking us was agonizing and we had not the heart to retaliate, but the scouts kept up a desultory fire until Captain Crawford, whom we had left lying by the camp fire, shouted to us to stop. In about fifteen minutes the firing ceased and it now became known that the attacking party were Mexicans, a detachment of whom, about thirteen, were seen approaching, four of them coming toward the rocks where we were. As I spoke Spanish, I advanced about fifty or seventy-five yards to meet them and was followed by Captain Crawford. I told them who we were and of our fight with the hostiles, that we had just captured their camp, etc. Captain Crawford, who did not speak Spanish, now asked if I had explained all to them. I told him I had. At this time we were all standing within a few feet of each other.

The officer commanding the Mexicans was Major Corredor, a tall, powerful man over six feet high, and he acted as spokesman. Looking to the rocks we could see the heads of many of our Indian scouts with their rifles ready, and could hear the sharp snap of the breechblocks as the cartridges were inserted. I can well recall the expression on the faces of these Mexicans, for they thought our scouts were going to fire ; indeed I thought so myself. At the same time I noticed a party of Mexicans marching in a low ravine toward a high point which commanded and enfiladed our position, about four hundred yards distant. I called Captain Crawford's attention to this as well as to the aspect of our own scouts. He said, "For God's sake, don't let them fire !" Major Corredor also said, "*No tiras;*" — Don't fire. I said to him, "No," and told him not to let his men fire. I then turned toward the scouts saying in Spanish "Don't fire," holding my hand toward them. They nearly all understood Spanish while they did not speak it. I had taken a few steps forward to carry out the Captain's instructions, when one shot rang out distinct and alone ; the echoes were such that I could not tell where it came from, but it sounded like a death knell and was followed by volleys from both sides. As we all sought cover, I looked back just in time to see the tall Mexican throw down his rifle and fall, shot through the heart. Another Mexican, Lieutenant Juan de La Cruz, fell as he ran, pierced by thirteen bullets. The other two ran behind a small oak, but it was nearly cut down by bullets and they were both killed. About nine or ten others who were in view rapidly got close to the ground or in hollows behind rocks, which alone saved them as they were near, and formed a portion of the party that advanced. Upon reaching the rocks where I had sought shelter, I found Captain Crawford lying with his head pierced by a ball. His brain was running down his face and some of it lay on the rocks. He must have been shot just as he reached and mounted the rocks. Over his face lay a red handkerchief at which his hand clutched in a spasmodic way. Dutchy stood near him. I thought him dead, and sick at heart I gave my attention to the serious conditions existing. The fall of Captain Crawford was a sad and unfortunate event, greatly to be deplored, and cast a gloom over us which we could not shake off.

Being next in command, I hastened to send scouts to prevent the attack attempted on our right above referred to, and after an interval of about two hours the Mexicans were driven entirely away and the firing gradually ceased. They now occupied a strong line of hills, with excellent shelter, were double our strength, and were armed with calibre 44 Remington rifles, which carried a cartridge similar to our own. Our command was without rations and nearly without ammunition, the one beltful supplied to each scout having in many cases been entirely exhausted in the two fights. It was true that many of them had extra rounds, but I estimated that between four and five thousand rounds had been fired and that some of the men had none left.

The Mexicans now called to us saying they would like to talk, but they were too cautious to advance. When Mr. Horn and I went forward, to talk to them, three or four advanced to meet us about one hundred and fifty yards from our position. The brother of the lieutenant who had been killed was crying bitterly, and the whole party seemed a most forlorn company of men, and sincere in saying that they thought we were the hostiles. All their officers were killed, and I believe others besides, but how many we never knew. The fact that our command was composed almost entirely of Indians was a most unfortunate one. With regular soldiers all would have been clear. Our position at this time, confronted as we were by a hostile Mexican force, while behind us was the entire hostile band of Indians evidently enjoying the situation, is probably unparalleled. We had scarcely any ammunition, no food, and our supplies were with the pack-train almost unprotected — no one knew where — while we were many days' march from our own country, which could only be reached through a territory hostile to our Indians. The governor of Sonora

M.—27

had made serious charges against the Indians for depredations committed on the march down, and besides, there was a bitter feeling existing caused by this fight. If the Mexicans had attacked us in the rear, where we were entirely unprotected, our position would have been untenable. Had such an attack been made the result would probably have been the scattering of our command in the mountains, our Chiricahuas joining the hostiles.

It looked very serious, and my future course was governed by the condition. If it were possible I was bound to protect the lives of the white men of the command, the pack-train, and our Indian scouts. Lieutenant Shipp and I were in accord, he appreciating as I did our desperate position. The first attack had been a mistake, and the second had been brought on before the Mexicans could know what had been said to their officers who had been killed. The Mexicans deplored the affair and seemed sincere. I felt a pity for them. They asked me to go with them while they carried their dead away. A small detail took the bodies one by one to their lines, and I went with each body. They then asked me to send our doctor to care for their wounded, and to loan them enough of the captured stock to carry their wounded back. I agreed to do this, but could give them no food, which they also asked. Late in the day the doctor arrived, and after he had attended to our wounded I sent him to look after theirs, some of whom were in a dangerous way. He attended five of them.

The next day I decided to move on, as the surgeon said that the death of Captain Crawford was a matter of but a little time, and our condition made it necessary for us to try and reach our pack-train for supplies and ammunition. I was afraid that the Mexicans might take our pack-train, as it had but a poor escort of the weak and sick. Besides, most of the packers had been armed with calibre 50 carbines (Sharps), while they had been supplied with calibre 45 ammunition. I was in hopes that when away from the Mexicans I might succeed in effecting a conference with the hostile chiefs, and possibly a surrender. This could not be done while the Mexicans were near, and they would not move before we did, as they said they were afraid they might be attacked by the scouts. In order to move Captain Crawford, I had to make a litter and have him carried by hand. As there was no wood in the country, I sent to the river and got canes, which we bound together to make the side rails, using a piece of canvas for the bed.

While busy attending to the making of this, I heard someone calling, and going out a short distance, saw Concepcion, the interpreter, standing

GERONIMO.

with some Mexicans about two hundred yards away. He beckoned to me and I went forward to talk to the men, as I was the only one who could speak Spanish, Horn being wounded. I had sent Concepcion to drive back some of the captured Indian stock which had wandered off during the fight. As I advanced toward the Mexicans they saluted me very courteously, and in a friendly way said that before they left they wanted to have a talk. It was raining and they asked me to step under a sheltering rock near by ; this was the very point from which they had first fired. On stepping under the rock, I found myself confronted with about fifty Mexicans, all armed with Remington rifles, and a hard looking lot. I would here state that I had sent them, according to my promise, six of the captured Indian horses, which, however, they had not received, as they said the horses were no good, being wounded and worn out ; but of this I did not know at the time. Old Concepcion was detained by them. He was a Mexican who had been stolen by the Apaches when a boy, and was employed as an interpreter, as he knew the Apache language.

The manner of the Mexicans when they found me in their power had undergone a marked change. They became insolent, stating that we had killed their officers and that we were marauders and had no authority in their country. They demanded my papers. I explained that there was a treaty between Mexico and the United States, but that I had no papers, as Captain Crawford had left all our baggage with the pack-train. Their language was insolent and threatening. I now appreciated my position and realized that the consequence of my being away from the command with the interpreter was that there was no one with the scouts who could make himself understood by them. The Mexicans stated that I had promised them animals to take back their wounded, and had not furnished them, as those I had sent were worthless. I told them I would send them other animals on my return, and started to go, when they surrounded me, saying that I must remain until I had sent the mules.

By this time our Indians were yelling and preparing to fight. A few shots would have precipitated matters. The Mexicans called my attention to the action of my scouts, and I told them that the Indians evidently feared treachery and that I could not control them while away. They then said I could go if I would send them six mules, after which they would leave the country. This I promised I would do, but they would not trust my word of honor and held old Concepcion a prisoner till I sent them the mules. I demanded a receipt, which they gave, and afterward Mexico paid our government the full value of the animals.

It was now too late in the day to move, but the next morning I proceeded on the homeward march, carrying Captain Crawford by hand. The Indians, always superstitious, did not want to help, but were persuaded, Lieutenant Shipp and I also assisting. To add to the difficulty, it was the rainy season and the steep mountain sides were climbed most laboriously. It would be difficult to describe this march. With great effort, the first day we only made two or three miles. The wounded Indian was placed on a pony, and although

OUR INDIANS WERE YELLING AND PREPARING TO FIGHT.

badly hurt, seemed to get along very well. The two other wounded scouts and Mr. Horn were so slightly injured that they moved with no trouble.

An Indian woman came into camp that night and said that Geronimo wanted to talk. I concluded to meet him, and the next morning, after moving about two miles, I left the command and went with the interpreter, Mr. Horn, and five scouts, to a point about a mile or so distant. We went without arms as this was expressly stipulated by Geronimo as a condition. The chiefs did not appear, but I had a talk with two of the men, who promised that the chiefs would meet me the next day. They said I must come without arms. The next day I went to meet them and found Geronimo, Natchez, Nana and Chihuahua with fourteen men. They came fully armed with their belts full of ammunition, and as I had come unarmed according to agreement, this was a breach of faith and I did not think it argued well for their conduct. Apparently suspicious of treachery, every man of them sat with his rifle in an upright position, forming a circle nearly around me with Geronimo in the center. He sat there for fully a minute looking me straight in the eyes and finally said to me:

"Why did you come down here?"

"I came to capture or destroy you and your band," I answered.

He knew perfectly well that this was the only answer I could truthfully make. He then arose, walked to me and shook my hand, saying that he could trust me, and then asked me to report to the department commander what he had to say. He enumerated his grievances at the agency, all of which were purely imaginary or assumed. I advised him to surrender and told him if he did not that neither the United States troops nor the Mexicans would let him rest. He agreed to surrender to me Nana, one other man, his (Geronimo's) wife, and one of Natchez's wives, with some of their children, nine in all, and promised to meet General Crook near San Bernardino in two moons to talk about surrendering. With this understanding I returned to camp. In a short time he sent the prisoners with the request that I give him a little sugar and flour. This request I complied with, having in the meantime sent some of my scouts for the pack-train, which they had found and brought back. Here, almost at midnight, I was awakened by the scouts who had assembled saying that they had seen the Mexicans approaching to attack us, and that they must have ammunition. I had not intended to issue any more just then, as we only had about three thousand rounds left, but they begged so hard that I finally issued one thousand rounds, though I could hardly believe this report. No Mexicans appeared. The hostiles had plenty of money and it was afterward reported that our scouts had sold them ammunition at the rate of one dollar per round.

The next day we continued on our march, which was very difficult on account of our being encumbered with our wounded. On the 17th of January, while sitting with Captain Crawford, he opened his eyes and looked me straight in the face and then pressed my hand. No doubt he was conscious, and I tried to get him to speak or write, but he could not. I assured him I would do all in my power to arrange his affairs, and he put his arm around me and drew me to him, but could only shake his head in answer. This conscious interval only lasted about five minutes, and then the look of intelligence seemed to pass away forever. The next day he died while we were on the march, passing away so quietly that no one knew the exact time of his death. We wrapped the body in canvas and placed it on one of the pack

THE DEATH OF CAPTAIN CRAWFORD.

mules. We now moved morerapidly, but when we reached the Satachi River we could not cross it, as it was swollen by the late rains and was deep and turbulent. We were thus forced to go into camp and lose a day. In the meantime the body of Captain Crawford began to decompose, so we hurried on, crossing the river the next day and on the day following reached Nacori. Here we buried Captain Crawford, putting his body in charge of the Presidente of the town and marking well the place of his burial. I could only get four boards (slabs) in the town and used them in making a coffin, the body being wrapped securely in canvas.

The disposition of the people was decidedly unfriendly, and at Baserac and Bavispe about two hundred of the local troops were assembled with hostile intent. To add to the trouble, the scouts obtained mescal and were very unruly. I had to use great care to prevent a conflict at Baserac. I was obliged to pass through the town, as there was a mountain on one side and a river on the other. The officials refused at first to let me pass, but I moved some of the troops through, supported by the remainder, and avoided a conflict. At Bavispe the Indians obtained a large quantity of mescal, and the civil authorities tried to take our captured stock. I sent them out of the camp, and had they not left when they did I am sure the intoxicated Indians would have fired upon them. Here occurred a quarrel between a company of White Mountain Indian scouts and one of Chiricahuas. They loaded their rifles to fire upon each other, while the first sergeants of the two companies fought between the lines, but I finally succeeded in quelling the disturbance. The next day I hurried away, and without further difficulty reached Lang's Ranch, arriving there on the first day of February. Up to that time we had marched over one thousand miles.

I was ordered to return, February 5, to Mexico and look out for the hostiles, who had agreed to signal their return. I camped about ten miles south of the line on the San Bernardino River, and remained there until the 15th of March, when a signal was observed on a high point about twenty miles south. I went out with four or five scouts and met some messengers from Geronimo and Natchez, near the point from which the signal had been made. They informed me that the entire band of hostiles were then about forty miles away, camped in the mountains near Fronteras. I told them to return and bring Geronimo and his band at once, as the Mexicans were in pursuit and liable to attack them at any time. On the nineteenth the entire band came and camped about half a mile from my command. One more warrior with his wife and two children gave themselves up, and I now had thirteen prisoners. I endeavored to persuade Geronimo and his band to go into Fort Bowie, telling them they were liable to be attacked by Mexican troops, but could only induce them to move with me to the Cañon de los Embudos, about twelve miles below the border, where they camped in a strong position among the rocks a half a mile away.

I had notified the department commander upon the arrival of the messengers on the 15th, and on the 29th he arrived at my camp. In the interval, however, before General Crook arrived, Geronimo had almost daily come into my camp to talk to me and ask when the general would get there. On his arrival a conference was held and the hostiles promised they would surrender. General Crook then returned, directing me to bring them in. This I endeavored to do, but this surrender was only an agreement, no arms being taken from them, nor were they any more in my possession than when I had met them in the Sierra Madre Mountains. It was believed, however, that they would come in. Unfortunately, they obtained liquor, and all night on the 27th I could hear firing in their camp a mile or so away. I sent my command on, and, accompanied only by the interpreter, waited for the hostiles to move, but they were in a bad humor. They moved their camp at noon that day and I then left. I met Geronimo and a number of warriors gathered together near by on Elias Creek, many of them being drunk, and Geronimo told me they would follow, but that I had better go on or he would not be responsible for my life. I then proceeded to my camp. I had ordered the battalion to camp at a point ten miles on the way back on the San Bernardino. That afternoon the hostiles came up and camped about half a mile above me in a higher position.

I went into their camp and found trouble. Natchez had shot his wife, and they were all drinking heavily. I sent Lieutenant Shipp with a detail to destroy all the mescal at a ranch near by, where they had previously obtained all their liquor. During the day all seemed quiet, but at night a few shots were heard. I sent to find out the cause and found the trouble was over some women; this trouble soon ceased, however, and quiet was restored. I felt anxious about the next day's march, as I would then cross the line and be near troops. The next morning I was awakened and told that the hostiles were gone. I caused a careful search to be made, and ascertained that Geronimo and Natchez with twenty men, thirteen women and two children had gone during the night, and not a soul as far as I could ascertain, knew anything of the time they had gone, or that they had intended to go. Chihuahua, Ulzahney, Nana, Catley, nine other men, and forty-seven women and children remained. The herd was brought in, and only three of their horses were missing. I directed Lieutenant Faison, with a sufficient detail, to take the remaining hostiles to Fort Bowie; then, with all the available men left, Lieutenant Shipp and I at once started in pursuit.

About six miles from camp we struck the trail going due west over a chain of high mountains. This gave us a full view of the mountains in all directions, but the trail suddenly changed its direction to the south and went down a steep and difficult descent, across a basin so dense with chapparel

and cut up with ravines as to make travel very difficult and slow, especially as every bush was full of thorns which tore ourselves and animals.
Across this basin, about ten miles, the trail ascended a high mountain,
very steep and rocky. The trail of the one horse with the hostiles induced us to think it might be possible to ride; but after reaching the top
we found this horse stabbed
and abandoned among the
rocks; they were unable to
take it farther. Be-
yond, the descent
was vertical and of

solid rock
from fifty to
three hun-
dred feet high for miles
each way. Here the trail
was lost, the Indians having scattered
and walked entirely on the rocks.

APACHES WATCHING THE TROOPS WITH
GLASSES.

No doubt our pursuit had been discov-
ered from this point when we crossed the mountain on the other side of the
basin, ten miles away. These Indians were well supplied with telescopes
and glasses, and a watch had doubtless been maintained here according
to their usual custom. It is in this way, by selecting their line of march
over these high points, that their retreat can always be watched and

danger avoided.   In the same way they watch the country for miles in advance.   These never-failing precautions may serve to show how difficult is the chance of catching these men, who once alarmed are like wild animals, with their sense of sight and of hearing as keenly developed.

We could not descend here, so we were obliged to retrace our steps down the mountain and make a circuit of ten miles to again strike the trail beyond. This we did, but when the stream beyond was reached it was dark, and further pursuit that night was impossible. The next morning we moved down the creek, cutting the trails which had come together about four miles below, and we followed this for about ten miles to the south. The hostiles had not stopped from the time they had left, and now had made about forty-five miles and had good ten hours the start. The trail here split and one part, the larger, crossed over the broken mountains north of Bavispe, into the Sierra Madres, while the other crossed into the mountains north of Fronteras.

The scouts now seemed discouraged. Their moccasins were worn out by the constant hard work of the past five months, and the prospect of returning to the scenes of their last trials was not inviting. Besides, their discharge would take place in about one month. They appealed to me to go no further, telling me that it was useless, etc. This I appreciated and decided to return. We then retraced our way and continued the homeward march. While returning, two of the escaped hostiles joined me and gave themselves up. I arrived at Fort Bowie on the 3d of April. The results of the expedition were by no means unimportant as we had secured the larger part of the hostiles, seventy-nine in all, of whom fifteen were warriors.

I cannot speak too highly of the noble and soldierly qualities of Captain Crawford, killed by Mexican troops while doing all in his power to help them.   He was ever ready, ever brave and loyal in the performance of his duty, and his loss was indeed a serious one.

Lieutenant Shipp suffered all the hardships of the campaign, and his services are entitled to high consideration.

Lieutenant Faison showed much ability and energy in supplying the command and in handling the trains. While not with the command during the action with the Indians and Mexicans, his duty was not only a hard one, but full of danger and suffering.

Doctor Davis was very faithful and efficient.

I cannot commend too highly Mr. Horn, my chief of scouts; his gallant services deserve a reward which he has never received.*

Meanwhile, the closing scenes above described by Captain Maus, and the condition of affairs in Arizona attracted unusual attention.

One of General Crook's methods of dealing with the hostiles was to employ a certain number of the same tribe to act as scouts in their pursuit. Possibly, as there have been so many misrepresentations as to what his instructions actually were, the conditions he made with the surrendered Indians, and my own instructions, a better understanding will be obtained by presenting the official correspondence first published in 1886, that passed between the department commander and the higher authorities immediately prior to my assuming command of that department. This correspondence was as follows, General Crook having gone from Fort Bowie down to meet the hostile Apaches:

CAMP EL CANON DE LOS EMBUDOS, ⎫
20 MILES S. E. SAN BERNARDINO, MEXICO, March 26, 1886.— ⎭

LIEUTENANT-GENERAL P. H. SHERIDAN, Washington, D. C. :

I met the hostiles yesterday at Lieut. Maus' camp, they being located about five hundred yards distant. I found them very independent, and fierce as so many tigers. Knowing what pitiless brutes they are themselves, they mistrust everyone else. After my talk with them it seemed as if it would be impossible to get any hold on them, except on condition that they be allowed to return to their reservation on their old status.

To-day things look more favorable. GEORGE CROOK, Brigadier General.

CAMP EL CANON LOS EMBUDOS, MEXICO, March 27, 1886.

LIEUTENANT-GENERAL SHERIDAN, U. S. A., Washington, D. C. : *Confidential.*

In conference with Geronimo and the other Chiricahuas I told them they must decide at once on unconditional surrender or to fight it out. That in the latter event hostilities should be resumed at once, and the last one of them killed if it took fifty years. I told them to reflect on what they were to do before giving me their answer. The only propositions they would entertain were these three: That they should be sent east for not exceeding two years, taking with them such of their families as so desired, leaving at Apache Nana who is seventy years old and superannuated ; or that they should all return to the reservation upon their old status ; or else return to the war-path with its attendant horrors.

---

*This is quite true of Mr. Horn, but not more true than of the writer himself, and of Captain Crawford, Captain Wirt Davis, Captain Wilder, Lieutenant Gatewood and Lieutenant Clarke. Neither were Captain Baldwin and Captain Snyder rewarded, and the same is true of scores of others who have rendered most distinguished, laborious and heroic services in this most difficult and dangerous of all warfare. It is true that some of them have had some advance of rank in the regular course of promotion, but no more than others who have never engaged in such services. Yet they have the consciousness of having rendered to the government and their fellow countrymen most valuable and important services.

As I had to act at once I have to-day accepted their surrender upon the first propo-sition. Kætena, the young chief who less than two years ago was the worst Chiricahua of the whole lot, is now perfectly subdued. He is thoroughly reconstructed, has rendered me valuable assistance, and will be of great service in helping to control these Indians in the future. His stay at Alcatraz has worked a complete reformation in his character. I have not a doubt that similar treatment will produce same results with the whole band, and that by the end of that time the excitement here will have died away.

Mangus, with thirteen Chiricahuas, six of whom are bucks, is not with the other Chiricahuas. He separated from them in August last, and has since held no communica-tion with them. He has committed no depredations. As it would be likely to take at least a year to find him in the immense ranges of mountains to the south, I think it inadvisable to attempt any search at this time, especially as he will undoubtedly give him-self up as soon as he hears what the others have done.

I start for Bowie to-morrow morning, to reach there next night. I respectfully request to be informed whether or not my action has been approved, and also that full instructions meet me at that point. The Chiricahuas start for Bowie to-morrow with the Apache scouts under Lieut. Maus.   GEORGE CROOK, Brigadier-General.

––––––––––––

WASHINGTON, D. C., March 30, 1886.
GENERAL GEORGE CROOK, Fort Bowie, Arizona.

You are confidentially informed that your telegram of March 29th is received. The President cannot assent to the surrender of the hostiles on the terms that their imprison-ment last for two years, with the understanding of their return to the reservation. He instructs you to enter again into negotiations on the terms of their unconditional surrender, only sparing their lives; in the meantime, and on the receipt of this order, you are directed to take every precaution against the escape of the hostiles, which must not be allowed under any circumstances. You must make at once such disposition of your troops as will insure against further hostilities by completing the destruction of the hostiles unless these terms are accepted.   P. H. SHERIDAN, Lieut.-General.

––––––––––––

FORT BOWIE, A. T., March 30, 1886.
LIEUT.-GEN. P. H. SHERIDAN, Washington, D. C.

A courier just in from Lieut. Maus reports that during last night Geronimo and Natchez with twenty men and thirteen women left his camp, taking no stock. He states that there was no apparent cause for their leaving. Two dispatches received from him this morning reported everything going on well and the Chiricahuas in good spirits. Chihuahua and twelve men remained behind. Lieut. Maus with his scouts, except enough to take the other prisoners to Bowie, have gone in pursuit.

                                   GEO. CROOK, Brigadier-General.

––––––––––––

WASHINGTON, D. C., March 31, 1886.
GENERAL GEORGE CROOK, Fort Bowie, A. T.

Your dispatch of yesterday received. It has occasioned great disappointment. It seems strange that Geronimo and party could have escaped without the knowledge of the scouts.   P. H. SHERIDAN, Lieut.-General.

FORT BOWIE, A. T., March 31, 1886.

LIEUT.-GENERAL P. H. SHERIDAN, Washington, D. C.

In reply to your dispatch of March thirtieth, to enable you to clearly understand the situation, it should be remembered that the hostiles had an agreement with Lieut. Maus that they were to be met by me twenty-five miles below the line, and that no regular troops were to be present. While I was very averse to such an arrangement, I had to

APACHES IN AMBUSH.

abide by it, as it had already been entered into. We found them in camp on a rocky hill about five hundred yards from Lieut. Maus, in such a position that a thousand men could not have surrounded them with any possibility of capturing them. They were able, upon the approach of any enemy being signaled, to scatter and escape through dozens of ravines and cañons, which would shelter them from pursuit until they reached the higher ranges in the vicinity. They were armed to the teeth, having the most approved guns and all the ammunition they could carry. The clothing and other supplies lost in the fight with Crawford had been replaced by blankets and shirts obtained in Mexico. Lieut. Maus, with Apache scouts, was camped at the nearest point the hostiles would agree to their approaching.

Even had I been disposed to betray the confidence they placed in me, it would have been simply an impossibility to get white troops to that point either by day or by night without their knowledge, and had I attempted to do this the whole band would have stampeded back to the mountains. So suspicious were they that never more than from five to eight of the men came into our camp at one time, and to have attempted the arrest of those would have stampeded the others to the mountains. Even after the march to Bowie began we were compelled to allow them to scatter. They would not march in a body, and had any efforts been made to keep them together they would have broken for the mountains. My only hope was to get their confidence on the march through Kaetena and other confidential Indians, and finally to put them on the cars, and until this was done it was impossible even to disarm them.

GEORGE CROOK, Brigadier-General, Commanding.

WASHINGTON, D. C., April 1, 1886.

GENERAL GEORGE CROOK, Fort Bowie, A. T.

Your dispatch of March thirty-first received. I do not see what you can now do except to concentrate your troops at the best points and give protection to the people. Geronimo will undoubtedly enter upon other raids of murder and robbery, and as the offensive campaign against him with scouts has failed, would it not be best to take up the defensive and give protection to the people and business interests of Arizona and New Mexico. The infantry might be stationed by companies at certain points requiring protection, and the cavalry patrol between them. You have in your department forty-three companies of infantry and forty companies of cavalry, and ought to be able to do a good deal with such a force. Please send me a statement of what you contemplate for the future.   P. H. SHERIDAN, Lieut.-General.

FORT BOWIE, A. T., April 1, 1886.

LIEUT.-GENERAL P. H. SHERIDAN, Washington, D. C.

Your dispatch of to-day received. It has been my aim throughout present operations to afford the greatest amount of protection to life and property interests, and troops have been stationed accordingly. Troops cannot protect property beyond a radius of one-half mile from their camp. If offensive movements against the Indians are not resumed, they may remain quietly in the mountains for an indefinite time without crossing the line, and yet their very presence there will be a constant menace and require the troops in the department to be at all times in position to repress sudden raids, and so long as any remain out they will form a nucleus for disaffected Indians from the different agencies in Arizona and New Mexico to join. That the operations of the scouts in Mexico have not proven as successful as was hoped, is due to the enormous difficulties they have been compelled to encounter from the nature of the Indians they have been hunting, and the character of the country in which they have operated, and of which persons not thoroughly conversant with both can have no conception. I believe that the plan upon which I have conducted operations is the one most likely to prove successful in the end. It may be, however, that I am too much wedded to my own views in this matter, and as I have spent nearly eight years of the hardest work in my life in this department, I respectfully request that I may now be relieved from its command.

GEORGE CROOK, Brigadier-General.

WASHINGTON, D. C., April 2, 1886.

GENERAL N. A. MILES, Fort Leavenworth, Kansas.

Orders of this day assign you to command the Department of Arizona to relieve General Crook. Instructions will be sent you.

R. C. DRUM, Adjutant-General.

FORT BOWIE, A. T., April 2, 1886.

LIEUT.-GENERAL P. H. SHERIDAN, Washington, D. C.

The hostiles who did not leave with Geronimo arrived to-day. About eighty. I have not ascertained the exact number. Some of the worst of the band are among them. In my judgment they should be sent away at once, as the effect on those still out would be much better than to confine them. After they get to their destination, if they can be shown that their future will be better by remaining than to return, I think there will be but little difficulty in obtaining their consent to remain indefinitely. When sent off a guard should accompany them. GEORGE CROOK, Brigadier-General.

WASHINGTON, D. C., April 5, 1886.

GEN. GEO. CROOK, Fort Bowie, Ariz.

The present terms not having been agreed to here, and Geronimo having broken every condition of surrender, the Indians now in custody are to be held as prisoners and sent to Fort Marion without reference to previous communication and without, in any way, consulting their wishes in the matter. This is in addition to my previous telegram of to-day. P. H. SHERIDAN, Lieut.-General.

WASHINGTON, D. C., April 2, 1886.

GENERAL GEORGE CROOK, Fort Bowie, A. T.

General Miles has been ordered to relieve you in command of the Department of Arizona and orders issued to-day. Advise General Miles where you will be.

By order Secretary of War. R. C DRUM, Adjutant-General.

FORT BOWIE, A. T., April 3, 1886.

GENERAL N. A. MILES, Fort Leavenworth, Kansas.

Adjutant-General of the Army telegraphs that you have been directed to relieve me in command Dep't of Arizona. Shall remain at Fort Bowie. When can I expect you here? GEORGE CROOK, Brigadier-General.

FORT LEAVENWORTH, KANSAS, April 3, 1886.

GENERAL GEORGE CROOK, Fort Bowie, A. T.

The order was a perfect surprise to me. I do not expect to leave here for several days, possibly, one week.   N. A. MILES, Brigadier-General.

HEADQUARTERS OF THE ARMY, }
WASHINGTON, D. C., April 3, 1886. }

GENERAL NELSON A. MILES, Fort Leavenworth, Kansas.

The Lieutenant-General directs that on assuming command of the Department of Arizona, you fix your headquarters temporarily at or near some point on the Southern Pacific R. R.

He directs that the greatest care be taken to prevent the spread of hostilities among friendly Indians in your command, and that the most vigorous operations looking to the destruction or capture of the hostiles be ceaselessly carried on. He does not wish to embarrass you by undertaking at this distance to give specific instructions in relation to operations against the hostiles, but it is deemed advisable to suggest the necessity of making active and prominent use of the regular troops of your command. It is desired that you proceed to Arizona as soon as practicable.

R. C. DRUM, Adjutant-General.

I never had any desire to go to this section of country or to engage in a campaign of that character. Still I was aware that such an event might possibly occur.

Therefore, perhaps, I should not have been surprised when, at Fort Leavenworth, Kansas, April 2, 1886, I received telegraphic orders to proceed immediately to Arizona and take charge of that department. I did not welcome the order with any degree of satisfaction. In fact it was a most undesirable duty. Yet the order was imperative and required immediate action.

By special act of Congress general officers are allowed certain staff officers known as aides-de-camp. They are the personal staff of the general officer, and are expected to go with him to any field or any part of the country and be in constant readiness for any service that may be required of them in organizing, disciplining, mobilizing and commanding any military force. At that time I was entitled to two officers of that class though I had but one, Lieutenant O. F. Long. He having recently been relieved under a rule that had been newly inaugurated, and I, not having been able to name another to take his place, was compelled to leave Leavenworth practically alone. Still I had at that time a very efficient and faithful general service clerk, stenographer and secretary, Mr. J. Frank Brown, and under the rules existing at that time I had authority to discharge him from the service and reëmploy him in another department. I had requested to have this man transferred to the Department of Arizona and also had asked permission to take with me one other man, a faithful, intelligent messenger. But these official requests having been disapproved, in accordance with the authority then existing I discharged from the service the general service clerk, and took him at my own expense to the Department of Arizona, where I had him reëmployed. I started on the morning of the 7th of April and reached Bowie Station, Arizona, April 12.

Very few of the troops in that department had ever served under my command and therefore I was not as familiar with the *personnel* of the command as I would have desired. Arriving practically alone and undertaking a campaign in a territory of the topography of which I had no personal knowledge any more than I had of the habits and disposition of the merciless savages, the enterprise seemed to be quite difficult.

At Bowie Station, on the Southern Pacific Railroad, I found a battalion of the Second Cavalry encamped, and in a very unsatisfactory condition. They appeared to be not only discouraged but thoroughly disheartened. They had been in the field a long time doing most disagreeable and hazardous duty, and appeared to have very little hope of ultimate success. The citizens and settlers located in that district of country were the most terror-stricken people I had ever seen in any part of the United States. The settlers were afraid to travel during the daytime, and never felt safe either night or day unless within reach of their firearms. Many of the mines and settlements had been abandoned. The Apache was the terror that haunted the settlers by day and by night. For

FORT BOWIE, ARIZONA.

hundreds of years the Apache had been at war with the civilized races; first with the Spaniards, then with the Mexicans, and still later with the United States authorities.

M.—28

Under a treaty or agreement between our government and Mexico, permission was granted by the Mexican government for our troops to pursue hostile Indians into the territory of Mexico. This arrangement resulted most satisfactorily as it enabled our troops to pursue the Indians without giving them any rest and also to act in concert with the Mexican troops. I found Governor Louis Torres, governor of Sonora and subsequently a general in the Mexican army, a most agreeable gentleman and efficient executive. His assistance and coöperation was most agreeable and beneficial. I was also fortunate in having the friendship of the distinguished diplomat, Senor Don Matias Romero, who has so long and ably represented his government in Washington as minister of that republic.

I also wish to acknowledge the able assistance received from Governor Ross of New Mexico, formerly a United States Senator from Kansas, and Governor Zulick of Arizona, for assistance and coöperation, as well as that of Mr. L. P. Hughes, then a citizen of that territory and now its governor.

From Bowie Station I went to Fort Bowie, where I established my headquarters. This little military post was situated in a pass of the mountains formerly known as Apache Pass, near what was called Cochise's stronghold in the mountains, which was a favorite resort of the Apaches for many years. The cemetery near that military station contains the remains of a large number of people, both men and women, who had been killed in that vicinity. Among the victims were people who had traveled on the stage, prospectors, ranchmen, and soldiers who had been waylaid and killed, or captured and then tortured to a cruel and merciless death.

My first duty was to reorganize the commands, and if possible inspire activity and confidence in the troops, and give the settlers assurances of protection. To this end I divided the territory of New Mexico and Arizona into districts of observation, placing the territory near each military post under the supervision of its commanding officer, with instructions to make his immediate district untenable for any band of Indians that might invade it. The whole aspect of the country was that of cheerlessness, doubt and uncertainty. The territory roamed over by these Indians was at least six hundred miles in extent north and south and three hundred and fifty miles east and west. This territory, comprised within the Rocky and Sierra Madre Mountains, was the most barren and desolate region on the continent.

These Apaches were perhaps the most expert mountain climbers in the world. By their training, by their habits of life and the necessities of their existence they were a strong, lithe, powerful people, with a singular lung power which enabled them to climb those high altitudes without accident and with very little fatigue. The mountains were rugged and precipitous, and the valleys narrow and in many places destitute of water. If there had been a large number of Indians where a strong body of troops could have been brought against them, the problem would have been simple and easy of solution; but to undertake to subjugate a small band that moved with the greatest rapidity from one inaccessible point to another was more difficult.

CHAPTER XXXVII.

THE ARIZONA CAMPAIGN. (I.)

PROBLEM PRESENTED BY THE SITUATION — OPINIONS OF CITIZENS — THE OBSTACLES TO SUCCESS
PRESENTED BY THE NATURAL CONDITIONS — AID FROM THE SIGNAL CORPS AT WASHING-
TON — THE HELIOSTAT — ARRANGEMENT OF STATIONS — NUMBER OF MESSAGES SENT —
DISTRICTS OF OBSERVATION — CAPTAIN LAWTON — CAPTAIN WOOD —
OTHER OFFICERS OF THE COMMAND — BREAKING OUT OF HOSTILES
— DETAILS OF THE CAMPAIGN AGAINST THE APACHES.

UCH being the circumstances the problem that presented itself to me was this : There were forty thousand Indians in New Mexico and Arizona the main portion of whom were peaceable and well disposed, yet in nearly all the different tribes there were disaffected and turbulent elements ready to assume hostilities if an opportunity occurred, or if the hostiles then at large were not brought under control. Over a vast area of country of rugged mountains and narrow valleys, with water only at scattered points and difficult to find and obtain, roamed one of the most desperate, cruel and hardy bands of outlaws that ever infested any country, who were to be hunted down and captured. A few criminals will keep the entire police force of the great city of London occupied ; and, as a matter of fact, it has always been found most difficult to arrest the leaders in any particular field of crime.

The mountain labyrinths of the Apaches may be compared to the criminal dens and slums of London, though on an immensely greater scale, and the outlaws to be tracked and subdued, for cunning, strength and ferocity have never been surpassed in the annals of either savage or civilized crime. A band of Indians that had roamed over that country for generations believed themselves to be masters and unconquerable, and many of the white people living in that country also believed it to be impossible to run them down and capture them. I was advised by many well-informed people of the uselessness of undertaking to subjugate the hostiles as, they stated, it had been tried for so many years without success. "Those Indians could go over mountain country better than white men;" "they could signal from one mountain range to another;" "they could conceal themselves;" and "when they turned upon their enemy they were utterly ruthless and cruel."

I listened to all this with a degree of patience, and the only reply that suggested itself was that though all that was said about their skill and enterprise and energy was true, yet with our superior intelligence and modern appliances we ought and would be able to counteract, equal, or surpass all the advantages possessed by the savages. As to the rapidity of their movements, we had the power of steam to aid us in moving troops, munitions and provisions, and the telegraph for communication. As to their being able to signal by the use of fire and smoke and the flashes of some bright piece of metal for a short distance, I thought we could not only equal, but far surpass them in a short time.

I had it in my mind to utilize for our benefit and their discomfiture, the very elements that had been the greatest obstacles in that whole country to their subjugation, namely, the high mountain ranges, the glaring, burning sunlight, and an atmosphere void of moisture. I therefore requested the chief signal officer at Washington, General Hazen, to send me a corps of skilled officers and men, and the best instruments and appliances that were attainable. I also directed my engineer officer to block out the country in such a way that we might establish a network of points of observation and communication over that entire country. Posts were established over the country most frequented by the Apaches, a district some two hundred miles wide by three hundred miles long, north and south. On the high mountain peaks of this region, I posted strong guards of infantry supplied with casks of water and provisions enough to last them for thirty days in case of siege. They were provided with the best field glasses and telescopes that could be obtained, and also with the best heliostats.

The heliostat is a little invention of an English officer which had been used in India many years before. My attention was first directed to it nearly twenty years ago when in the office of the chief signal officer of the army, General Myer, who then had six of these instruments. As they were not being used, I suggested that he send them to me at the cantonment on the Yellowstone, now Fort Keogh, Montana, and I there established the first line in this country, from Fort Keogh to Fort Custer. I afterward used them experimentally in the Department of the Columbia between Vancouver Barracks and Mount Hood a distance in an air line of fifty miles. I now determined to test them to their full extent and make practical use of them in the Department of Arizona.

I was much gratified to receive the hearty support of General Hazen in sending me skilled men ; and within a short time these stations were fixed on the high mountain peaks. It was remarkable what advantage they gave us in observing the movements of the Indians or of the troops in the valleys below, and in reporting it promptly to the central station or headquarters; also in communicating with the various commands, posts and stations in the field. At one time, when the system was in full operation, to test its efficiency a message of twenty-five words was sent from the extreme eastern to the extreme western station, over a zigzag course of four hundred miles, and the answer was received in four hours, the total distance traversed being about eight hundred miles. Between these two points for a part of the distance there was telegraphic communication, yet the

HELIOGRAPH STATION.

message could not have been sent by telegraph and courier and answer received as quickly as it was by this method.

The importance of the work done by the heliostat in the Apache campaign makes it worthy of a more extended notice than has as yet been accorded it. The method of signaling by it is very simple. By alternately interposing and removing some object in front of the mirror which forms the principal part of the instrument, long or short flashes of light are made which indicate words and letters to the eye in the same way the telegraph indicates them to the ear. The mirrors are usually mounted on a tripod, and the distance through which this method of communication may be carried depends on the clearness of the atmosphere and the size of the mirrors.

At the beginning of the campaign, Lieutenant A. M. Fuller of the Second Cavalry was placed in charge of the division of Arizona, and Lieutenant E. E. Dravo of the Sixth Cavalry, in charge of the division of New Mexico for the purpose of establishing heliograph stations at suitable points, and the success of the system was largely due to the able and judicious manner in which these officers performed their duties. The stations were generally situated on high mountains, some of them being six or seven thousand feet above the level of the sea. They were manned by two or three operators according to the amount of work to be done, and were usually provided with from one to five guards, according to the dangers of the situation. Couriers were also furnished wherever needed. Sometimes it was necessary to establish these stations a mile or two from water, which in that case was brought to them on the backs of mules. Rations were usually supplied by the month from the most convenient military post.

Besides the heliographs these stations were fitted out with field glasses, and usually also with a telescope, and all day long the lookout scanned the country for signals from undetermined points. Whenever possible the station was so situated as to afford a dark background, as it was found that a flash from such a station could be much more easily seen than from one where the sky formed the only background.

In the division of New Mexico there were thirteen of these stations, and in that of Arizona there were fourteen. The work was systematized from the very beginning. All details, changes and instructions were made by regular orders, and each station was provided with the necessary material for keeping records. Weekly reports were rendered by each station as to the number of messages sent and received, and weekly reports of the weather were also required. As the number of members of the signal corps was limited, much work was performed by enlisted men, who proved themselves to be very intelligent and apt, some of them being competent to go on a station after but two weeks' instruction. Naturally, telegraph operators found it much easier to learn the system than others did.

Some of these stations communicated with but one other, while some communicated with as many as five, as in the case of the one at Bowie Peak, Arizona Territory, or the one at the extreme northern point of the Swisshelm Mountains. The average distance between these stations was in a direct line about twenty-five miles, but Fort Huachuca, which communicated with three other stations, was thirty-one miles distant from the nearest.

In the division of Arizona the total number of messages sent from May 1, 1886, to September 30, of the same year was 2,264. The greatest number of messages from one station (802) was from Fort Bowie, and the next greatest numbers (284 and 241) were from the stations at Rucker Cañon and at Antelope Springs, near the south end of the Dragoon Mountains.

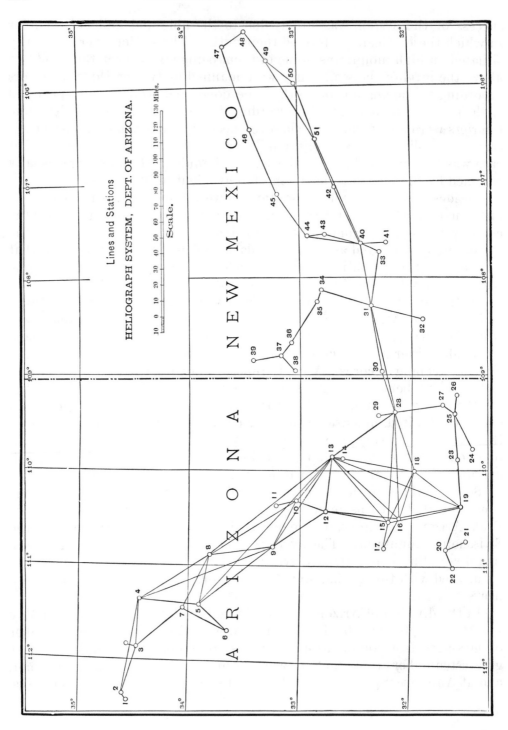

Lines and Stations
HELIOGRAPH SYSTEM, DEPT. OF ARIZONA.

Scale.

From Cochise's stronghold on the west side of the Dragoon Mountains, there were only eighteen messages sent, though this station repeated one hundred and twenty-five messages. The station at Bowie Peak repeated 1,644 messages, and the whole number of messages repeated was 4,463. The average number of words contained in these messages was about fifty, though there were cases where there were more than two hundred.

The country was subdivided into districts of observation, and each district was occupied by an efficient command fully supplied with transportation, field equipment, guides, scouts, trailers, etc., and Captain Thompson, of the Fourth Cavalry, an experienced and efficient officer, was appointed adjutant-general in the field.

For the instruction of the troops in the department, I issued the following orders:

HEADQUARTERS DEPARTMENT ARIZONA, IN THE FIELD,
FORT BOWIE, A. T., April 20, 1886.

GENERAL FIELD ORDERS No. 7.

The following instructions are issued for the information and guidance of troops serving in the southern portions of Arizona and New Mexico.

The chief object of the troops will be to capture or destroy any band of hostile Apache Indians found in this section of country; and to this end the most vigorous and persistent efforts will be required of all officers and soldiers until the object is accomplished.

To better facilitate this duty and afford as far as practicable protection to the scattered settlements, the territory is subdivided into Districts of Observation as shown upon maps furnished by the department engineer officer, and these will be placed under commanding officers to be hereafter designated.

Each command will have a sufficient number of troops and the necessary transportation to thoroughly examine the district of country to which it is assigned, and will be expected to keep such section clear of hostile Indians.

The signal detachments will be placed upon the highest peaks and prominent lookouts to discover any movements of Indians and to transmit messages between the different camps.

The infantry will be used in hunting through the groups and ranges of mountains, the resorts of the Indians, occupying the important passes in the mountains, guarding supplies, etc.

A sufficient number of reliable Indians will be used as auxiliaries to discover any signs of hostile Indians, and as trailers.

The cavalry will be used in light scouting parties, with a sufficient force held in readiness at all times to make the most persistent and effective pursuit.

To avoid any advantage the Indians may have by a relay of horses, where a troop or squadron commander is near the hostile Indians he will be justified in dismounting one-half of his command and selecting the lightest and best riders to make pursuit by the most vigorous forced marches, until the strength of all the animals of his command shall have been exhausted.

In this way a command should, under a judicious leader, capture a band of Indians or drive them from one hundred and fifty to two hundred miles in forty-eight hours through a country favorable for cavalry movements; and the horses of the troops will be trained for this purpose.

All the commanding officers will make themselves thoroughly familiar with the sections of country under their charge and will use every means to give timely information regarding the movements of hostile Indians to their superiors or others acting in concert with them, in order that fresh troops may intercept the hostiles or take up the pursuit.

Commanding officers are expected to continue a pursuit until capture, or until they are assured a fresh command is on the trail.

All camps and movements of troops will be concealed as far as possible, and every effort will be made at all times by the troops to discover hostile Indians before being seen by them.

To avoid ammunition getting into the hands of the hostile Indians every cartridge will be rigidly accounted for, and when they are used in the field the empty shells will be effectually destroyed.

Friendly relations will be encouraged between the troops and citizens of the country, and all facilities rendered for the prompt interchange of reliable information regarding the movements of hostile Indians.

Field reports will be made on the tenth, twentieth, and thirtieth of each month, giving the exact location of troops and the strength and condition of commands.

By command of Brigadier-General Miles:

WILLIAM A. THOMPSON, Captain Fourth Cavalry, A. A. A. G.

In making these dispositions the argument in my mind was that no human being and no wild animal could endure being hunted persistently without eventually being subjugated. Therefore in establishing these districts of observation, and making each one of them untenable, I believed that it would also be necessary to have a force to continue the pursuit when the Indians should retreat south of the Mexican boundary. At that time our government had a treaty with the Mexican government by which our forces were authorized to follow the trail of the hostile Indians or continue the pursuit in their territory, and that they would afford us whatever facilities they could in the way of information and assistance against these hostiles.

For some time I was undecided as to the personnel of this pursuing command. I visited several military posts—Fort Bowie, Fort Grant, Fort Huachuca and other stations,—before I fully made up my mind as to the officers and men I should choose to constitute such a force. At length I selected from Fort Huachuca an officer by the name of Captain H. W. Lawton, Fourth United States Cavalry, who, I thought, would fulfill all the requirements as commander. First of all, because he believed that these Indians *could* be subjugated. Officers who do not believe in success and are always ready to show how a thing cannot be done and give labored and logical reasons and arguments why it would be useless to attempt to accomplish a purpose, as a rule are not the kind of men to be selected for any hazardous enterprise. While some men may be over zealous and unduly confident, yet where you find a man of sterling ability and clear strong will power who believes that a thing can be accomplished, the chances are that, given an opportunity, he will be more likely to succeed than one who has no faith in what he may be called upon to do, or required to undertake.

Captain Lawton was of that class who believed that the Indians could be overcome. Although he recognized their great skill, cunning and physical strength, he believed they could be met and defeated by studying and improving upon their own methods. He had made himself a splendid record during the war of the rebellion, had also a fine record on the frontier, had been one of General Mackenzie's most zealous supporters, and possessed all the experience necessary to the command of such a force. He was physically, perhaps, as fine a specimen of a man as could be found. He weighed at that time two hundred and thirty pounds, was well proportioned, straight, active, agile, full of energy, stood six feet five inches in height and was without a superfluous pound of flesh. His bone, muscle, sinew and nerve power was of the finest texture. It was said that he could at that time take up an ordinary man and throw him a rod. A giant in stature, he had a bright handsome face, and was in the prime of life. I informed him of what I desired and he was delighted at the opportunity for making the effort and undertaking the enterprise, although it involved hardship and labor and required reckless courage to meet the dangers to be encountered.

I also found at Fort Huachuca another splendid type of American manhood, Captain Leonard Wood, Assistant Surgeon, United States Army. He was a young officer aged twenty-four, a native of Massachusetts, a graduate of Harvard, a fair-haired, blue-eyed young man of great intelligence, sterling, manly qualities, and resolute spirit. He was also perhaps as fine a specimen of physical strength and endurance as could easily be found. He had a perfect knowledge of anatomy and had utilized this knowledge of physiology in training himself and bringing every part of his physique to its highest perfection, and seemed to have the will power and energy to keep his own physical mechanism in perfect condition and activity. I said to him:

"We have heard much said about the physical strength and endurance of these Apache Indians, these natives of the desert and mountain. I would like to have you accompany Captain Lawton's command, and as you are probably in as good a condition as anyone to endure what they endure, you can make a careful study of the Indians at every opportunity and discover wherein lies their superiority, if it does exist, and whether it is hereditary, and if hereditary, whether the fiber and sinew and nerve power is of a finer quality, and whether their lungs are really of greater development and capacity to endure the exertion of climbing these mountains than those of our best men."

Captain Wood entered into the spirit of this most heartily, and his services and observations and example were most commendable and valuable and added much to the final success of the enterprise.

The other officers of the command were selected for similar considerations.

Captain Lawton's picked infantry, Indian scouts and cavalry were at times under the immediate command of Lieutenants Henry Johnson, Jr., Eighth Infantry, H. C. Benton, R. A. Brown, R. S. Walsh and A. L. Smith, Fourth Cavalry, and Leighton Finley, Tenth Cavalry. Lieutenant Finley, now dead, rendered very efficient service in command of the scouts during the first two months of the campaign. He was a gallant officer and had distinguished himself the preceding year (1885) in an affray with the hostiles in Arizona during an attack which they had made upon a command to which he was attached. Lieutenant Brown commanded the scouts during the last two months of the pursuit and rendered valuable service. They are all entitled to great credit for the zeal, judgment and fidelity with which they carried out his instructions.

The soldiers of this command were also carefully selected and I doubt whether there was ever a finer collection of men and officers, for the number, gathered in one command. It was a question of fidelity, of endurance, of tenacity of purpose; for when the troops north of the boundary had driven the hostiles over the border, this command was expected to take up the chase and continue it until the hostiles were either worn down and brought to bay, or driven back again to our territory. Well did they accomplish this duty, as will be seen by every reader who follows to the end the narrative of this five months' campaign.

The command was perfectly equipped and abundantly supplied, and in such a way as to be independent of wagon transportation. The pack-train was the best in the country, and, in addition to the supplies carried by it, I moved by trains down the valleys practicable for wagons. abundant supplies, in order that this movable command could have a movable base for their stores and military supplies.

Before we were fairly ready the hostiles themselves precipitated the campaign. They could have quietly remained in their mountain fastnesses in the Sierra Madres and forced us to hunt them, which might have consumed from twelve months to two years, but with reckless bravado they opened the campaign by committing depredations south of the boundary in northern Mexico. This was to us a welcome signal, for it gave us a positive knowledge of their whereabouts, and enabled me to immediately put my plans into effect and initiate the operations I had blocked out for their subjugation.

The hostiles were under the leadership of the chiefs Geronimo and Natchez, the last named being the hereditary chief of the Chiricahuas, and their raid spread t e r r o r throughout that district of Mexico. They then swept northward, and on the 27th of April invaded our territory, passing up the Santa Cruz Valley, stealing stock and killing a few citizens, including the Peck family. Of this family the mother and one child were murdered, and a girl, some ten years of age, was captured and subsequently recaptured by the troops. The Indians, dis-

MOUNTAIN FASTNESS—COCHISE'S STRONGHOLD.

regarding their usual custom, released the father after holding him in captivity for several hours.

Although at this time they struck a section of country further west than they had appeared in for many years, yet Captain T. C. Lebo, an energetic officer, and almost an ideal leader for such service, with his troop, Tenth Cavalry, was quickly on the trail, and after a hot pursuit of two hundred miles brought the Indians to bay in the Pinito Mountains, some thirty miles south of the boundary in Sonora, Mexico. In spite of the fact that he was obliged to meet the enemy on ground of their own choosing, and with every natural obstacle against him, this officer made a good fight, and while he sustained very little loss himself, inflicted considerable upon his opponents. During this fight a brave soldier, Corporal Scott, was so severely wounded as to be completely disabled. As he lay on the ground under a sharp fire from the Indians, Lieutenant Powhatan H. Clarke, a gallant young officer fresh from West Point, dashed forward to the rescue of the disabled soldier, and at the imminent peril of his own life, lifted and carried the veteran to a place of safety. Though knights clad in armor have long since faded away into the dim past, and the clash of sword on shield is heard no more, with deeds like this before us who shall say that the days of chivalry are no more? We could write a volume describing the heroism of this splendid young officer previous to his untimely death, but must pass on to other events and heroic deeds.

After this engagement the Indians continued their retreat, and the trail was soon after taken up by Lieutenant H. C. Benson of the Fourth Cavalry. They were then pursued south and west, until their trail was again taken up by Lebo's command, and later by that of Captain Lawton. The command of Captain C. A. P. Hatfield, Fourth Cavalry, had been placed to intercept them, east of Santa Cruz, Sonora, and on the 15th of May succeeded in completely surprising the savages at that place. In the engagement which followed, the hostiles lost their entire camp equipage and about twenty horses, as well as their first deserter, who, having been wounded and having had his horse shot under him, crawled into the rocks and continued his retreat for forty-five days, surrendering at last at Fort Apache, 250 miles to the north, on the 28th day of June. This man was afterward of value to us, as will be explained when an account is given of the condition of the Indians, he being used to aid in opening communications by which their ultimate surrender was effected.

Unfortunately while passing west through a deep and narrow cañon towards Santa Cruz, embarrassed with his captured horses and other Indian property, Captain Hatfield's command was in turn attacked by the hostiles and a sharp fight ensued. In this fight there were numerous instances of conspicuous bravery. John H. Conradi, one of the soldiers of the troop, lay severely wounded on the ground, and though unable to move himself beyond the fire of the Indians, continued to use his rifle with telling effect. Two of his comrades, First Sergeant Samuel Adams and citizen packer George Bowman, seeing his helpless condition bravely exposed their own lives in the effort to reach him. But just as they were bearing him to a place of safety he received another and this time a mortal wound, thus meeting the very death to save him from which his comrades had risked their lives. Many heroes have died, yet there are many still living.

After Hatfield's fight Lieutenant R. A. Brown, Fourth Cavalry, struck the trail and pursued the hostiles in an easterly direction. The Indians then divided into two bands. One, moving north, was intercepted by Lieutenant Brett of the Second Cavalry, who displayed great energy and determination in his pursuit. The Indians going over the roughest mountains and breaking down one set of horses, would abandon them and pass straight over the highest ranges and descending to the valleys below would steal others and continue their retreat, while the troops in order to pursue them were obliged to send their horses around the impassable mountain heights and follow the trail on foot, climbing in the ascent and sliding in the descent. On this occasion, at one time the troops continued the pursuit for twenty-six hours without a halt, and were without water during eighteen hours in the intense heat of that season. This was the second occasion in which a part of my commands were suffering so intensely from thirst—an agony fortunately unknown to the mass of mankind—that the men opened their veins to moisten their burning lips with their own blood. This band of hostiles under Natchez swept north as far as Fort Apache, then turned south pursued by one commanding officer after another who took up the pursuit. The Indians were turned to the south again, and finally recrossed the Mexican boundary.

The other band was followed west by Lieutenant Brown, until their trail was struck by Captain Lawton. The Indians were first driven north and then south, and in passing through the Patagonia Mountains were intercepted by Lieutenant Walsh, of the Fourth Cavalry. He surprised their camp on the evening of June 6, and captured nearly all their animals, baggage and supplies. The hostiles scattered, and by the time the scouts could work out the trail it became too dark to follow. At daylight the pursuit was again taken up and carried on so vigorously that the Indians were obliged to abandon all the remaining animals they had with them and scatter again on foot. Captain Lawton, who had meanwhile joined this command, was convinced from the fact that the Indians had entirely disappeared from the border, and from the direction in which their trail led, that at last they were going toward their stronghold, the Sierra Madres, and a pursuit was at once inaugurated for a campaign in those excessively rugged mountains. The infantry command was at this time replaced by another detachment of equal strength and with these new troops Captain Lawton pursued the savages from one range of mountains to another for three months, sometimes scaling peaks nine thousand or ten thousand feet above the level of the sea, and then again descending into the depths of the cañons where the heat was almost intolerable. During this time the troops marched 1,396 miles. Most of the country had been burned over leaving no grass, and water was so scarce that the troops frequently suffered intensely. One portion of the command was without food, with the exception of such game as they could kill, for five days. At one time when the pack-train had been delayed by the roughness of the trail, the troops were obliged to subsist on two or three deer killed by the scouts, and on mule meat without salt.

Sonora, the part of Mexico in which the operations of the troops were now being carried on, is a rough, mountainous country, presenting obstacles of an extremely serious nature. It is a succession of rugged mountains, broken here and there by a steep cañon, and producing nothing but a few wild fruits, cacti, and some game. There is but little water and that often of a poor quality. Grass is almost entirely wanting during the dry season.

This section of country was very thinly populated, but here and there would be found a small town built within a walled enclosure. Inside this wall were one story adobe houses and scores of children and adults who wore but little superfluous clothing. Nothing could speak more eloquently of the fear and dread in which the Mexicans held the Apaches than these little walled towns; but in spite of the many lessons they had received, they were still poorly armed and in a condition to fall ready victims to the hostiles. The intelligent and liberal construction given by Governor Louis E. Torres, of Sonora, to the terms of the compact between the two governments was of very great assistance to our officers in moving troops and supplies through that portion of the country, and was acquiesced in by other Mexican officials. Every assistance within his personal and official powers was rendered by the governor to aid in arresting the common enemy that had for many years disturbed the peace of the two republics.

During the early days of the expedition much of the difficult work was done by the cavalry in southern Arizona and northern Sonora. Forage could then occasionally be obtained, but as the mountains grew more and more impassable that arm proved inadequate, and the chief dependence was necessarily placed upon the infantry. In some of the companies there were men who had seen service in India and in South Africa, and in their opinion this campaign in Arizona and far down in southern Sonora was the hardest, most exacting service they had ever endured. The heat was so intense at times that the men could not place their hands on the metal work of their guns. Pack-trains could, in the middle of the day, move only five or six miles before the animals became overheated and unable to travel. The food was not what it should have been to sustain the strength and vitality of men under long-continued fatigue.

By the 5th of July the Indians had been driven south of Oposura, Mexico. A supply camp had been established at that point, and the command was equipped ready to continue operations. Until now the hostiles had been accustomed to separate into small parties which would make sudden and bloody raids upon settlements when unexpected, but after this time they were so closely pursued that they could derive no further benefit from their raids, as they were obliged to abandon their animals or else fight to protect them, which latter alternative they carefully avoided. Sometimes the Indians would scatter, but in that case the trail of a single man was followed until he again joined the rest of the band. The march was taken up toward the mouth of Tepache Creek where it was learned that the hostiles had passed, committing depredations on their way. But after a couple of hours' march in that direction the command was overtaken by a courier with the information that a man had been wounded by the Indians at Tonababu the evening before. Captain Lawton immediately changed his course and on reaching the place discovered the trail of the savages who had been doing the shooting.

The scouts under Lieutenant Brown were pushed ahead of the command, and on the 13th of July a runner was sent back to say that the Indian camp had been discovered, that the scouts would attack it at once, and asking that the infantry be sent forward to their support. Unfortunately the surprise was not an entire success for the Indians escaped, but their animals, camp equipage, a large amount of dried meat, and other provisions fell into the hands of the troops. The trail was again followed until supplies were nearly exhausted, when a halt was reluctantly called. After a short rest scouts were sent out to discover the whereabouts of the hostiles, and on the 13th of August information was received that they were moving toward the Terras Mountains. Captain Lawton immediately started to head them off, and by making forced marches arrived in the neighborhood of Fronteras on the 20th, where he learned that the hostiles had communicated to the Mexicans a desire to surrender.

M.—29

CHAPTER XXXVIII.

The Arizona Campaign. II.

HILE preparations and movements were in progress which in time were to subjugate the Indians in active hostility, great care was taken to prevent the other Indians at the agencies from affording them any assistance in men, munitions or provisions. Soon after I assumed command of that department in April, 1886, I became convinced that there could be no lasting peace or permanent settlement of the chronic condition of warfare that had for many years afflicted the people of the territory now comprised in Arizona, New Mexico and the bordering Mexican States, until the Chiricahuas and Warm Spring Indians had been removed from that mountainous region. The trails they had made during past years showed that their raids had been from the agencies through the settlements south to old Mexico, and then back again to the same beginning. Every few years a new generation of their boys and young men had grown to manhood and become full fledged warriors and their only hope of achieving distinction according to the traditions, practice and influence of their fathers, was in committing acts of cruelty and devastation. All they knew of their own history appeared to be confined to this field. It was taught them from their earliest infancy and practiced until their old age.

Early in the month of May, I went as far north as Fort Thomas, Arizona, and there met by appointment Captain F. E. Pierce, who had charge of the San Carlos agency. This officer has had a most remarkable career. He commanded a brigade during the war with distinction, lost an eye in the service, and was a most earnest and zealous officer. He had charge of some of the worst Indians in the country. Three different tribes were located at the San Carlos agency (the San Carlos, the Yumas, and the Mohaves), and as they were friendly to the Chiricahuas and Warm Spring Indians, one of my objects in going there and meeting Captain Pierce was to make all the arrangements possible to keep these Indians from joining the hostiles, and to prevent them from giving assistance to those who were then out. I also met Colonel J. F. Wade who was then commanding at Fort Apache. Both of these officers were directed to use every means possible to prevent any communication between the hostiles and the Indians under their charge. Colonel Wade was also directed to, as far as possible, bring the Chiricahua and Warm Spring Indians entirely under his control, so that they could be removed from the Territory if it became necessary. I informed him at that time that I believed such a measure was the only means of bringing about a permanent peace, and that I would some time in the near future send him an order to remove them from the country. Captain Pierce, who as I have stated, had charge of the San Carlos Indians, fully agreed with me on this subject and actively coöperated in the enterprise. The conversation was to be considered strictly confidential.

Previous to my taking command of the department a large number of Apache scouts had been employed for the purpose of hunting the hostile Apaches. I had no confidence in their integrity and did not believe they could be trusted. I believed that they were naturally more friendly to their own blood relatives than they could be to our service, and took measures to have nearly all of them discharged. In their stead I hired other Indians who were more hostile to the Chiricahua Apaches. What few scouts were with the troops we used principally as trailers.

In July, while the troops were actively employed in pursuing the hostile Indians, a chase which had then been on for several months, I turned my attention to the serious question of the final disposition to be made of the Apaches, and determined to visit Fort Apache in person and make an examination of affairs at that agency. In order that there might be perfect harmony between the military department and the Department of the Interior, I wrote to Mr. L. Q. C. Lamar, Jr., a special agent of the Interior Department, whose father, the then Secretary of the Interior, I knew personally, asking him to accompany me to Fort Apache. We met at Albuquerque, New Mexico, and with my aid-de-camp Lieutenant Dapray,

thence journeyed west together to Holbrook, Arizona, and from there to
Fort Apache. This last named post is situated in the White Mountains,
in a beautiful and picturesque country of lofty mountains, pine and cedar
forests, and near a great rushing, roaring mountain river full of trout. The
country teemed with an abundance of game — bear, deer, antelope, wild
turkeys and small game.

I found at Fort Apache over four hundred men, women and children,

DRUNKEN INDIANS IN CAMP.

belonging to the Chiricahua and Warm Spring Indians, and a more turbulent, desperate, disreputable band of human beings I had never seen before and hope never to see again. The Apaches on this reservation were
called prisoners of war, yet they had never been disarmed or dismounted.
Some of them had a little land under cultivation on which they raised barley, out of which they manufactured " tiswin," a most intoxicating liquor,
which has the peculiar characteristic of rousing all that is turbulent and

vicious in the individual who had been imbibing; and the more barley they raised the more tiswin riots occurred. When I visited their camp they were having their drunken orgies every night, and it was a perfect pandemonium. It was dangerous to go near them, as they were constantly discharging pistols and rifles. The amount of land they had under cultivation in 1886 was altogether only about a hundred acres. The women did nearly all the work, though a few men condescended occasionally to assist. One of the most prominent among the Indians was Chatto, who at one time had led what was, perhaps, the bloodiest raid ever made in that country. The young men were insolent, violent and restless, and anxious to go on the warpath. They employed their time in riding about the camp with firearms, to the terror of everyone with whom they came in contact. The people of Arizona had frequently sent strong petitions to Washington praying that these Indians might be removed from that Territory, and at the time I now write of I received reliable information that another outbreak was contemplated by the Indians and was then being arranged among them.

After fully considering the condition of affairs in all its bearings, and after a thorough personal examination in company with Mr. Lamar, I became more fully convinced than ever of the necessity of removing that band of Indians to some region remote from Arizona, where they could not at any moment resume hostilities and terrorize and devastate the country. As it was supposed that this removal could be effected much more easily with than without their consent, I urged upon them the importance of the benefits to be obtained by removing to another part of the country. I also requested and obtained from the authorities at Washington permission to send a delegation thither for the purpose of securing their consent. This delegation was placed under the charge of Captain Dorst, of the Fourth Cavalry, an experienced and accomplished officer.

I was of the opinion at that time that a removal to the Indian Territory would be the most advisable, the climate of that country being similar to that in which they were accustomed to live. There they would also be near another band of Apaches that had been living in that Territory for a very long time. However, it was found impossible to remove them immediately to that locality owing to a law that had been enacted by Congress prohibiting the sending thither of any more Apaches. Still I thought they could be removed to some adjacent country in New Mexico, Texas or Kansas, and on a representation of the facts of the case I believed that the law would be repealed by Congress, and so it subsequently proved.

The delegation went to Washington, where other influences were brought to bear upon them, and they eventually determined to make no terms, but insisted on returning to the mountains of Arizona. The delegation was ordered back without anything having been accomplished. Learning of this I sent a most earnest appeal to have the delegation stopped at Fort Leavenworth, Kansas, stating that in my opinion if they returned to Arizona in defiance of the military authorities and the appeals of the people of that Territory, outbreaks and disturbances might be expected for the next twenty years. Finally, in deference to this appeal, they were ordered detained at Fort Leavenworth, where they became defiant and exceedingly troublesome.

The authorities had by this time become fully convinced that these Indians would make no peaceful agreement for their removal, which had now come to be regarded as an absolute military necessity. When the delegation was stopped at Fort Leavenworth, I telegraphed Captain Dorst to report to me in Arizona and inform me of the disposition of these Indians. After he had made his report he was ordered to return to Fort Leavenworth and inform the Indian delegation that they could, if they chose, be considered friendly treaty Indians, in which case they must conform to the wishes and directions of the government and consent to the peaceable removal of all their people from the Territory of Arizona, or else they must be considered as individuals, responsible for the crimes they had committed, and they were reminded that indictments were then pending in the courts of Arizona charging them with murder and various other crimes. They were also reminded of the murders they had perpetrated, and told that the warrants for their arrest were awaiting them, and that they could not expect the military to shelter them in the civil courts from the legal consequences of their acts.

The effect of this plain talk was an agreement on their part to accept any disposition the government might conclude to make of them. They agreed to go to any place I might select, there to remain until the government should furnish them with utensils, stock and provisions by which they could become self sustaining. My object was then to eventually have them located in the Indian Territory, but I desired especially to place them far enough away from Arizona to render it impossible for them to resume hostilities whenever they might be so disposed.

The importance of the removal of this large and troublesome body of Indians was patent to all conversant with the situation, and was vitally necessary to the welfare of the country. The President had been advised that any failure of such an attempt would result in one of the most serious wars that had ever occurred in the southwest country; that if it could not be accomplished peaceably, and that if even a few should escape and take to the warpath the results would be altogether serious. Still I regarded it as an imperative necessity, and after consulting with Colonel Wade, who had been requested to meet me again at Albuquerque, New Mexico, and who also had confidence that it could be done, the following telegram was sent to Washington:

ALBUQUERQUE, N. MEX., August 20, 1886.

ADJUTANT-GENERAL, U. S. ARMY, Washington, D. C.:

Captain Dorst reports that the Indians that are now at Fort Leavenworth received some kind of certificate in Washington that appeared to give them great assurance, and that when he parted with them their conduct was defiant and insolent. Should they return with the feeling that they were entirely independent of the military authorities as well as the civil government, their control would be most difficult and their presence more dangerous to the peace of this country. I have directed him to inform them on his return that they can either be *treaty Indians* or that they must be regarded as prisoners of war and must abide by what disposition the government deems best for the welfare of all concerned. I have given him a memoranda to propose to them as the just and liberal terms of the government, practically as stated in my letter of July 7, viz.: to move to such place as the government deems best and await such time as a reservation or a place of of residence shall be provided for them outside of the Territories of Arizona and New Mexico. Should they accept it, a part can remain at Leavenworth and a part return to accompany the balance of the tribe. Colonel Wade, commanding Fort Apache, who is now here, informs me that he can move those at Apache without difficulty, and arrangements have already been considered. The discomfiture of the hostiles renders the time favorable, and as the measure is of vital importance, I pray that it may receive the approval of the government.

MILES, Commanding Department Arizona.

(Indorsement on foregoing.)

HEADQUARTERS OF THE ARMY, WASHINGTON, August 21, 1886.

Respectfully submitted to the Acting Secretary of War, with copy for information of the Department of the Interior.

P. H. SHERIDAN, Lieutenant-General, Commanding.

The above dispatch from me was telegraphed by the Acting Secretary of War to the Secretary of War, Salem, Massachusetts, August 21, 1886, and to the President, Saranac Inn, Bloomingdale, Essex County, New York, August 21, 1886.

he following further official action resulted:

WAR DEPARTMENT, WASHINGTON CITY, August 24, 1886.

SIR:—Having transmitted by telegraph to the President and Secretary of War General Miles's telegram of the twentieth instant, the inclosed are their replies. As it is of importance that General Miles should have the President's views at the earliest practicable moment, I beg to request your opinion as to the President's views as soon as you can conveniently furnish it.

Very respectfully, your obedient servant,

R. C. DRUM, Acting Secretary of War.

The Secretary of the Interior.

Then comes the letter from the Secretary of War to the Adjutant-General and Acting Secretary of War, of which the following is an extract:

Now, as to the telegram you have sent the substance of, from Miles. I understand him to say that there is no trouble now at Fort Apache, and arrangements have already been considered — that is, he can capture them all and send them away from the Territories of Arizona and New Mexico, and those on their way from here, now at Leavenworth, can a portion remain at Leavenworth, and the balance be taken away with the others; but he does not say where he proposes to take them, though he must have been informed by Captain Dorst what the views of the President were in that regard, viz., that the place of confinement should be Fort Marion, Florida. The only hesitation the President had in regard to this course arose from his desire to be assured by General Miles that all of this dangerous band could be secured and successfully conveyed away; for if a few should escape and take to the warpath the results would be altogether too serious. If, therefore, General Miles can accomplish this, and take them to Fort Marion from Arizona, the course approved by the President can be carried out so far as that part of the band at Fort Apache is concerned.

As to Chatto (then at Fort Leavenworth), and those with him, it was thought proper that he should be taken back to Arizona, to be sent to Marion with the others, and not taken directly there.

As before stated to General Miles, there is no other place available, the Indian Territory being out of the question for many reasons. They are to be treated as prisoners of war, and no hopes can be held out to them in regard to the Indian Territory.

General Sheridan and Mr. Lamar, or both, I presume, are in Washington. I wish you would show them the above so far as the Apaches are concerned, and unless some suggestion of disapproval is made by them I think a final order to carry out the original intention should issue — to take the whole band of Chiricahuas at Fort Apache, and Chatto's people on their return, and convey them to Fort Marion to join those already there.

(Indorsement on foregoing.)

HEADQUARTERS OF THE ARMY, August 24, 1886.

I concur with the views of the Secretary of War.

P. H. SHERIDAN, Lieutenant-General, Commanding.

While I believed that some point not too far distant from Arizona and New Mexico should be chosen for the purpose of concentrating the Indians then at Fort Apache and those that might surrender or be captured as prisoners of war, still, as it was decided by the goverment that Fort Marion should be the place in which to concentrate all the Indians for the time being, I assented as a matter of course. The fact that Fort Marion, Florida, had been decided upon as the place of confinement for not only those at Fort Apache, Arizona, but also for those who might surrender or be captured, is clearly indicated in the following official communication :

WAR DEPARTMENT, WASHINGTON CITY, August 24, 1886.

SIR : Seeing that Fort Marion appeared to be agreed upon as the place at which to hold the Apaches on their capture or surrender as prisoners of war, and having no data here from which to judge of its capacity, &c., I sent the following telegram to the commanding officer at Saint Augustine, Fla. :

" What number of Indians — men, women and children — can, in addition to the number now at Saint Augustine, be accommodated there ? Should it be determined to increase the number by some four or five hundred, what preparation would be necessary and what probable expenditure required ? "

In reply I received the following :

" Can accommodate seventy-five men, women and children, in addition to those now here. Fort Marion is a small place ; all must live in tents. Have tentage by taking battery tents. Need no particular preparation, but will have to expend $200 for additional tent floor and lavatories. Would recommend no more Indians be sent here. More details by mail." Very respectfully,

R. C. DRUM, Acting Secretary of War.

THE LIEUTENANT-GENERAL OF THE ARMY.

It will be seen that this was the understanding not only with the Lieutenant-General and the acting Secretary of War, but also with the Secretary of the Interior.

Seventy-seven Indians mentioned, men women and children, had been sent to Fort Marion in March previous, as stated in a former chapter, and as it was the final determination of the authorities at Washington that the remainder of the Chiricahua and Warm Spring Indians should be sent there also. I gave my most earnest attention to the matter. Let it be observed that the removal of both the dangerous and turbulent Indians at Fort Apache, and the hostile Indians whom the troops had been hunting since April, occurred at about the same time.

In the meantime one troop after another had been moved to the vicinity of Fort Apache until I had succeeded in placing in the immediate neighborhood, under the command of Colonel Wade, nine troops of cavalry, a sufficient force I believed, to handle that entire body of Indians.

Before returning to Fort Bowie I had several conversations with Colonel Wade as to the duty he was to perform and the methods of its performance. From Fort Bowie I went to Wilcox Station on the Southern Pacific Railroad, which was about twelve miles from Fort Bowie, and in

direct telegraphic communication with Fort Apache. There in the telegraph office I opened communication with Colonel Wade and directed him
to secure the entire Indian camp at Fort Apache and move them north to
the railroad, and thence east to Florida.

The result proved that no mistake had been made in the selection of an
officer for this duty. Colonel J. F. Wade is "a chip of the old block," a son of
that eminent statesman, the late Benjamin F. Wade of Ohio, who for many

ON THE WAY TO FLORIDA.

years represented that State in the Senate of the United States. He inherited
the sterling qualities of his illustrious father. As a boy of eighteen he was
a distinguished soldier during the great war, and has since fulfilled all the
requirements of his positions from lieutenant to that of one of the senior
colonels of the army of to-day. It was only necessary to give him an
order, and he could be left to execute it according to his own best judgment. Yet I was extremely anxious at this critical moment of the campaign, because I so fully realized how disastrous it would be should he

take any measures which would cause an outbreak among the Indians, or put a large additional body on the warpath by allowing them to escape, for there was a very large hostile element in the camp. It would have resulted in the sacrifice of many innocent lives, as well as serious censure upon the management of the affair. There are occasions when a commanding officer is obliged to trust the fortunes of the campaign, either for weal or woe, to his subordinate. This was such a case. Of course he is responsible for the selection of the subordinate to carry out his wishes, but when so selected, if the subordinate fails the entire responsibility and blame must rest upon the principal.

In this case I felt the utmost confidence that the duty was left in safe hands, yet so anxious was I not to disturb Colonel Wade by any official inquiry or by calling for official reports, that I went down to the telegraph office and asked the operator on duty, a bright and intelligent young man, if he would not open communication with the operator at Fort Apache, and in his own name, without mentioning my presence, ask for the news of what

GENERAL MILES AT TELEGRAPH OFFICE.

was going on. He did so, and the operator at Fort Apache, whose office occupied a high point so that he could overlook the whole scene from his window, replied that he observed that all the Indians had been gathered in to be counted as was the custom on Sunday. Also, as was their usual practice, the troops had gone through their Sunday inspection, and after they had performed their ordinary duties, had taken certain positions that commanded the position of the Indians.

All this merely served to increase my anxiety while I awaited results. Then the operator at Wilcox said to the other one at Apache, two hundred miles distant:

"Let me know fully what is going on."

And he replied:

"I will."

Though not aware of the significance and importance of what was going on under his eyes, he watched events and kept us informed of all that occurred. He saw the troops suddenly take position surrounding the large body of Indians, and absolutely commanding the position of the Indian camp. He saw some commotion among the Indians. All the warriors took a standing position ready for immediate action. He saw Colonel Wade quietly walk down to their vicinity and command them all to sit down. The Indians realizing the folly of resistance in the presence of this strong body of troops, and that there was no avenue of escape for them, were entirely within the control of the troops, and quietly obeyed the command of Colonel Wade. All this was flashed over the wires to the operator at Wilcox, who, as little realized the importance of it as the other operator did who sent the messages.

I received the information with infinite delight. I was prepared to receive news of a desperate fight, of a bloody encounter, or possibly the escape of the entire body of Indians, and, therefore, when the electric spark flashed the gratifying news which I knew meant peace, and I hoped eternal peace, to that whole territory, I was greatly gratified.

I waited for another dispatch which said that Colonel Wade had commanded the warriors to leave the camp and to go into one of the large buildings adjacent to the body of troops. A fourth dispatch stated that Colonel Wade had directed a certain number of the women to return to their camps and bring in their goods and all that they required to carry with them, as they were about to be removed. When this information was received I was entirely satisfied that Colonel Wade had that entire camp—which was the arsenal, the breeding place, the recruiting depot, the hospital, the asylum of the hostiles, and had been so for years,—entirely under his control, and that we had seen the last of hostile Indians coming to and going from that camp.

I did not wait for Colonel Wade's official report. I knew that when he had time he would send it. Again I turned my attention to the hostile element still out and still being hunted, pursued, harassed and run down by the troops under Lawton and those acting with him. I went back to Fort Bowie that night, and for several days remained there in communication with the troops a hundred miles south of us who had for months been pursuing Geronimo's band.

CHAPTER XXXIX.

INCIDENTS OF THE APACHE CAMPAIGN.

THE STORY OF THE WOUNDED APACHE—CAPTAIN WOOD'S STORY—CHARACTER OF APACHE RAIDS—
THE CASE OF THE PECK FAMILY—INDIAN IDEAS ABOUT INSANE PERSONS—FIGHT BETWEEN
APACHES AND MEXICANS, AND SOME OF ITS RESULTS—MEETING THE MEXICAN TROOPS—
FINDING THE MURDERED MEXICANS—FINDING DEAD BODIES ON THE MARCH—INDIAN
MANNER OF RIDING HORSES TO DEATH—THE OLD MINES OF MEXICO—HOW THE
SOLDIERS MARCHED, ATE AND SLEPT—SURPRISING AN INDIAN CAMP—PRE-
LIMINARIES OF SURRENDER AT FRONTERAS—GERONIMO COMES IN—
AGREEMENT TO SURRENDER—MEETING WITH THE MEXICAN SOL-
DIERS—GERONIMO'S FRIENDLY OFFER TO ASSIST—MEXICAN
NERVOUSNESS—LOSING A COMMAND—A NEW RIFLE—A
STAMPEDE—MEXICAN TOWNS—EXTREME HARDSHIP OF
THE CAMPAIGN—THE PROPORTION OF SURVIVORS
—GERONIMO'S PHILOSOPHY OF SURRENDER.

IN July, while at Fort Apache, I had found the Indian before referred to, who had been wounded in Hatfield's fight, and who had worked his way north to Camp Apache. He had avoided the troops by traveling along the crests of the mountains, and had contrived to subsist on field-mice, rabbits, the juice of the giant cactus, and whatever he could find to sustain life. He reported that when he left the camp of the hostiles they were much worn down and disheartened, and that some of them were disposed to surrender. I was satisfied from his story that this was the time to demand a surrender, and that he could be made useful in opening communication with the hostiles. I, therefore, decided to send him with one other Indian, under the charge of Lieutenant Gatewood, to seek out the hostile camp and demand a surrender.

Captain Leonard Wood, the only officer who was with Captain Lawton during the entire campaign, is at present stationed at Washington, D. C., and gives me the following interesting account of the Apache campaign south of the border, from notes taken by him during the time.

CAPTAIN LEONARD WOOD'S STORY.

As illustrating the character of the raiding done by these Apaches, I may mention the case of the Peck family. Their ranch was surrounded by Indians, the entire family was captured, and several of the farm-hands were killed. The husband was tied up and compelled to witness indescribable tortures inflicted upon his wife until she died. The terrible ordeal rendered him temporarily insane, and as the Apaches, like most Indians, stand in great awe of an insane person, they set him free as soon as they discovered his mental condition; but otherwise he would never have been allowed to live. He was afterward found by his friends wandering about the place.

His daughter, who was about thirteen years old, was captured by the Indians and carried by them three hundred miles, hotly pursued by Captain Lawton's command, when they met a party of Mexicans consisting of sixty or seventy men. The Mexicans fired a volley on the Indians, killing a woman and wounding the man who carried the little girl, thus enabling her to escape. This Indian's horse was killed at the same time, thus making it impossible for him to follow the remainder of the party as they retreated, so he took to the rocks, and stood off the entire sixty or seventy Mexicans, killing seven of them, each of whom was shot through the head. Our command had followed the outfit that had the little girl, and on the same day that this skirmish occurred with the

CAPTAIN LEONARD WOOD.

Mexicans we had been able to get near enough to fire at them, but it was too late in the day to accomplish anything, and the next morning at daybreak we were again on their trail following as fast as possible, when our scouts came rushing back, saying they had met a large body of Mexican troops. Captain Lawton, Lieutenant Finley, and myself went on foot as rapidly as we could to try to overtake them but they were in full retreat and we had to follow them about six miles before we could catch them. As we approached, the whole party covered us with their rifles and seemed very much excited. They proved to be the very party who had recaptured the little girl, and they now delivered her over to Captain Lawton, who sent her back to the United States where she was taken in charge by friends.

The Mexicans explained their fright at our appearance in this way. They had descended into the cañon where the fight had taken place to bring out the bodies of the seven men who had been shot, when they saw our five scouts advancing down the cañon. They mistook them for the friends of the Indian woman who had been killed coming to recover her body, and as they had had all the fighting they cared for with that particular band, they proceeded to retreat as rapidly as possible.

It was on this same expedition after the little girl, but a few days pre-

FINDING THE MURDERED MEXICANS.

vious to the events just related, that I was out hunting, trying to get some fresh meat for the command, when I noticed far down in the ravine five or six little Mexican bush huts. I approached them and discovered the bodies of five Mexicans, all shot through the head. Some of their faces were powder-burned, showing that the shots were very close. They proved to be the placer miners, who had been working in the creek when the Indians crept stealthily upon them and killed them all, probably at the first volley. On one occasion the Indians rode right through a wood-chopper's camp, killing seven, and there were forty or fifty instances of similar atrocities. In one day we picked up as many as ten bodies, and the governor of Sonora reported the number of Mexicans killed during the whole campaign to be as high as five or six hundred.

The Indians would start out with fifty or sixty horses, and after one had been urged as far as possible, his rider would kill him and then select a fresh animal and hurry on. When our troops got anywhere near them they would simply scatter like quail, to meet again four or five days later at some designated point. The general drift of the trail was about the headwaters of the Yaqui River, and in a country that was absolutely unknown. In this vicinity are situated those famous old lost mines of north Mexico, about which every Mexican town is full of stories. Just south of the boundary line is the only east and west trail for a hundred or two miles. All the trails of this region are of the very faintest kind, and can be followed only with the greatest difficulty by daylight and at night not at all, unless unusually good. Even in the daytime they are often lost. These old mines just referred to had long been abandoned, and as the Apaches have run over this region during the last two or three hundred years, they have never been rediscovered, but are supposed to be fabulously rich. One day while on the Yaqui River a man came to us who had been lost for sixty-one days. He was an American and almost demented. He had been following the course of the river, trying to find his way out of this wilderness. He had frequently seen signs of the Indians, but had not been molested by them. He had come across one of these old mines and gave a very complete description of it, which agreed with the recorded description given us by the old priest of Oposura.

When we reached the Yaqui River country it was found impossible to make use of the cavalry—the mountains, volcanic in their character, being almost impassable. The heat was intense, and the command was reduced to deer meat for food. There were absolutely no vegetables, and in fact very little even of the meat mentioned. Our supply of bacon had hair on both sides of it. So thin had it become that nothing was left but the hide. One day Captain Lawton was made violently ill by eating some canned corned-beef, which had fermented soon after being opened, and for a few hours his life hung in the balance. At one time I was in command of the scouts on a trip across the main divide of the Sierra Madre to "cut sign" of the hostiles, and we were without rations for seven days with the exception of game. We slept in the bushes, and were without blankets or bedding. Our Indian scouts were always very loyal and ready for duty. They would follow a trail for days where there was not a sign that white men could see. Their sight was remarkable, and every movement of a bird or insect was noted by them.

M.—30

On the 13th of July we effected the surprise of the camp of Geronimo and Natchez which eventually led to their surrender, and resulted in the immediate capture of everything in their camps except themselves and the clothes they wore. It was our practice to keep two scouts two or three days in advance of the command, and between them and the main body four or five other scouts. The Indian scouts in advance would locate the camp of the hostiles and send back word to the next party, who in their turn would notify the main command; then a forced march would be made in order to surround and surprise the camp. On the day mentioned, following this method of procedure, we located the Indians on the Yaqui River in a section of country almost impassable for man or beast, and in a position which the Indians evidently felt to be perfectly secure. The small table-land on which the camp was located bordered on the Yaqui River and was surrounded on all sides by high cliffs with practically only two points of entrance, one up the river and the other down. The officers were able to creep up and look down on the Indian camp, which was about two thousand feet below their point of observation. All the fires were burning, the horses were grazing, and the Indians were in the river swimming, with evidently not the slightest apprehension of attack. Our plan was to send scouts to close the upper opening, and then to send the infantry, of which I had the command, to attack the camp from below.

Both Indians and infantry were put in position, and advanced on the hostile camp, which, situated as it was on this table-land covered with cane-brake and boulders, formed an ideal position for Indian defense. As the infantry advanced the firing of the scouts was heard, which led us to believe that the fight was on, and great, accordingly, was our disgust to find, on our arrival, that the firing was accounted for by the fact that the scouts were killing the stock, the Apaches themselves having escaped through the northern exit just a few minutes before their arrival. It was a very narrow escape for the Indians, and was due to a mere accident. One of their number who had been out hunting discovered the red head-band of one of our scouts as he was crawling around into position. He immediately dropped his game and notified the Apaches, and they were able to get away just before the scouts closed up the exit. Some of these Indians were suffering from old wounds. Natchez himself was among this number, and their sufferings through the pursuit which followed led to their discouragement and, finally, to their surrender.

From this point they made a big detour to the south of the Yaqui River, captured a Mexican pack-train, remounted themselves, and started north with our command hard after them. When we were about a hundred miles south of Fronteras we learned from some Mexicans whom we met that the Indians were in the vicinity of that place. Two of the Indian women had been in the town, and to the house of one Jose Maria, whom they knew well as he had been a captive among them for seventeen years. These two women had been sent to get him to open communications with a view to surrender. Jose was at the time with Captain Lawton, acting as interpreter for the scouts; but his wife was at home, and when she heard some one calling her husband, went to the window and discovered the two Indian women on a neighboring hill. They told her they had been sent to ask Jose to open negotiations with the Americans. This was the first really direct intimation of their intention to surrender.

The news of their being in Fronteras had also reached several military commands in Arizona, and we found on our arrival that Lieutenant Wilder of the Fourth Cavalry had found these Indian women, and had sent a message by them to the hostiles, demanding

"You Are the Man I Want to Talk With."

their surrender. In the meantime Lieutenant Gatewood who had joined Captain Lawton's command about ten days before on the Yaqui River, the two Indians, his escort, interpreters, packers, etc., were sent to the hostile camp to discover the state of mind of the hostiles. The two Indians entered the hostile camp. One stayed all night, but the other returned and said that Geronimo wanted to meet Lieutenant Gatewood in the open and unattended, for a talk. Gatewood had this talk with him, found his tone friendly, and afterward with his party went into their camp. Lawton was with his scouts in advance of his main command and near the Indians' camp. Gatewood, after his visit to the Indians returned to Lawton's camp very much discouraged, saying that the Indians had declined to recognize him and that he had no faith in their surrendering. Lawton replied that the Indians were not waiting there for nothing, and that he believed they meant to surrender.

The next morning at daybreak Geronimo, Natchez and twelve or thirteen other Indians came into our camp, and Geronimo rushed up to Lawton, threw his arms around him, and giving him a hug said:

"You are the man I want to talk with."

They had a short conversation, and as a result the entire body of Indians came down and camped within two miles of us, and later in the day moved still nearer, so that they were only half a mile away, and finally they agreed to accompany Lawton to where they could meet General Miles and formally surrender.

Under these conditions we had advanced a day's march, when we were very much surprised one morning before we had left our camp at the sudden appearance of a party of 180 Mexicans, commanded by the prefect of Arispe. Lieutenant Smith and Tom Horn, chief of scouts, jumped on their mules and rode down to meet them in a dense canebrake, and found them extremely hostile. They insisted that they were going to attack the Indian camp in spite of the fact that we assured them that the Indians were our prisoners, were peaceably on their way to the United States, and that we could not permit them to be attacked. They finally stopped advancing, Lawton came up and agreed to allow ten of their number to go into our camp and receive proof that the Indians seriously intended to surrender. During the time that an attack seemed imminent, Geronimo sent word to Captain Lawton that he held his Indians in readiness to attack the Mexicans in the rear while we attacked them in front.

As soon as the Mexicans halted I went on and overtook the Indians, who in the meantime had been instructed by Captain Lawton to "pull out, and keep out of the way." Walsh of the Fourth Cavalry and Gatewood were sent with them to protect them in case they came in contact with any of our own troops. Captain Lawton sent me to them to assure them that we would stand by them under any circumstances, and would not allow them to be attacked. Towards night some of their scouts came in with the report that ten Mexicans were with our people, which created considerable excitement among the Indians. This showed how well they kept posted regarding events that were transpiring around them. I hastened to assure them that there were only ten Mexicans, and that there could not possibly be any treachery on our part. This satisfied them, and Captain Lawton came up soon after and went into camp close by them. He then sent a message to Geronimo to bring down his Indians as it was necessary to assure the Mexicans that they were going in to surrender.

Geronimo immediately complied, and came down with nearly all his men. As they advanced toward the tree under which the Mexicans were standing, one of the latter nervously moved his revolver in his belt. In an instant every Indian weapon was drawn, and the only thing that saved the lives of the Mexicans was the fact that we jumped in between and held up our hands to prevent the Indians from firing. The Mexicans now appeared to be perfectly satisfied, and from this time we saw no more of them.

The next day after this exciting episode, when Lieutenant Smith started off with the cavalry and pack-train, there must have been some misunderstanding about the designated camping place, for he took a direction different from that taken by the Indians, who were accompanied by Lawton, Gatewood, Clay and myself. It was necessary for some of us to travel with them in order that in case we ran into any of our troops an explanation might be made before a fight ensued.

About two o'clock in the afternoon Lawton became anxious about the disappearance of the command, and after arriving at an understanding with the Indians in regard to the camping place for the night, he started out to find it. Gatewood had with him his interpreter, a man named George Wratton, and about four o'clock we sent him out to search for the command. But unfortunately he did not reach the command until the next day, having wandered around all night and ridden his mule to death. This left only Gatewood, Clay and myself in the Apache camp, and entirely at the mercy of the Indians. Instead of taking advantage of our position, they assured us that while we were in their camp it was our camp, and that as we had never lied to them they were going to keep faith with us. They gave us the best they had to eat, and treated us as well as we could wish in every way. Just before giving us these assurances, Geronimo came to me and asked to see my rifle. It was a Hotchkiss and he had never seen its mechanism. When he asked me for the gun and some ammunition I must confess I felt a little nervous, for I thought it might be a device to get hold of one of our weapons. I made no objection, however, but let him have it, showed him how to use it, and he fired at a mark, just missing one of his own men, which he regarded as a great joke, rolling on the ground, laughing heartily and saying "good gun."

Late the next afternoon we came up with our command, and we then proceeded toward the boundary line. The Indians were very watchful, and when we came near any of our troops we found the Indians were always aware of their presence before we knew of it ourselves.

After the surrender at Skeleton Cañon, the Indians who remained with our command were very quiet until we were within four miles of Fort Bowie. On the morning of the day we reached the fort, just before daylight, an officer rode suddenly down upon the Indian camp and stampeded it; and when daylight came we found seven of them had disappeared. The party consisted of three men, three women and a child, one of the men being the brother of Natchez. Lieutenant Johnson and myself were sent with small parties in pursuit of them, but though we each traveled about two thousand miles — going far down into Mexico, he on the east and I on the west of the Sierra Madre — we could not even learn their fate, though Johnson heard rumors of their being killed in Mexico.

During our pursuit of the Apaches, which lasted from April to August, we were sometimes very near them without seeing them. One day Horn and myself were out after deer, in the hope of being able to obtain something to eat, and while we were climbing the side of a cañon, we were both shot at and our faces filled with dust. Doubtless our unseen assailants were hostiles. Again, on another occasion, while going across the mountains to a Mexican town in quest of information, I found tracks of the Indians not over thirty minutes old. I knew this was so because they had been made since a heavy rain, which had occurred only a few minutes before. Two men had been killed on this trail shortly before, and the body of one was being taken into town as I came in.

The little Mexican towns that we passed were usually walled; every ranch was fortified, as well as every village, and the houses were loopholed for musketry. The people were primitive to a degree, many of them scarcely knowing whether Mexico was a republic or an empire, and nearly every family had lost some relative or friend through the Apaches. The Indians always chose this section of country when endeavoring to make their escape from the United States troops, and pursuit was especially difficult from the fact that the region was entirely unknown to us and almost impassable. The Indians would purposely lead us into places where there was no water, and sometimes all of that liquid that we had to drink would be as thick as jelly — stuff that had stood in rock tanks for

LAWTON'S PURSUIT OF GERONIMO.—See Page 486.

months. At other times they would set fire to the grass and bushes. Although the men for this expedition were picked with the greatest care, only about one-third of them endured the long fatigue, and we had practically three sets of officers. Only Lawton and I of the whole command went through the entire campaign from beginning to end.

One who does not know this country cannot realize what this kind of service means — marching every day in the intense heat, the rocks and earth being so torrid that the feet are blistered and rifle-barrels and everything metallic being so hot that the hand cannot touch them without getting burnt. It is a country rough beyond description, covered everywhere with cactus and full of rattlesnakes and other undesirable companions of that sort. The rain, when it does come, comes as a tropical tempest, transforming dry cañons into raging torrents in an instant. The small white-tail deer abounded and served us well as a meat ration. It was no unusual sight to see half a dozen brought into camp and disposed of in as many minutes. "Meat, and lots of it," that was the cry while we were doing our hardest work, and it seemed to be required to make good the waste. We had no tents and little or no baggage of any kind except rations and ammunition. Suits of underclothing formed our uniform and moccasins covered our feet.

There can be no doubt that the terms of surrender were fully understood by all the Indians. In all the talks at which I was present they seemed to comprehend perfectly that the surrender was to be unconditional, and they were told from the very first that the intention was to send them away. Geronimo only said:

" If you will tell me that the General will do all he can to save our lives, we will come in; but if we are going to be killed anyhow, we might just as well fight it out right here, because, in that case, a few of us might possibly get away."

The only assurance that was given him was that American soldiers did not kill their prisoners.

In the vicinity of Fronteras in their interviews with Captain Lawton the Indians asked terms and privileges similar to those they had before enjoyed. They sent me two messages through the interpreters, and made most urgent appeals to see the department commander. I replied to Captain Lawton that their requests could not be granted, and that he was fully authorized to receive their surrender as prisoners of war to troops in the field. They were told that the troops were brave and honest men, and that if they threw down their arms and placed themselves at the mercy of the officers, they would not be killed, but held as prisoners of war subject, of course, to higher legal authority.   They promised to surrender to me in person, and for eleven days Captain Lawton's command moved north; Geronimo's and Natchez' camp moving parallel with it and frequently camping near it.

CHAPTER XL.

END OF THE APACHE WAR.

EVERAL messages were received by me from Captain Lawton reporting his progress and success, and I also understood from him that the Indians desired to see me in person. He was convinced that they were worn down to the point of submission. I did not intend to have any failure or deception, or a pretended surrender that would give them a chance to escape. I therefore sent word to Lawton that he was authorized to receive their surrender at any time, and that that was all the authority the troops had. We had not the pardoning power, and we had no jurisdiction as to the punishment of their crimes. They were regarded as outlaws and hostile to the government. They had been making war against the peace of the Territory, and they must surrender as prisoners of war without any assurances as to the future. He replied that they were anxious to surrender, but only to the highest authority, and wanted me to go down and meet them. I informed him that I did not care to do so unless they gave me some assurance of their purpose to surrender, and that they were acting in entire good faith, and stated to him that the best way was for them to send some hostage as a guarantee of their intention. On receiving this message Geronimo sent his own brother to Fort Bowie to remain there as a hostage.

Captain Lawton notified me that this hostage had started, and in consideration of this fact and in compliance with Lawton's earnest appeal I made arrangements to start on September 2, and moved south sixty-five miles with Lieutenant Dapray, A. D. C., and a suitable escort. I must confess that I went with some forebodings, though I still had hope that the promises of Geronimo would be fulfilled. I had received information that the Indians had gone into Lawton's camp, and that some of his officers had, at a very great risk and with a daring that was perhaps somewhat reckless, gone into the camp of the savages. I knew that they were expert riflemen and good pistol shots, and would sell their lives very dearly if the Indians attempted to take advantage of them. At the same time I would not have sacrificed one of those valuable lives for the whole Apache camp.

This state of affairs gave me much uneasiness as I made the long journey to meet Captain Lawton. I took with me both saddle horses and wagons, and made the journey riding sometimes in the saddle and sometimes with the driver on the box. I had with me a heliostat operator, and as we occasionally came in sight of a mountain peak on which was one of our stations, I would open communication with it and through it with Fort Bowie and Captain Lawton, and with other stations. I received communications from Lawton and sent cautionary dispatches to him, directing his officers not to place themselves where the Indians could take advantage of them to seize them and hold for a ransom, or for enforcing such terms as they might dictate, or kill them.

The first night out we camped at Rucker Cañon, a rugged, desolate region named for the gallant young officer, Lieutenant Rucker, who lost his life in crossing the treacherous torrent that sweeps down the cañon that now bears his name. His father, General Rucker, the aged and distinguished veteran of four score years, still lives in the capital of the nation.

The next day we journeyed on, and joined the camp of Captain Lawton at Skeleton Cañon on the evening of September 3. This cañon had been a favorite resort of the Indians in former years, and was well suited by name and tradition to witness the closing scenes of such an Indian war.

Soon after my reaching Lawton's command, Geronimo rode into our camp and dismounted. He was one of the brightest, most resolute, determined looking men that I have ever encountered. He had the clearest, sharpest, dark eye I think I have ever seen, unless it was that of General Sherman when he was at the prime of life and just at the close of the great war. Every movement indicated power, energy and determination. In everything he did, he had a purpose. Of course after being hunted over these desolate valleys, mountain crests and dark ravines until he was worn down, he was anxious to make the best terms possible. His greatest anxiety seemed to be to know whether we would treat him fairly and without treachery, or, as soon as he and his followers were in our hands, order them shot to death, as had been the fate of some of his people. He first wanted to surrender as they had been accustomed to surrender before, by going back to Apache and taking their property, arms, stolen stock, and everything with them. I replied to this proposal that I was there to confirm what Captain Lawton had told them, and that was that they must surrender absolutely as prisoners of war. They could not go back to Fort Apache as they had done on previous occasions, but whatever we told them to do that they must conform to. "And more than that," I said, "it is of no use for you to ask to go back to Fort Apache, for there are no Apaches there now."

"What, no Apaches in the White Mountains?" he asked in surprise.

"No," I said.

"Where have they gone?" he asked.

"I have moved them all out of the country," I replied. "You have been at war with the white people for many years, and have been engaged in constant hostilities. I have thought it best that you should be removed from this country to some place where these hostilities cannot be resumed."

This seemed to dishearten him more than any other fact of the situation. The idea that there were no Apaches in the White Mountains was something that he had not anticipated, and he seemed to be wholly unmanned. He then said :

"We are going to do whatever you say and will request but one condition."

"What is that?" I asked.

"That you will spare our lives."

I saw at once that he still entertained the idea that we might kill them if they surrendered, and said to him :

"It is not the custom of officers of the United States army to misuse or destroy their prisoners. So long as you are our prisoners we shall not kill you but shall treat you justly. After that you must look to the President of the United States, who is the great father of all the Indians as well as of all the white people. He has control especially over Indians. He is a just man, and will treat you justly and fairly."

I did not try to explain to this savage the fact that I had no pardoning power; that I had no authority to mitigate the punishment for their crimes, or if they were tried and convicted to pardon them, but that that authority was one of the prerogatives of the chief magistrate alone. Therefore, I merely told him that he must rely upon the President for the character of

his treatment, and that I was going to move him, as I had already moved the other Indians, out of the country. I explained to him that his people were then in three places. Part of them in Florida, part had recently been at Fort Apache, and part were then with him; but that we were going to move all to some one place. To illustrate this to him, I picked up from the sand three pebbles in front of me, and placing them on the ground separated them so as to form the three points of a triangle, each representing a part of the tribe, and showed him that we were moving two portions of the tribe toward the third pebble which formed the apex of the triangle; I showed him that I could not tell what their future would be, but that one thing was positive: he must do whatever he was directed to do. He assented to this and said he would bring his camp in early the following morning.

EXPLAINING THE SITUATION.

He impressed me with a belief in his sincerity, and I allowed him to return to his camp, not far distant. It was one of those times when one has to place confidence even in a savage. When he mounted his horse and turned his back to us I realized we had very little control over him; still, he had placed his brother in our hands as a pledge of his good faith.

True to his word he brought in his band next morning. But Natchez, who was a younger man and the hereditary chief of the Apaches, still remained out. Why he had done so I did not know, and it gave me some concern. I had a conversation with Geronimo in which I induced him to talk quite freely, and then tried to explain to him the uselessness of contending against the military authority of the white race, owing to our many superior advantages. I told him that we had the use of steam, and could move troops with great rapidity from one part of the country to another; that we also had the telegraph and the heliostat, both superior to any of their methods of communication. He wanted to know what that was, and I said I would explain it to him.

We were then near a pool of water with no cover overhead. The operator had placed his heliostat on an extemporized tripod made by placing three sticks together. I said to Geronimo:

"We can watch your movements and send messages over the tops of these mountains in a small part of one day, and over a distance which it would take a man mounted on a swift pony twenty days to travel."

Geronimo's face assumed an air of curiosity and incredulity, and he said:

"How is that?"

I told him I would show him, and, taking him down to the heliostat, asked the operator to open communication with the nearest station which was about fifteen miles away in an air line. He immediately turned his instrument upon that point and flashed a signal of attention. As quick as thought the sunlight was flashed back again.

VICTORIO, APACHE CHIEF.

As I have previously had occasion to remark, when an Indian sees something that he cannot comprehend, he attributes it to some superior power beyond his knowledge and control, and immediately feels that he is in the presence of a spirit. As those stalwart warriors in Montana in using the telephone for the first time had given it the name of the "whispering spirit," so this type of the wild southern savage attributed the power he saw to something more than a mere human being. He told me that he had observed these flashes upon the mountain heights, and believing them to be spirits, had avoided them by going around those points of the mountains, never realizing that it was a subtle power used by his enemies, and that those enemies were themselves located upon these lofty points of observation and communication. I explained to him that it, the instrument, was not only harmless, but of great use, and said to him:

"From here to that point is a distance of nearly a day's march. From that point we can communicate all over this country. I can send a message back to Fort Bowie. sixty-five miles away, or to Fort Apache, nearly three hundred miles from here, and get an answer before the sun goes down in the west."

He comprehended its power and immediately put my statement to the test by saying:

"If you can talk with Fort Bowie, do this: I sent my brother to you there as a guarantee of my good faith; now tell me if my brother is all right." I said to the operator:

"Open communication with Fort Bowie and ask the officer in command. Major Beaumont, or Captain Thompson, my Adjutant-General, if Geronimo's brother is at Fort Bowie.

"Now," I said to Geronimo, "you must wait, for that inquiry with the reply will have to be repeated six times."

In a short time the answer came back that Geronimo's brother was there, was well, and waiting for him to come. This struck the savage with awe, and evidently made a strong impression upon him. I noticed that he said something to one of the warriors close by him, at which the warrior quietly turned upon his heel, walked back a short distance to where his pony was lariated, jumped on his back, and rode rapidly back in the direction of the mountains from whence Geronimo had come. This excited my curiosity, and I asked the interpreter, who was standing near by, what

GERONIMO AND THE HELIOGRAPH.

Geronimo said to that young warrior. The interpreter replied: "He told him to go and tell Natchez that there was a power here which he could not understand; and to come in, and come quick."

The heliostat had performed its last and best work, and in a few hours Natchez came riding down from the mountains with his band of warriors and their families and came into camp, though with much hesitation and reserve. They dismounted within a short distance of the camp and Natchez with an elastic, active step came forward, with an expression on his face of awe and uncertainty, and yet expressing a desire to do what was expected of him. All his acts were graceful and courtly. He exhibited a dignified reserve, and though he appeared to be anxious, yet seemed always conscious that he was the hereditary chief, and son of the great Cochise. His father had been one of the most noted men in that country, and had been at the head of the Apaches for many years. Natchez was a tall, slender, lithe fellow, six feet two, straight as an arrow, and, I judge, was of about the age of thirty or thirty-five years, suspicious, watchful and dignified in every movement.

The Indians that surrendered with Geronimo have probably never been matched since the days of Robin Hood. Many of the warriors were outlaws from their own tribes, and their boys of from twelve to eighteen were the very worst and most vicious of all. They were clad in such a way as to disguise themselves as much as possible. Masses of grass, bunches of weeds, twigs or small boughs were fastened under their hatbands very profusely, and also upon their shoulders and backs. Their clothing was trimmed in such a way that when lying upon the ground in a bunch of grass or at the head of a ravine, if they remained perfectly silent it was as impossible to discover them as if they had been a bird or a serpent. It was in this way that they were wont to commit their worst crimes. An unsuspecting ranchman or miner going along a road or trail would pass within a few feet of these concealed Apaches, and the first intimation he would have of their presence would be a bullet through his heart or brain. The Indians, when captured, were abundantly supplied with stolen property and were well mounted on Mexican horses. One difficulty that would have been found in case they had been turned over to the civil courts for trial and punishment would have been this: Indictments would probably have been found against the principal Indians, but the young men and boys who had undoubtedly committed the larger number of crimes would have escaped, and remaining in that country would have returned to the warpath. Many of these were afterward sent to the Carlisle school, and their improvement was very marked and of a permanent character.

But what a change had come over the brave fellows who had run them down! When I had last seen Lawton he was in full form, but with a grave aspect of countenance. Now, he was gaunt and lean, having lost forty pounds in weight, but his face was lighted up with the sparkle and joy of the conscious victor, as much as to say, "I present you the trophies of the hard, though fairly won, chase." His counterpart in transformation was Captain Wood, his faithful and true assistant through it all, who had lost nearly thirty pounds in weight.

The early part of the day, September 4, was occupied in gathering in the Indians, in explaining to them what was expected, and what would be required of them, and, as has been related, in receiving the surrender of Natchez and preparing for the morrow. As I did not wish to make another camp I arranged for an early start the next day. Thus the afternoon soon wore away; the intense heat was followed by dark, threatening clouds and a fierce thunder storm that I have rarely, if ever, seen equaled in the volume of the tempest or the explosion and roar of the electricity with which the atmosphere was charged. It was a strange scene when enemies—victors and captives—sought shelter from the fury of the elements. Geronimo, Natchez, Dapray, Lawton and myself were in a small canvas-covered wagon; others were under the wagon, and officers, soldiers and

APACHE WAITING FOR A VICTIM.

Indians were huddled together as best they could under the spare shelter of a few pieces of canvas. It was a fit ending to the tragedies that had been enacted over those fields and amid those cañons, and I could but hope that there was in truth a silver lining to that war cloud.

The next day after the surrender of Natchez I started with escort of a troop of cavalry for Fort Bowie, accompanied by Geronimo, Natchez, and four other Indians. We reached that post, a distance of sixty-five miles, shortly after dark, and Captain Lawton, following with the remainder of the Indians, arrived there three days later. On our way to the fort, as we were riding along, Geronimo, looking toward the

Chiricahua Mountains, referred to the raids of his band in that country. He said:

"This is the fourth time I have surrendered." Upon which I answered:

"And I think it is the last time you will ever have occasion to surrender."

As we moved along at a rapid trot, and occasionally at a gallop, I directed Lieutenant Wilder to ride forward to Fort Bowie and notify the commanding officers of our approach, in order that he might arrange for room at the garrison, and have accommodations prepared for the prisoners, and provide the necessary guards.

At Fort Bowie was a small garrison, and, like all the posts in that country, it had been in great anxiety, and practically besieged. No one could leave there unless armed or under strong escort, and the families of officers had waited day after day and week after week for tidings from those in the field. Lieutenant Wilder's family was there, and about the time he arrived, his wife, an accomplished gentlewoman, was taking a walk with her little children. It so happened that her little boy had run some distance ahead and out of her sight, to the outer edge of the post, just outside the buildings. As the gallant young officer dashed up to the post the first object he discovered was his little boy, and leaping down, the child and the hero were quickly clasped in each others arms. Lifting his boy to the saddle, he remounted, and with his son in front of him, rode into the post carrying the good news, the first joyful tidings to the young wife and mother being the sudden appearance of her husband and son together, the boy proud to bring home his father, the father proud that he, with others, could bring in their old enemies as prisoners. The news was almost too good for the garrison to believe, for it meant rest and peace, and the end of the terrible dangers through which they had passed.

On arriving at Fort Bowie, in order not to be disturbed by the civil authorities, or have any contest with them, I put a strong guard around the reservation, which was quite an extensive tract of land. The Indians were dismounted, disarmed, and placed under a strong escort, and on the 8th of September, under the charge of Captain Lawton, were started east from Bowie Station on the line of the Southern Pacific Railroad. As the procession was about to move from Fort Bowie, the band of the Fourth Cavalry was stationed on the parade ground, and, partly it is to be presumed through sentiment, and partly through derision on the occasion of the final adieu of the troops to the Apaches whom they had been hunting and fighting for so many years, it struck up "Auld Lang Syne:"

M.—31

> " Should auld acquaintance be forgot,
> And never brought to mind ? "

The humor of the situation was evidently not apparent to the Apaches, and they could not understand what occasioned the mirth of the soldiers.

So intense was the feeling of the citizens of that community that when they heard the Apaches had been captured they consulted among themselves along the line of the railroad about destroying the supports of some of the bridges, and thus throwing the train down some precipice. But mindful of the fact that such a course would also cause the death of many brave officers and soldiers who were guarding the Apaches, they refrained from carrying out their purpose of revenge. Instead, they gathered in large numbers at the different stations to see their old enemies pass out of the country forever.

Many people who had lost comrades and relatives, seeing these savages *en route* to the far eastern country, were overcome by their feelings and their faces were bedewed with tears of grief or joy. A very great change immediately occurred in the values of property in that country. People who had abandoned their mines and had not seen them for months or years returned to them again. The value of horse and cattle ranches increased fifty per cent., as it was then safe for men to travel without arms.

These Indians were for a time detained at San Antonio, Texas, but were subsequently forwarded to their destination in Florida.

I left Fort Bowie on the 8th of September, at the same time as the Indians, and accordingly did not receive a telegram concerning their disposition that arrived at that station on the afternoon of that day, and had no knowledge of it until the Indians had passed out of my department and were east of El Paso, Texas, *en route* to Florida, and I had turned north to go to Albuquerque, New Mexico, to conduct the removal of the Indians from Fort Apache who, under instructions received, had been ordered to be moved direct to Fort Marion, Florida.

While the above described movements were in progress, Colonel Wade was quietly moving the Indians from Fort Apache over a mountainous country, a distance of nearly a hundred miles, to Holbrook on the Atlantic and Pacific Railway. At Holbrook he found a train of twelve cars and two locomotives which I had sent him, and put the Indians on board these on the 13th of September. Twenty-four hours later I had the pleasure of meeting him at the depot at Albuquerque, and of seeing the long train loaded with the worst element that ever infested that country glide slowly past on its way to the East.

Thus far Colonel Wade had not lost a single Indian and did not lose one until he was east of the Mississippi River. Just after they passed St. Louis one Indian contrived to make his escape from the train, despite all the precautions that had been taken. True to his wolfish nature he succeeded in avoiding settlements and people who would be likely to arrest him, and though it took him a year to work his way back to the San Carlos reservation, he finally succeeded in doing it. Like a hyena he occasionally, at long intervals, stole down upon the Indian camp at San Carlos, captured an Indian woman, carried her back up into the mountains, kept her for several months, then cruelly murdered her and returned to repeat the same crime. This he did several times, and his movements were as secret and stealthy as those of a reptile. One Indian girl

APACHE BRIDE.

whom he had captured made her escape and told of his habits and cruelty. This man was afterwards reported killed by United States troops.

The Indians on board the train had not the remotest idea whither they were being transported, and though every effort was made to reassure them and convince them that they would receive proper treatment, yet they had great misgivings and were in a constant state of alarm.

They had never been on a train, and some of them had never seen a locomotive. As they passed into a long tunnel in going eastward they conceived the idea that they were going into the earth, and uttered shrieks of terror. When the train passed out at the other end of the tunnel many of them were found under the benches.

LITTLE MIKE, INDIAN BOY REARED BY WHITE PEOPLE.

After the surrender of Geronimo and Natchez, a small band of hostiles under a chief named Mangus, who had not been with the other hostiles, still remained out, and to secure them I organized a force under Lieutenant C. P. Johnson, who followed them down through parts of old Mexico and back up into and through New Mexico. On the 14th of October, the Indians having been reported in the region of the eastern border of Arizona, Captain Charles L. Cooper, of the Tenth Cavalry, with twenty enlisted men and two scouts, in obedience to orders, left Fort Apache to proceed in search of them. About dark on the 17th, he found a trail going west. The next morning he took up this trail, following it as rapidly as the extremely rugged nature of the country would allow, and after going about thirty miles obtained sight of the Indians, and was at the same time discovered by them. He was then at the base of an almost perpendicular mountain, two thousand feet high, over the top of which they were just passing. He pursued them over this mountain and over five others equally as high, and after a hard chase of about fifteen

OFFICERS WHO WERE ENGAGED IN THE CAPTURE OF GERONIMO AT FORT BOWIE, ARIZONA.

miles the Indians were obliged to abandon their stock, and again take to the mountains. But the troops were so close to them that their movements were discernible, and one after another was hunted down until all were captured but three, and these were soon induced to surrender.

The Indians captured consisted of Chief Mangus, two warriors, three women, two boys capable of bearing arms, one girl and four children of various ages. On the 30th of October this party left Fort Apache for Florida, Mangus and the two other men being sent to Fort Pickens, and the women and children to Fort Marion. One of the men died on the way but the remainder reached Florida safely early in November.

On his way east Mangus made a desperate attempt to escape from the train. It is almost impossible to handcuff an Indian securely, as his hands are smaller than his wrists, and on this occasion Mangus succeeded in removing his handcuffs without being observed. Then watching his

INDIAN WEAPONS AND GARMENTS.

1. Bow.
2. Arrows.
3. Sioux Flageolet or Flute.
4. Cheyenne Flute.
5. Cheyenne Rattler.
6. Bow Case and Quiver, made of Panther Skin.
7. Sioux Rattle, made from Ends of Buffalo Toes.
8. Cheyenne Moccasins, Beautifully Embroidered with Beads.
9. Cheyenne Tobacco Pouch.
10. Cheyenne Beaded Cradle.
11. Cheyenne Squaw Dress.

opportunity he jumped through the glass of the window by which he had been sitting, though he must have known that the chances of suicide were many to one of his escaping alive. The train was stopped, and he was found in a stunned condition, though not seriously injured. He is still alive and with the tribe, now in the Indian Territory.

On the 8th of November, 1887, I was presented by the citizens of Arizona with a very beautifully ornamented sword in token of their appreciation of my services in ridding their country of the Apaches. The ceremonies attending the presentation were long and interesting, commencing with a street parade at 12.30 and ending with a grand reception and ball at the San Xavier Hotel, Tucson, in the evening.

I cannot close this chapter without a more special tribute to Lawton, Wood, Hatfield, Benson, Wilder, Brown, Clarke and the other officers who so zealously, courageously and persistently pursued the hostiles to the end. Their services, like those of Bennett, Hale, Biddle, Baldwin, Snyder, Baird, Maus, Casey and others who supported me in former campaigns, were invaluable to the country. They have passed years on the remote frontier, some of them with their families, refined and gentle people, experiencing all the hardships and enjoying few of the ameliorations of army life, and their services and those of many like them cannot be too highly appreciated.

CHAPTER XLI.

HOW THE REGULARS ARE TRAINED.

REDUCED EXPENSES ON THE CESSATION OF INDIAN HOSTILITIES — THE NOGALES DISTURBANCE —
TROUBLES AT SAN CARLOS RESERVATION — THE EMERGENCIES OF PRESENT MILI-
TARY SERVICE — WHY INDIANS ARE DIFFICULT TO CAPTURE — FIELD SERVICE
AND ITS VALUE — THE FIELD MANEUVERS OF 1887 — ORDERS FOR
THE SAME — THEIR SUCCESS, VALUE, AND RESULTS.

FTER the cessation of hostilities in 1886, the expenses of the Department of Arizona were reduced at the rate of over a million dollars per annum. The troops belonging to the Departments of Texas and California were returned to their respective stations, and over four hundred enlisted scouts were discharged. In December, 1886, California, south of the thirty-fifth parallel was added to the Department of Arizona, and the headquarters were fixed at Los Angeles, California.

In March, 1887, a disturbance occurred at Nogales, Arizona Territory. This town is situated on the national line between the United States and Mexico, and at that time the population was about equally divided between Americans and Mexicans. Several officers belonging to the Mexican army crossed over to the American side of the town, and engaged in a shooting escapade with certain local civil officers. Prompt action was taken by the Mexican authorities, and the offenders were speedily punished; but as Nogales was an important place and other difficulties were likely to occur at any time, I stationed a company of infantry in the vicinity of the town, with the most gratifying results. During this same month, a young Indian named Nah-diz-az became

SAN CARLOS MILITARY CAMP.

dissatisfied with the division of farming land made by Second Lieutenant Seward Mott, Tenth Cavalry, who was on duty at the San Carlos reservation, and in charge of Indian farming on the upper Gila River. Owing to this dissatisfaction and the fact that his father had been confined by Lieutenant Mott for disobedience of orders and using threatening language, the Indian shot this young officer on the 9th of March, wounding him so severely as to cause his death the following day, and thus one more brave soldier, the victim of savage passions, found a last resting place

"Beneath the low green tent
Whose curtain never outward swings."

On the San Carlos reservation, in a mountainous, arid country, were more than five thousand degraded, barbarous Indians divided into various tribes, chiefly San Carlos, Yumas, Mojaves, Pimas and White Mountain Indians.

Captain Pierce, who had charge of the reservation, managed their affairs well, and was wonderfully successful considering the circumstances in inducing them to work. Nevertheless, for some time they had been a menace to the white settlers in the country. Several disturbances had occurred, and there had been a general demand for their removal on the part of the principal white people of the territory. Early in the summer of 1887 an outbreak took place that threatened to be of the most serious nature.

It occurred in this way. About six months previous to this time there had been a "tiswin drunk" among the Indians at San Carlos, in which a very popular chief, Toggy-da-shoose, was killed. The friends of the victim in their turn quickly and unhesitatingly despatched the murderer, and in this way a deadly feud was created between two bands. On the evening of May 28, five enlisted

TONTO WARRIOR.

Indian scouts belonging to the same band with Toggy-da-shoose, after another carouse of tiswin, went without permission to Arivaypa Cañon, and there killed an Indian named Rip, who, they claimed, had been the cause of the chief's death. In addition to this they threatened the life of a young warrior named Kid who formed one of the attacking party.

Five other Indians accompanied the scouts, and they were all absent about five days.

On their return they went to the tent of the chief-of-scouts, followed by some eight or ten other Indians, to await the arrival of the commanding officer. When Captain Pierce appeared he ordered them to lay down their arms and take off their cartridge belts. They had already complied with this command when some commotion arose and one of the Indians in the rear fired a shot. At this the chief-of-scouts stepped back into his tent and seized his rifle, a general breakout occurred, and a fusilade of shots was fired. The Indians continued to fire as they ran, some scouts about the camp returning the fire. The insurgents then fled to the mountains east of the agency, where they were quickly followed by a detachment of troops under Lieutenant Hughes.

MOQUI INDIAN GIRL.

Upon news of the affair reaching headquarters, troops from the various posts were ordered to occupy the country through which it was likely the rebellious Indians would pass. There were at first only ten men in the party, two or three of whom were on foot, but these were afterward joined by others. They were pursued rapidly and incessantly over the most rugged and mountainous region on the continent; no matter in what direction they turned they found that troops had made the country unsafe for them, while a pursuing command was always close behind them. In some respects this raid varied greatly from all previous ones, as the Indians stole but very little, frequently passing through herds without molesting the cattle, and only two white men were killed during the entire time they remained outside the reservation. On one occasion, while camped on the crest of the Rincon Mountains at a height of about seven thousand feet above the sea level, their camp was surprised by the troops under Lieutenant Carter P. Johnson and all their property, including their horses, was captured. But the Indians themselves escaped by sliding or crawling down over ledges of rock. From this point they traveled along the mountain ranges on foot, crossing the narrow valleys at night, and endeavored to take refuge in the Indian camps on the reservation, but were trailed and hunted down by the troops to their retreat.

On the 13th of June I left my headquarters to·visit San Carlos, in order to personally inquire into the circumstances attending the disturbance, and to direct the movements of the pursuing forces. I found that from a thousand to twelve hundred Indians had left their camps, abandoned their fields, and had congregated at a place called Coyote Holes, where they assumed a most threatening attitude. Here they held their nightly orgies and Indian dances and were harangued by their medicine men, whose influence was decidedly prejudicial to peace. But no actual outbreak occurred, as troops were stationed at proper points to check any further disturbance.

On the 18th of June one of the renegades surrendered. As he had been absent nineteen days, I sent him to the guardhouse for the same length of time, but on the second day following he practically turned State's evidence and gave information concerning the movements of himself and others, so I remitted his sentence. On the 22d eight others surrendered, followed by Kid with seven companions on the 25th. It was believed that a Yaqui Indian named Miguel was the instigator of the whole affair. According to the best obtainable evidence he had fired the shot that opened hostilities, and with his own hand had killed the two men who had been murdered. The outbreak was evidently unpremeditated on the part of most of the Indians, and this, added to the fact that they had committed such a small number of depredations, entitled them to some consideration. Although the scouts did not fully comprehend the responsibility of their obligations as enlisted men, I ordered an investigation by a general court-martial as if they had been white soldiers. One of the culprits was afterward condemned to suffer death but this sentence was afterwards remitted, and the others were given sentences of from two to twenty years' imprisonment. The disaffected and hostile element were finally persuaded and forced to return to their former camps without serious hostilities, and thus once more it was found better to avoid war than to end one.

Two tribes on the San Carlos agency, the Yumas and Mojaves, had for years been pleading to be allowed to return to their former homes. The place where they were located along the Gila River was so intensely hot, arid, desolate and sickly that the troops on duty there were obliged to be changed every few months in order to preserve their health. The excitement of these Indians over the general condition of affairs was greatly increased by the earthquakes which occurred in that vicinity about this time. Part of these Indians were anxious to be returned to the Colorado

River to join others of their own tribes at Yuma and Mojave, while still others desired to go to the vicinity of their former home on the Fort Verde reservation.

The White Mountain Indians who had been forced to go to the Gila Valley declared they would rather die than live there. They were told that they could not have rations if they did not remain, and they said they would rather go back to their own country, if they had to starve. They did go back, and for years made a most heroic struggle to live without receiving rations from the government. They cut wood and hay for Fort Apache, and I have seen their women go long distances and cut grass with knives and pack it on their backs to the post, although the amount of money they received for their labor was exceedingly small.

The Navajo Indians of New Mexico were among the largest and most powerful of all the tribes, numbering twenty thousand souls, with at least four thousand men capable of bearing arms, while they were at the same time rich enough to supply themselves with the most improved rifles, with an average of one thousand rounds of ammunition per man. This being the case, even though they were practically at peace, I deemed it best to concentrate as many of the cavalry as possible in that vicinity.

Whenever emergencies had arisen, requiring active field service, it was a common occurrence for requests or reports like the following to be

MOJAVE RUNNERS.

received at headquarters: "Request authority to employ scouts;" "Guides;" "Experienced trailers;" "Men familiar with the habits of the Indians and topography of the country," etc.; "Trail scattered;" "Lost trail and command returned to station;" "Misled by guides," etc. The condition of affairs indicated by such applications and reports ought not to exist. Troops serving any considerable length of time in a department should themselves excel in an accurate and thorough knowledge of the country and in skillful pursuit of the enemy. While garrison duty, target practice, drills and parades in garrison are important, yet there is another service of vital importance the moment a command takes the field, and to this all other duties are really preparatory. In order to render this service entirely effective I required the troops to devote special attention to field service for a number of years, and with the most gratifying results.

The element of strength that was possessed by the Indians against which the troops found it most difficult to contend, was their skill in passing rapidly over the country, noting every feature of it, and observing the movements and strength of their enemies, without allowing themselves to be discovered. This faculty was the natural outgrowth of the fact that generation after generation of the Indians had followed the life of the hunter and warrior. The superior intelligence of the white man renders him capable of acquiring the same art in an almost equal degree if given the opportunity.

While the chief motive of drill in this field service was to give the troops practice that would enable them in times of actual hostility to render the country untenable for the Indians, yet it was also a training invaluable to the officers in case they should be called upon for service in civilized warfare; for, owing to the small size of the regular army, the same officers that might in this practice or in actual Indian campaigning be in command of a small detachment of troops, are liable at any time to be suddenly required to lead a division or a corps, should the necessity suddenly arise for greatly increasing the army.

For these reasons I determined to give special attention to field maneuvers, and, therefore, while in command of the Department of Arizona in 1887, I issued the following orders:

HEADQUARTERS DEPARTMENT OF ARIZONA, }
LOS ANGELES, CAL., August 20, 1887. }

GENERAL ORDERS No. 24:

I. During the months of September and October of this year the troops of this Department will be considered as on field duty, and will be instructed and exercised in all that pertains to the practical requirements of field service. During those months all other drills and duties will, as far as practicable, be suspended, except the target and signal practice required by orders of the War Department, which will be regulated so as to admit of this field service.

II. On September 1st, post commanders will occupy their districts of observation by the location of outposts, signal and heliograph stations, and establish communications with the nearest signal stations of the adjacent posts.

III. During the first fifteen days of that month post commanders will, if necessary, make themselves familiar with the topographical features of the district of country within their charge, and give such instructions to the troops of their commands regarding every detail of field service as will render them most efficient and afford them a knowledge of the general features of the country in which they are serving, and give to them that general knowledge of the geography and topography of the country as will enable them to pass over it readily without the aid of guides, compass or maps.

IV. Cavalry troops will be specially instructed in movements by open order formations. To this end care will be taken to make the trooper and his horse the unit rather than to adhere constantly to the close formation of a troop, with a view of training the horses to act separately and independently of the close column.

V. After two weeks of this kind of practice, the commanding officer of Fort Huachuca, Arizona, is hereby directed to send out a detachment of troops to march from that post to Fort Apache, Arizona, and return, via. the route indicated in this order. This raiding party will consist of two officers and twenty enlisted men, well mounted and provided with extra horses, and sufficient pack animals to carry the necessary baggage and camp equipage. Pack animals will not be required to carry more than one hundred pounds per mule, all superfluous articles being left in the post, including sabers, revolvers, curb bridles, hobbles, nose bags, extra horse equipments and camp equipage of every kind that can be dispensed with. The detachment will be properly rationed and is authorized to obtain necessary supplies en route in the usual form and to carry forty rounds of ammunition per man, with the necessary clothing. It will start from Fort Huachuca at noon on September 17th and will march east of Fort Bowie, west of Fort Grant, touching the limits of the Fort Lowell district, east of Fort Thomas, west of Apache to a point north of that post, should they reach that point without being captured.

The commanding officer will then notify the commanding officer, Fort Apache, by courier, of the presence of his detachment. He will then select an agreeable camp and send to Fort Apache for supplies. After remaining there ten days they will return, passing east of Fort Apache, west of Fort Thomas, east of Fort Grant, and west of Fort Bowie, and east of Dragoon Station, on the Southern Pacific railroad to Fort Huachuca. In starting from Fort Huachuca they will be allowed from 12 M. September 17, until 6 A. M. the day following, before being followed by the troops from Fort Huachuca. After 6 A. M. September 18, they will remain in camp until 12 M. of that day, and after that time they will be limited in marches to the hours between 12 M. and midnight of each day. The commanding officer of the detachment will select (within the above described limits) his own line of march and conceal his men and camps according to his own judgment. Both officers and men of the detachment should fully understand the course to be taken and places of rendezvoux, in order to assemble again, whenever it becomes necessary to separate because of close pursuit, or to avoid discovery.

VI. Post commanders will conceal their troops and establish lookouts in such way as to discover, surprise and capture the detachment above mentioned, if possible, and in any event they are directed to have the raiding party pursued until a fresh command is on the trail. Information concerning the party to be pursued will be communicated with the least possible delay by heliograph, telegraph or courier to the different post commanders and to all troops placed to intercept them.

VII. Reports will be made by post commanders by telegraph to these headquarters daily, of any observation of the raiding party, their movements and efforts made to capture them. The party or any portion of them will be regarded as captured whenever another detachment or command of equal numbers gets within hailing distance or within bugle sound.

The Commanding Officers at Forts Bowie and Grant, will send one officer or non-commissioned officer, provided with two horses each, to accompany the party and act as witnesses in case any question should arise as to the rules to be followed or results. In case of capture the detachment will march to the nearest post and another raiding party will be immediately ordered from these headquarters.

Similar movements will be made in the District of New Mexico by a detachment of cavalry from Fort Wingate, N. M., moving around Fort Bayard and returning to its station; also one from Fort Stanton around Fort Bayard and return to its station, each going at some time within ten miles of that post and orders for marching and concealment of each will be the same as those directed for Fort Huachuca.

Care will be taken to avoid breaking down either the troop horses or pack animals, or stampeding or injuring any stock or property of citizens.

At the close of the period for field practice, post commanders will call for suggestions from officers and men of their commands, and make brief reports of results and mention any defects in the equipment of their command or anything that would tend to promote their efficiency.

Post Commanders will retain communication with their detachments sufficient to enable them to recall them to their stations without delay in case of necessity.

By command of Brigadier-General MILES:

J. A. DAPRAY, Second Lieutenant Twenty-third Infantry, A. D. C.
A. A. A. General.

An officer in command of a raiding force was credited with the capture of a military post if he succeeded in getting his command during daylight within one thousand yards of the flagstaff of that post.

The movements directed during the months of September and October were continued during parts of October and November, and embraced the country between Fort Huachuca, Arizona, and Fort Stanton, New Mexico, and between Fort Wingate, New Mexico, and Fort Apache, Arizona, a mountainous region three hundred miles in extent east and west, and nearly the same distance north and south.

This series of practical maneuvers, considering their initiatory or experimental nature were in the main very satisfactory, and the experience gained by officers and troops engaged in them were of incalculable value. The results of ten distinct field maneuvres covering an area of hundreds of miles in extent may be stated in brief as follows: On five different occasions the raiding parties were overtaken and captured by the troops in pursuit, commanded respectively by Captains Chaffee, Wood and Stanton, and Lieutenants Scott and Pershing, notwithstanding that every device was adopted to annoy and deceive the pursuers by dispersing, destroying trails by having herds of cattle driven over them, by false maneuvers, etc.

On five occasions different detachments commanded by Captains Wint, Wallace and Kendall, and Lieutenants Richards and McGrath, misled and eluded their pursuers, but were discovered and intercepted by the troops in advance who were lying in wait for them.

Captain Wallace started from Fort Bayard, New Mexico, captured the command sent in pursuit of him, and avoiding the troops in advance succeeded in reaching Fort Stanton, New Mexico, but was captured by Lieutenant Pershing in endeavoring to return.

Captain Wint started from Fort Lowell, Arizona Territory, and escaping from his pursuers and eluding the troops sent to intercept him, remained several days in their vicinity in the Graham Mountains, and finally succeeded in reaching Fort Apache, with the loss of but four men, captured. Returning, he skillfully misled and avoided the command in pursuit, capturing a second command endeavoring to intercept him, but was finally captured by a third command to which one of his captives had deserted and given information of his presence. This was one of the longest and most successful expeditions of the series.

Lieutenant C. P. Johnson made one of the most successful and remarkable raids, exhibiting much originality in planning and skill in executing.

He started from Fort Grant to circle or capture Fort Lowell (distance approximately one hundred miles to the south of west); to accomplish this same with Fort Huachuca (distance approximately one hundred and twenty miles), and also Fort Bowie, forty-two miles south of Fort Grant.

Starting from Fort Grant he scattered his command, partially obliterating his trail by getting his command upon a heavy, sandy road that ran north and south but a few miles west of the fort; under cover of night he moved north instead of southwest, as he was expected to do. This sandy road was used by heavy teams hauling copper ore from Globe to Wilcox on the Southern Pacific road.

The troops that were put in pursuit from Grant moved west and southwest, lost the scattered trail and spent two weeks in endeavoring to find some trace of this lost command.

The commanding officer went to Fort Lowell for supplies and finally gave up the pursuit in despair.

Notwithstanding troops were on the lookout for Lieutenant Johnson from Grant, Lowell, Huachuca and Bowie, he was for three weeks as completely lost as if he had disappeared in a cavern in the earth, or in mid-air. Instead of going in the direction of Fort Lowell, as he pretended to do, he reversed his course, struck the Globe and Wilcox road, moved past his own station (Grant), and within a few miles of it, going north about thirty-five miles to the crossing of the Gila River, then moved down the river for about twenty miles, leaving no more trail behind him than a bird in the air. This skillful movement brought his command a long distance to the northwest and in a broken, mountainous country.

In this section he concealed his command, moving still further to the west under cover of the Santa Catarena Mountains and timber and the darkness of the night with as much celerity and secrecy as an Indian or a panther. Gradually bearing south, in the gray of the morning he passed to the west and south of Fort Lowell, thus encircling that military post as he rode rapidly through the town of Tucson, about eight miles from Fort Lowell, while the occupants of that town were wrapped in blissful slumber.

Knowing he would be pursued by troops from Lowell he made rapidly to the southwest for twenty-five miles to the Santa Rita Mountains, where he again scattered his command and by a series of false movements, decoys and skillful maneuvers, threw his pursuers off his trail and threatened Fort Huachuca, and while pretending to circle that post to the south he suddenly disappeared and, moving west a good distance, made a forced march across country and surprised Fort Bowie.

Under the rule he was allowed to remain ten days for rest. The colonel commanding Fort Huachuca reported this young officer as having disregarded his orders and that he had not circled that post, little thinking that the maneuvers were intended as a blind.

After quietly resting ten days Lieutenant Johnson apparently made all preparations to move north from Bowie to Grant. After leaving the former post he suddenly reversed his course and moving rapidly and secretly across the country, succeeding in getting his command within a thousand yards of the flagstaff of Fort Huachuca, surprised and captured the post and garrison of six troops of cavalry.

It is needless to say that the chagrin and envy felt by the officers of the garrison was very great, for they were a proud, spirited and enterprising class of men. In fact, the feeling amounted almost to hostility against this officer, though they were very gracious to him and extended to him every civility and hospitality during his stay of ten days for rest and recuperation.

He had still a most difficult problem to solve. He was more than one hundred miles from his own station, and when once he started from Huachuca he was sure to be pursued by the picked troopers from that garrison, and in addition to this he must contend against the vigilance of those on the lookout from Bowie and Grant, for he must return to his own post either as victor or captive.

After a good rest and ample time to study the maps and topography of the country between Huachuca and Grant, Lieutenant Johnson marched out at twelve o'clock, noon, for his movement against Fort Grant. Under the rule he was allowed eighteen hours before he could be pursued—six hours of day and twelve hours of night.

Sleuth hounds never tugged harder at the leash, thoroughbred racers never champed the bit with more impatience than did those Fourth Cavalry troopers to be set loose on the trail or in pursuit of the successful raiders, while there was the wildest excitement concerning its success on the part of the pursued party, and the most intense enthusiasm on the part of the pursuers. Fortunately the command was entrusted to an able and experienced cavalry officer, Captain A. Wood, who demonstrated his skill and good judgment, who instead of following the circuitous trail and false maneuvers, with the disadvantage of a stern chase, moved directly across country by a forced march of seventy miles to a pass in a range of mountains that he believed Lieutenant Johnson would pass through but not where any of his trails would indicate he was going. Towards this gap Captain Wood's troop marched at a rapid pace and reached it as the sun was low in the afternoon. Now the thing to be accomplished was to find if Lieutenant Johnson's command was concealed in the vicinity.

In these maneuvers it was not uncommon for the commanding officer to bribe the citizens to make false reports, or to give them erroneous information in order that they might convey the same misleading intelligence to their pursuers.

Lieutenant Johnson had evidently missed one civilian for, as Captain Wood was looking for signs of the pursued party or for some trace of the raiders, he discovered a lone missionary traveling through that country, who, on being questioned whether he had seen anything of a command of soldiers, stated that he had passed a small company just going into camp in a little pocket of the mountains about five miles away. This was a revelation and a boon for this accomplished cavalry leader and within a very short time his bugles sounded the command for Lieutenant Johnson's surrender after his very long and very successful raid.

Thus, Captain Wood's good judgment, enterprise and hard ride of seventy-five miles was rewarded with most gratifying and most creditable success.

This ended one of the most skillful of the interesting practical field maneuvers. Lieutenant Johnson is a fair representative of those Virginians like Stuart, Ashby and other brilliant cavalry leaders. He informed me that while a part of his plan was to capture the department commander, in which he was, however, not successful, he believed if he could destroy the telegraph lines he could make a successful raid from

M.—32

Arizona to the Atlantic seaboard and avoid the troops in the intermediate districts of the country.

It is to be regretted that the untimely death by a cruel and painful disease has deprived the service of so accomplished an officer as Captain Wood, whose record, during the great war, on the Western frontier and in the field of military literature was most creditable and valuable.

The results attained in this field maneuvering were most pleasing. The excellent judgment and intelligence displayed by the commanding officers of the districts of observation in the disposition of their troops, the use made of the means of observation and communication, the zeal and skill exhibited by officers in the field, and the very great interest taken in these operations by the troops, were all most gratifying.

CHAPTER XLII.

The Arid Region and Irrigation.

The Conditions of the Arid Region — A Rich Soil, But a Lack of Rainfall — What the
Arid Belt Includes — Area and Proportion Irrigated — The Sub-Humid Region — The
Standard of Humidity — Science and Personal Experience — Idea of Farming
by Irrigation New to the Saxon — The Instance of California — Irriga-
tion in History — Universal Efficiency of the System — The
Measures Taken by the Government — The Action of States
— Cost — Reasons for Further Government Action.

HAVING crossed the imaginary line which divides the old and well-known farming region, to which we are all accustomed, from the newer West, we instantly encounter new conditions, requiring a system of farming new to the ideas of the Saxon.

There is a vast tract there where the rainfall is so small that it imposes new conditions, though the soil is rich and the climate much more favorable to agriculture than that of New England, or even that of the Middle States. This region is now known as the "arid belt," and its boundaries are well defined. Its extent is enormous. It includes Montana, Wyoming, Colorado, Utah, Idaho, Nevada, Arizona, and New Mexico, with those portions of North and South Dakota, Kansas, and Nebraska which lie west of the one hundredth meridian, with large portions of southern and western Texas, and all of California south of the thirty-ninth parallel. The eastern two-thirds of Oregon are also included, with one-third of Washington.

The area of this vast territory includes 1,340,000 square miles. In 1890 the irrigated portion of it was about one-half of one per cent of the whole.

Associated with the lack of rainfall is a dryness of the air which desiccates the foliage of vegetation, and in much of this region a scanty growth, accustomed to the vicissitudes of the climate, alone survives. The clouds evaporated from the Pacific are precipitated on the western coast. Those of the Atlantic rain themselves out on the eastern. Those formed by the Great Lakes and the Gulf seldom pass beyond one hundred miles westward of the west line of Missouri.

There is a sub-humid region lying on the borders of the area given. The standard of humidity which has been fixed for aridness is twenty inches of rainfall, or less, annual average for a period of years. There is no region within the boundaries of the United States where it may be said never to rain at all. Sometimes, at irregular intervals, on the high plains of the west the rainfall within a few hours is of immense volume. There is a want of seasonableness and regularity, and many months, or even sometimes an entire year, may pass without a copious rain. There are, therefore, in the sub-arid area fine crop-years occasionally. These fruitful years come still more frequently in the eastern portions of the belts. An entire failure of all crops does not often occur in the latter region, and a full crop may at long intervals be made in all except the dryest areas of the vast territory named.

During the past thirty years most of the facts stated have been learned experimentally by actual settlers. The universal American enterprise carried thousands of families at least to the edge of the arid region, and many hundreds of them into its very heart. There is an unwritten history of these enterprises. Meantime science has not been idle, and the labors of practical meteorologists have defined and mapped the boundaries of aridness, and have discovered its causes. There is but one remedy —irrigation.

As stated, the idea of farming by irrigation is new to the Saxon mind,

ARTESIAN WELLS.

though it is one of the oldest arts of civilization. With this man, to whom it is new, it is more successful when once he has adopted it than it is in any other hands. Southern California, a new land to Americans from the east, is an example. Within the memory of most readers it was a hopeless desert, with an oasis here and there around which all there was of the Spanish civilization had clustered. American ingenuity, tempted by a climate which has, perhaps, no parallel in the world, found new sources of water. The highest resources of modern engineering science were applied, and mechanical skill of the first order was brought to bear. Artesian wells were sunk where the existence of water beneath the surface had never before been suspected, and flowing wells, which surprise the eye and seem miraculous, water hundreds of the richest acres of the world. Tunnels have been bored into the mountains. Ditches were lined with cement to prevent the seepage which had wasted half the water in all old systems. Miles of piping have been laid. Mountain springs have been found and their waters carried long distances at vast expense. The results are now known to all the world as something marvelous in an age of marvels. The work has not yet come to an end, and the time may come when hardly an arable acre in all that wonderful region will be unwatered and idle.

This is but an instance, though perhaps the foremost one, of the practical results of modern irrigation. Yet systems even still more colossal have been made, used, and have passed away, upon American soil. The most extensive of these remains are found in Arizona, a region then and now almost the heart of aridness, and yet one that was once occupied by choice by the unknown people of an unknown time, who lived and toiled in those valleys which have not since their time been occupied, and which have long since reverted to the primeval desert.

History makes it clear that irrigation has entered largely into the story of all the older races. The great canal which connected Pelusium with the Red Sea was an irrigating ditch. The greatest work of the kind ever made was in Arabia. It existed before the time of Solomon, and was fed by a dam two miles long and two hundred and fifty feet high, and it endured for two thousand years. The historic plains of Assyria and Babylon were all irrigated. The Hebrews lived in Goshen under Pharaoh, and grew wealthy and numerous as farmers under a system of irrigation. The ancient Peruvians and Mexicans had an immense irrigation system. Lombardy, in Europe, has at the present time an extensive system which the modern Lombards inherited from the Romans, and in which the distribution of the waters is a function of the government. Some of the oldest lands of history are now all arid, having in their day grown rich and powerful solely because they farmed these arid lands from choice, and with a water supply altogether artificial. Historically considered, the moist lands and the humid regions were the last to be occupied by a high civilization, and among the original enterprises of mankind was the making certain of the food supply without reference to the uncertain rainfall of any given year.

Historic irrigation had two ends, one was to secure regularity of supply in regions where the natural rainfall was almost, or quite normal, the other to redeem lands absolutely arid. Almost all the irrigation of modern Europe is of the first class. It has been practiced in England for a long period, but mainly with the purpose of increasing the yield of hay on low-lying meadows. There is in fact no agricultural region where an artificial means of watering the fields would not be of immense advantage. There are times in all lands where the rain which is needed does not come, and where when not needed, there may be a heavy fall. Stimulated by the example of irrigation in the far West, the time is coming when systems will be established in the regions of greatest rainfall, where unused streams abound, for the purpose of establishing a control over the water supply for growing crops. Instances of irrigating systems exist now in nearly all the arable fields lying near our great cities, where vegetables are grown for market. The light, cheap and efficient American windmill is seen whirling in all the summer breezes, though it is often the case that in the aggregate there is rather too much than too little rainfall.

Rice, rather than wheat, is the staple food of the majority of mankind. Millions subsist upon it as the staple, almost the only food. There are varieties that grow without irrigation, but that necessity exists in nearly all rice-growing regions, and is used in the production of all of that grain that reaches the market. This fact alone is an index of the age and wide extent of a system that until recently has been quite ignored by us, though we are even now one of the greatest agricultural nations of the world.

The question of irrigation in the United States has in recent years become a topic of absorbing interest. The public lands which are arable and lie in the humid and sub-humid regions are practically all now occupied, and the process of spreading out and occupying has had its first check. Yet, the soil of the arid region is very rich. There is every inducement to settlement if there were only a certainty of even a half supply of water. So recently has the emergency confronted us that no action has as yet been taken by the general government beyond the appointment of a commission to investigate general facts, and establish boundaries, and whose final report has never been acted upon. The various States and Territories have locally interested themselves. The instances of successful irrigation in southern California have been mentioned, and exist elsewhere in localities far apart over a wide area. But they may be said truly to hardly affect the general situation, which is one of great magnitude and vast importance. These beginnings have led to investigation and imitation, and the following are some of the facts that now appear.

According to the census of 1890 Colorado had under irrigation 4,068,409 acres, or about 6,337 square miles. Arizona had 65,821 acres; New Mexico, 91,745 acres; Wyoming, 229,676 acres; Montana, 350,582 acres. California exceeds the largest of these figures, and there is a still smaller acreage in Idaho, Washington and Oregon. It will be seen how small a proportion of the area of these regions is at this date under the dominion of the plow.

The cost is at present great. In California the cost, including all necessary ditches, is from ten to twenty dollars per acre. In the same State at least twelve inches depth of water per annum are required for raising cereal crops. One cubic foot of water every second for twenty-four hours covers two acres with nearly twelve inches of water. At this rate of flow it requires one hundred days to cover two hundred acres with the requisite aggregate depth, given at intervals, to raise a cereal crop.

SWEETWATER DAM.

Comparing this with the average rainfall in the humid regions will convey some idea of the relative situation. In the grain States of the Mississippi Valley the farmer has upon his land an annual rainfall almost never less than thirty inches, and often reaching fifty inches. But it often comes when it is not wanted, and very often fails when it is. The great crop years are distinguished not by volume of rainfall, but by equable and timely distribution.

It is rapidly becoming a settled conviction that individual enterprise can never entirely and adequately solve the problem of Western irrigation. The task is a vast one, extending far beyond State lines and individual interests. In view of the fact that there are vast areas of the public domain still remaining unoccupied, which seem to require an intelligent and judicious system of improvement by the government in order that the best results may be obtained in their settlement, and, in order to prevent a small percentage of the people from taking possession of the water-courses and holding them exclusively for their own benefit, thereby shutting out all others from the occupation of a much larger portion, and practically controlling the use of thousands of square miles of the public domain, it might be well for the government to devise some system by which these lands may be utilized and colonized for the benefit of the home-builders who constitute our best population.

There is another view of this matter which should not fail to be duly considered. Within the last few years we have witnessed the terrible results occasioned by drought, and half crops or total failures have been reported throughout many of the States and Territories. We have also noticed that this has resulted in a very large percentage of the land in several of the States and Territories referred to being placed under very heavy mortgages, and should this evil continue for a series of years no one can anticipate what result may follow. That good results can be produced by a scientific and judicious control of the water-courses of the Western country is a fact so well established that it does not require argument. We have reached that period in which attention should be drawn to this important subject, and it is not surprising that the question of water-storage and irrigating works in the arid regions of our Western country has been engrossing the attention of the citizens residing west of the one hundredth meridian more in the past few years than ever before.

While the people of nearly every State and Territory west of that meridian have carefully considered the question, and while their legislators have enacted various local laws bearing upon it, the federal government but recently took up the matter by an act of Congress authorizing the investigation of the subject to ascertain to what extent the arid regions of the United States can be benefited by irrigation. It stipulated that $100,000 be appropriated for topographical surveys for the fiscal year ending June 30, 1889, or any part thereof, to be used by the Director of the Geological Survey, Major Powell, with the approval of the Secretary of the Interior, for the purpose of ascertaining the feasibility of providing reservoirs of water with a view to the establishing of a system of irrigation of the lands in question, and Major Powell was directed to make his report to Congress at as early a date as was practicable. Upon his report, and the recommendation of the Secretary of the Interior, the $100,000 was supplemented by an additional appropriation of $250,000 during a succeeding session of Congress, and by the passage of an act authorizing a further investigation of the arid region. A committee of senators was appointed to visit the arid regions of the different western States and Territories the following summer. It completed its work of investigation, was on the road some fifty days, traveling in that time about twelve thousand miles, and taking the testimony of hundreds of witnesses.

These were the first steps taken by the general government toward the utilization of what is commonly called desert land. The bill reserves all lands that may hereafter be designated for reservoirs and ditches, and the lands to be reclaimed by irrigation from such reservoirs, from the date of the passage of the act, and provides that the President may, from time to time, remove any of the reservations made by the bill, and in his discretion, by proclamation, open any portion or all of the lands reserved by the provision to settlement under the homestead laws. This, however, might, with benefit, be modified so as to fix the price of such lands, so improved by the general government, at such a rate per acre as will compensate it for the expense of such improvement. The sums appropriated, it is hoped, are but the commencement of necessary appropriations for irrigating purposes, as they will scarcely cover the amount requisite for preliminary investigations, without, in the least, considering the vastness and extent of the work to follow. The engineers employed in the work were required to measure the various streams and sources of water supply, select sites for reservoirs and other hydraulic works necessary for storage and utilization of water, make maps of arable lands surveyed, and furnish full information for the use of Congress in considering further legislation on the subject.

This has been becoming more and more a prominent question in

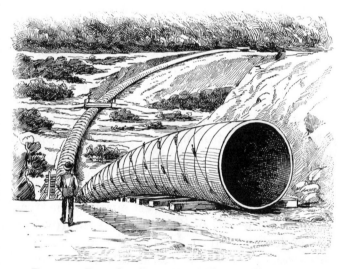

REDWOOD PIPE, SAN BERNARDINO COUNTY, CALIFORNIA.

the history of all the Western States and Territories, and by being brought to the attention of the general public, the necessities and usefulness of irrigation may in time be extended to all parts of the country where needed. In some parts the system would prevent the desolating effects of drought, and in others, by the use of reservoirs and dams for storing the waters, the disastrous floods that almost periodically destroy growing crops and injure routes of travel and commerce would be rendered less frequent and destructive. There is not now a piece of land sold in the dry regions where the judicious purchaser does not look well into the question of how many inches of irrigating water goes with the land, that being the most important factor to be considered. The water right, the number of miner's inches that can be used, and the cost price per foot per acre, are all matters that are duly considered.

The following resolution was presented in the platform of one of the political parties in a Western State some time ago as an important measure:

"Resolved, That the waters of the State belong to the land they irrigate, and we favor and will aid in maintaining a broad and comprehensive system of irrigation that looks to the benefit of the irrigator as primary to the assumed rights of the riparian and appropriator; a system controlled by the government, free to all, under the control of no class of persons, and established and maintained by a revenue derived from those whom the system will benefit.

"We believe the water is the property of the people, and that it should be so used as to secure the greatest good to the greatest number of people."

The government of our country has an important mission to perform, now that it has once taken charge of the work, and it is presumed that it will continue until a time when the entire irrigation system will be under its control, with one simple law governing it alike in all the Western States and Territories. As to whether the work will ever be taken energetically in charge of by the federal government remains to be seen. The enormous amount of money required to place the desert lands in a productive state would have to be furnished by the government, as it would be impossible for the States and Territories to complete so vast a system as must be undertaken; and the funds expended should, by a well-matured and comprehensive plan, revert again to the treasury of the general government from the sale of its lands thus improved.

The feeling that it is the work of the federal government is almost universal. In some States resolutions like the following have been passed:

First. The declaration that every natural stream and water source is public property.

Second. That the appropriation for beneficial uses of any such stream must be made under legislative enactment.

Third. That all water so appropriated in the State is declared to be a public use.

Fourth. Rates and rents for use are to be fixed by public authority, but must not exceed seven per cent. on capital actually expended in constructing irrigating works."

The legislature of Wyoming has adopted the water legislation of the State of Colorado, which is considered the best in use by any of the States and Territories. The subject has been discussed at length in the various reports of the governors, and all the Western States have fostered and cared for irrigating enterprises, and their citizens have invested millions of dollars in the same, the revenue from which makes it a very profitable investment and which benefit the people and the country adjacent to the plant.

The precipitation of water in the mountainous portions of the arid belt averages not more than twenty inches yearly, although in parts, in some years, as much as seventy-five inches has fallen in a short time, causing floods in the streams, frequently creating destruction in the arable low land, and the most of it disappearing in the sandy wastes where the average rainfall is scarcely five inches. The lesser amount falling on low desert lands and the greater in the mountains, the plan of building dams across the mountain valleys or cañons, wherever it can be done to advantage and at small cost, should in all cases be pursued to completion. Where natural catchment basins exist—and there are any number of them in the mountains,—the government should reserve them for future irrigation purposes.

Private enterprises, mindful of the advantages and large returns for the the money invested and the indifference shown by the federal government, have taken up many important sites for reservoirs which drain areas many square miles in extent, and control the water for vast districts. On the general surface of the arid region it is estimated that about fifteen inches of water falls annually, much of which can be utilized. All of the arid region embraces arable lands favorable for agriculture in all its phases, from the cultivation of the products of the north temperate zone to those of the tropics. Where irrigation is used in the north, the season for watering is generally not longer than three months, but in the south it embraces at least eight or nine months of the year. As much water is used at a time as would result from a day's copious rain. A practical experience is requisite, as too much water is liable to produce more injury than benefit. While the irrigated farms are larger generally in Colorado and Utah, in southern California twenty acres is as much as one family can well care for when devoted to the cultivation of vines, fruits, vegetables, or alfalfa.

The eminent English writer and traveler, Sir Edwin Arnold, recently passing across the continent, made this observation:

" Nothing has struck me more in my visit to America than the slope of your sierras. Your orchards and vineyards were a revelation to me. You will be the wine growers of the world. Then in your sagebrush plateaus you only need irrigation to make them fruitful. The land I saw in Nevada is almost exactly like what I saw in India and Arabia, which has been made so productive."

The streams of the West find their sources near the summits of the mountain peaks that are covered with eternal snow, and derive their main supply from the rains and snows that fall within the great basin through which they course to the sea, and it is in this mountain region that the lowlands and foot-hills will have to depend for the water to make them fruitful under cultivation. The cañons can be formed into great catch-basins for retaining the rains in their season, while natural lakes are numerous throughout the region.

The State of California is blessed with prosperity derived from its

FLUME BUILDING. SPRINGING IN THE BOTTOM PLANK.

irrigating works, and is fast being populated with a prosperous class of agriculturalists who have been brought thither mainly through the success of irrigation, combined with the unequaled climate. The changes wrought in places in California which not long ago were considered valueless have been briefly mentioned. Where once it was thought nothing but sage brush and cactus could grow the land has been cleared, ditches have been made, trees have been planted, crops cultivated, and the land placed in a higher state of cultivation than in many favored localities of the Eastern and Southern States. In ten years villages and cities have sprung up where before coyotes starved. In fact, it is impossible for one to conceive how much a country supposed to be utterly worthless can be benefited by the use of water, unless he has seen such effects. To pass from the hot, arid regions into the fertile valleys of California is as gladdening to the eyes of the beholder as the sight of an oasis is to the traveler in the desert. To see the countless acres of trees with their ripening fruit, the unlimited acres of grapes, fields of wheat, barley and alfalfa, and everything breathing life and health, is to see the blessed use of water, husbanded and cared for and appreciated in all its worth. Land originally valued at less than a dollar per acre has increased through the benefit of a sure supply of water until one acre is worth as much as one hundred would have been had not the systems of irrigation been established. Without irrigation, except in certain moist lands, these beautiful valleys and lowlands would once more revert to desert wastes.

It is a well-known fact that after land has been thoroughly cultivated by irrigation less water is required; and it is safe to assert that thousands of acres of so-called desert land may become adapted for agricultural purposes without the quantity of water at first necessary. Immediately following the establishment of an irrigation district, after the canals, with their lateral ditches have been completed and the cultivation of crops has commenced, the planting of trees should be encouraged. The eucalyptus variety is mostly planted in California, and the cottonwood in Arizona and New Mexico. The former has a very rapid growth, and as a wind-break and a protection to crops it is used extensively. This tree planting would in a short time not only change the appearance of the country and supply the wood which is necessary for fuel, but would also modify the climate. It would hardly be possible to estimate the value of trees in their usefulness toward reclaiming arid lands, and too much cannot be said in urging the profuse planting of them. In fact, it would be well for the government in selling land reclaimed through any irrigation system to be established, to make it compulsory on the purchaser to plant a portion of his acreage in forest trees. They would only require thorough irrigation during the first year, less of it the second, very little the third, and possibly none at all thereafter. Tree culture, especially the planting of trees indigenous to the country, should by all means be encouraged.

As we review the past, we notice the action of the unscrupulous and the insatiable in following in the wake or hanging upon the flanks, and very often seen in a position far in advance, of any humane, progressive measure which may be adopted for the benefit of mankind, or to promote the welfare of the people. It is wonderful how difficult it is to ward off the schemes of avaricious men, and in a measure of this kind, which has in view the welfare of the entire people, safeguards cannot be too strongly applied to protect the general public. It is a fact to be regretted that many of our most commendable measures, whether municipal, State or National, which have given us avenues of commerce, works of art, and many improvements for the public good, whether patriotic or beneficent, have been embarrassed and contaminated by the touch of speculation, and the purpose of the designer has often been marred and debased by the influence of those who see nothing in any public or progressive measure other than the opportunity to gratify their selfish desires.

Moreover, it should be distinctly understood that there are hundreds of square miles of our public domain where it would be utter folly to spend more money than the amount necessary to definitely ascertain the fact of their worthlessness. Extravagance in expenditure should be avoided, and the government should systematically improve only its lands which will repay the expenditure, and divide the same in such manner that it can never be monopolized by a few, but shall be cultivated by an industrious, enterprising, and intelligent people, who will build for themselves and their posterity homes that will enrich and beautify the region, thus sustaining and promoting the general welfare.

TUNNEL PORTAL, SAN DIEGO FLUME.

It may be added, finally, that early action by the general government upon the irrigation question is earnestly to be desired. The reservations made under the surveys alluded to have not been utilized, and it is being urged that they could be used with great advantage to the country by others, syndicates and corporations, if those reservations were annulled. In view of the magnitude of the work, and its steadily growing necessity, it seems very desirable that private schemes looking to the acquirement of the actual control of immense tracts of valuable land, should be discouraged, or even rendered impossible, by early action by the government in pursuance of the plan under which these surveys and reservations were originally made.

There are many practical difficulties to be overcome, and the highest engineering skill will be required. Holland was won from the sea with an immense expenditure of time, toil and money. Our task is the opposite one, but attended with difficulties almost as great. The work to be done must be widely distributed, and must cover an immense area, and when done constant vigilance will be the price of permanence. The dams and catch-basins will fill with silt, the washings of the mountain sides. The ditches will wash and break; the first cost will be enormous; the care will be costly and continuous. But the question is one that must nevertheless be met. We have grown to more than seventy millions. The waste and idleness of any of our natural resources will soon come to be regarded as a culpable negligence, if not a crime. The richest soil and the most favorable climate lie within the arid regions. To utilize all the water that the sky yields is unquestionably within the genius of a nation that thus far has been daunted by no obstacles and deterred by no circumstances.

A long residence in the West in contact with its people, have turned the writer's attention to such features of the irrigation problem as are here set down, and as such they fall within the scope of the present volume. Aridness, a condition of nature, is, indeed, the only bar to the complete victory of that vanguard which the soldiers led. It must be conquered now by science, and under the law of the greatest good to the greatest number.

CHAPTER XLIII.

TRANSPORTATION.

THE UNBRIDGED SPACE BETWEEN THE EAST AND THE WEST — EARLY RAILROADS — EARLY RAIL-
ROADS OF THE UNITED STATES — CHANGE IN RATES OF SPEED — PROPHECY OF SIMON CAMERON
— VAST AND RAPID INCREASE IN MILEAGE — THE SLEEPING CAR — THE OLD PASSENGER
CAR — THROUGH TICKETS AND TRANSFERS — THE ORIGIN OF THE IDEA OF A
TRANS-CONTINENTAL LINE — THE UNION AND CENTRAL PACIFIC LINES —
THE NORTHERN PACIFIC — THE THIRTY-FIFTH PARALLEL ROUTE —
THE SOUTHERN PACIFIC — LAND GRANTS TO THE PACIFIC LINES
— SUM OF LAND GRANTS TO ALL LINES — GROSS INCOME
OF THE RAILROADS OF THE UNITED STATES.

IN the preceding chapter I have described the vast country which lies between the region which now by universal consent is the East, and that which in recent times has become the actual West; the West which lies beyond the supposed possibilities of even a few years ago, and which is now bounded not by an idea of comparative locality, but by the Pacific.

This arid region had not within it the inducements to rapid settlement and remarkable growth which had already made rich and populous all the splendid commonwealths which were once called Western States; which had dotted them with cities and had crossed them in all directions with railroad lines. Yet, beyond it lay the beautiful State, which I shall describe in the last chapter of this volume, and in its center lay gems like Colorado, with vast resources as yet only surmised along its length and hidden in its nooks and corners. More than fifteen hundred miles of mountain and plain lay almost uninhabited between the most eastern settlements of the western coast and the western borders of the Valley of the Mississippi.

With a brief glance at the history of the small beginnings of the vast railroad system of the United States, I shall in this chapter describe how this arid and then unproductive region was bridged, how the farther East was united with the utmost West, and the means by which all that lies between was made accessible to the energy of the American people, with the vast results, some of whose beginnings have been sketched in these pages.

The locomotive with its long attendant train of cars has now become such a familiar feature of our landscape that it attracts but little notice. Still it is less than the three score and ten years that are the allotted span of human life since, through the magic power of steam, was evolved so potent a factor in our civilization. A journey that once might have consumed weeks can now be performed in a day; and a journey, which in winter, could only be accomplished at the cost of exposure to cold and storms and the suffering entailed thereby, can now be taken with as much comfort as if we remained in our own homes. Now the products of each respective section are no longer enjoyed merely in that particular portion of the country, but are obtainable everywhere; and in our new West are populous cities, that seem to have sprung up almost in a night, which never could have been born, much less attained such a growth if they had not been connected with the older portions of the country by the shining bands of steel over which glides the swift train.

The idea of a graded or artificial roadway is not a new one by any means, for as far back as when Rome was mistress of the world, her people, who were always famous road builders, constructed ways of cut stone. About one hundred and fifty years ago what were known as tramroads were built in England to facilitate the conveyance of coal from the mines to the place of shipment, and here iron was used instead of steel for rails, as at the present day.

Railways would be of little value without some power of rapid transportation, so when James Watt invented the steam engine in 1773, earnest thinkers began to conceive the idea of a locomotive, and the tropical imagination of Erasmus Darwin led him to make in 1781 his famous prediction:

> " Soon shall thy arm, unconquered steam! afar
> Drag the slow barge or drive the rapid car."

The first locomotive that was successfully used was the " Puffing Billy" built in 1813, which can to-day be seen in the museum of the English Patent Office. In 1821 the Stockton and Darlington Railroad in England used a steam locomotive, built by the Stephensons, but it was only used to haul freight over a road twelve miles long. In 1825 a locomotive drew the first passenger train over this road, making the distance of twelve miles in two hours. In order that no one might be injured by their indulgence in this swift rate of speed the kind-hearted manager sent a horseman ahead to ride down the track in front of the engine and warn people to get out of the way.

The Carbondale Railroad in Pennsylvania was the first road in this country on which a locomotive was used. This engine was known as the "Stourbridge Lion," and was built in England by Horatio Allen, who went there for that express purpose.

The locomotives invented by the Stephensons could not go around sharp corners, and vast sums were therefore expended to make the line as straight as possible and to obtain easy grades. When the Americans first began to build railways in 1831, the English designs were followed for a time, but our engineers soon found that their money would not be ample if such a course was pursued, and so were either forced to stop building or find some way to overcome these obstacles. The result was that the swivelling truck was invented, and also the equalizing beams or levers, by which the weight of the engine is always borne by three out of four or more driving wheels. These two improvements, which are absolutely necessary for the building of roads in new countries, are also of the greatest value on the smoothest and straightest tracks. Another American invention is the switchback. By this plan the length of line required to ease the gradient is obtained by running a zigzag course instead of going straight up a mountain. This device was first used in Pennsylvania to lower coal cars down into the Neshoning. Then it was employed to carry the temporary tracks of the Cascade Division of the Northern Pacific Railroad over the Stampede Pass with grades of 297 feet per mile, while a tunnel was being driven through the mountain. This device has now reached such perfection that it is quite a common occurrence for a road to run above itself in spiral form.

PLAINS TRAVEL BEFORE THE RAILROADS CAME.

The Old and the New Way. (561)

The first cars were built in the form of stagecoaches with outside and inside seats; then they were built like two or three coaches joined together, and finally assumed the rectangular form now commonly in use. The first time-table in this country was published in Baltimore about 1832, and referred to the "brigade of cars" that would leave the depot at a certain time.

The rate of speed attainable by railroad trains is wonderfully increased. In 1835 when the road was chartered to connect Philadelphia with Harrisburg, there was a town meeting held to discuss the practicability of the scheme. The Hon. Simon Cameron, who advocated the measure, was so carried away by his enthusiasm that he predicted that there were persons present at the time who would live to see a passenger take his breakfast in Harrisburg and his supper in Philadelphia on the same day. After he had finished speaking, a friend took him aside and said:

"That's all right Simon, to tell the boys, but you and I are no such infernal fools as to believe it."

They both lived to make the distance in but little more than two hours. The fastest record was made in 1893 on the New York Central when a mile was made in thirty-two seconds or at the rate of one hundred and twelve and one-half miles an hour.

In 1830 there were but twenty-three miles of railroad in the whole United States. In 1840 the number had increased to 2,818. During the next twenty years the increase was more rapid, making a showing of 30,635 miles of road in 1860. During another score of years the number was increased more than threefold, giving a total of 93,450 miles in 1880. The building of the trans-continental roads advanced the rate of increase, and in 1893 the whole number of miles of railroad in the United States was 173,433. The greatest yearly increase was in 1882, showing an advance of 11,596 miles in a single year. The length of the world's railways in 1894 was 410,000 miles, or more than sixteen times the greatest circumference of the earth.

The first passenger car which showed a radical departure from the old model, was built by Mr. Pullman, after a number of years devoted to experimenting, and was designated by the letter "A," evidently no one having the idea that the twenty-six letters of the alphabet would not be sufficient to furnish names for the cars that would afterward be built. The Pullman and Wagner companies have introduced the hotel-car, and the dining-car has started on its travels. Several ingenious inventions have been patented for heating the cars with steam from the engines. At the present time, on the same train may be found sleeping-cars, dining-cars, smoking-saloon, bath-room, barber shop and library with books, desks and writing materials. There is free circulation of air throughout the train and the electric lights and steam heating apparatus all serve to make traveling comfortable.

All this is in strong contrast to the methods that prevailed during the first fifteen or twenty years after traveling by steam was introduced. At that time the car ceilings were low and without ventilation; there were stoves at either end of the car but they had little effect on the temperature of the middle seats, while the cars were filled with cinders in a way that seemed marvelous in contrast to the difficulty of introducing fresh air. Tallow candles were used for illumination purposes and were chiefly noticeable for their odor. The roughness of the track and the jarring of the train made conversation impossible. The flat rails used were cut at an angle and with lapped edges so they were occasionally caught by the wheels and driven up through the floor, impaling the unfortunate passenger who might happen to be sitting directly over the spot. Through tickets were unknown, and at the end of each short line the passenger had to purchase a new ticket, change cars, and personally attend to the transfer of his baggage.

Railways have so cheapened the cost of transportation that it is said that while a load of wheat loses all its value by being hauled one hundred miles over a common road, meat and flour enough to support a man a year can be hauled fifteen hundred miles over a railroad for one day's wages of a skilled mechanic. The number of people employed in constructing, equipping and operating our railways is approximately two millions.

The first man to advocate a trans-continental railway is believed to have been Doctor Barlow, of Massachusetts, who began in 1834 when the railroad business was still in its infancy to write articles for the newspapers advocating the undertaking by the general government of the construction of a railroad from New York city to the mouth of the Columbia. But Asa Whitney was the first man to put the idea into practical shape and urge it upon the attention of Congress. He had lived for a number of years in China, and being familiar with the conditions of the Chinese and the East Indian trade, and carefully calculating the distance from Liverpool to the point where that trade centered, he found that a route across the United States by rail, and by sea by the way of Puget Sound, would be considerably shorter than the all sea route around the Cape of Good Hope.

In December, 1845, he appeared in Washington with a scheme for a railroad from Lake Michigan to the Pacific Coast, to be built by him with the proceeds of a grant of land for thirty miles on each side of the track. At first his scheme received nothing but ridicule, but nothing daunted he returned again and again to the attack until in 1847 he obtained a favorable report from the Senate committee on public lands. He spent his entire fortune in his efforts in behalf of this project, but achieved no tangible results. Still his agitation of the subject did much good, for it brought the subject prominently before the people, and in 1853 Congress authorized the survey of various possible routes.

There was much rivalry between the different sections of the country to secure the route most favorable to their especial interests. Under the provisions of a bill passed in 1862 the Union Pacific, starting at Omaha, received a subsidy in government bonds of $16,000 per mile for the portion of its line traversing the great plains; $48,000 per mile for the one hundred and fifty miles across the Rocky Mountains, and $32,000 per mile for the remainder of the line. The aggregate of this subsidy for the 1,033 miles of road was $27,226,512. The Central Pacific received at the same time a similar subsidy in bonds, the total amount being $27,855,680, or a little more than that of the Union Pacific. Each company obtained at the same time a grant of public lands of 12,800 acres per mile of road. This route was naturally the first selected, as it closely followed the overland trail to California made by the gold hunters and was the route that was traversed by the overland mail and passenger coaches, and the thrifty agricultural settlements of the Mormons in the valley of the Great Salt Lake were also on the way.

Stimulated by the aid bestowed by the federal government the Union Pacific and the Central Pacific, which together formed the first transcontinental line, made rapid progress. The Central Pacific was the first to begin operations, the work of grading being commenced at Sacramento in January, 1863, though but few people had faith in its ability to complete such an undertaking. A notable feature in the construction of this road was the employment of Chinese labor. At first there were many discouragements to be encountered in the work of construction, but after a time public confidence was secured, the company became more prosperous, and its monthly earnings increased.

Work was not begun at the eastern end of the road by the Union Pacific Company for eighteen months after it was inaugurated at the western terminus, but fast time was made after it did commence, as it was able to carry the work on during the winter while the Central was delayed by the deep snows. It had, besides, the advantage that there was a level plain over which to lay its tracks for five hundred miles. The Northwest Railroad between Chicago and Missouri was completed by this time so the Union Pacific was enabled to transport all its supplies by rail while the Central Pacific had to wait until its materials were brought around by the way of Cape Horn. By the summer of 1867 the Central Pacific had reached the summit of the Sierras, fifteen tunnels were far advanced toward completion, and ten thousand men and thirteen hundred teams were working on the grade down the eastern slope. The Union Pacific had a still larger force at work and was now well on to the foot-hills of the Rocky Mountains.

As the work began to near completion, it was pushed forward by both companies to the utmost limit of their ability. Twenty-five thousand workmen and six thousand teams were ceaselessly at work on the road, and six hundred tons of material were daily forwarded from either end of the track. At one time there were thirty vessels *en route* around Cape Horn with rolling stock for the Central Pacific, besides what was transported across the isth-

AT THE 100TH MERIDIAN.

mus. The Union Pacific showed equal energy, and the fact is recorded that "more ground was ironed in a day than was traversed by the ox teams of the pioneers of '49."

The work progressed so rapidly that by the 10th of June, 1869, the last spike in the last rail was to be driven. Governor Stanford and Vice-President Durant, the two great leaders, shook hands over the last rail as it was laid in place. Arrangements were made with the superintendents of telegraph lines to connect with all the fire alarm bells in the various cities all over the country, that they might be struck as the last spike was driven. Two gold spikes were sent from California and two silver ones from Nevada and Arizona respectively. At the final ceremonies the two silver spikes were driven first, after which Vice-President Durant drove one of the golden spikes, and then Leland Stanford stood with uplifted arm waiting the moment that should give the signal that the work was accomplished; the blow fell, the last spike was driven, and the East was united in closer ties with the West than had ever before been possible.

The advocates of the Northern route did not venture to compete with the schemes described, but they did get a charter and land grant, although they did not ask for money or credit, and their bill was passed through Congress at the same time with the Union and Central bill and was signed by President Lincoln July 2, 1864. The land grant, instead of being twenty sections to a mile of track, was twenty in Minnesota and Oregon and forty for the remainder of the way, but there was no provision for a subsidy in government bonds. The passage of this act was largely due to the efforts of Mr. Perham, who had previously advocated a road from the Missouri River to the Bay of San Francisco. He gained the favor and friendship of Thaddeus Stevens, of Pennsylvania, who did much to aid the passage of the bill.

Thus the great enterprise was launched but made very little progress for the next few years. The franchise was transferred, a new board of directors was elected, and Congress was applied to for aid. The time for commencement should have been in July, 1866, but the new company obtained an extension of time, and not succeeding in getting financial aid from Congress determined to wait no longer, but obtained the passage of an act authorizing the company to issue its bonds and secure them by a mortgage upon its railroad and telegraph line. The services of the great banking house of Jay Cooke and Company were secured for the sale of the bonds, which under their management soon became a favorite form of investment for the small savings of mechanics, farmers and tradesmen, as well as for the larger accumulations of capitalists.

The construction of the Northern Pacific began in the summer of 1870, but the first ground was broken during the winter about a mile west of the present town of Northern Pacific Junction, where the St. Paul & Duluth Railroad joins the Northern Pacific. The night before this occurred a large number of people drove out from the neighboring cities and slept on the floor of a log house so as to be on hand early the next morning. A fire of logs had been built the day before to melt the snow and thaw out the frozen earth in order that it might be penetrated by a spade. Citizens from Minnesota and Wisconsin were appointed to fill the first wheelbarrow with earth; they did so, wheeled the load a few steps, dumped it, and the assemblage then dispersed with cheer upon cheer for the Northern Pacific.

During the summer of 1870 and the whole of the year of 1871, money poured into the treasury of the Northern Pacific Company, but it was severely crippled in the financial panic of 1873. The newspapers commenced to ridicule it, and called it a scheme to build a railroad from "nowhere through no man's land to no place." However, the company was reorganized, and was soon placed on a firm footing under Mr. Billings of Vermont.

Henry Villard, a German by birth, although he came to the United States when very young, became interested in some of the Western railroads, and during the six years following the panic of 1873, gradually obtained control of the transportation lines in the State of Oregon. He then conceived the scheme of uniting his own lines with the Northern Pacific, and in 1881, with this end in view, he organized the "blind pool" in New York and in a short time, with no other security than that of his own personal obligation, obtained $8,000,000. With this and other means he secured a controlling interest in the stock of the Northern Pacific, and was elected president of that company in September of the same year.

The construction of this road was a series of remarkable engineering feats. Two of the great tunnels, one at Bozeman's Pass in the Belt range and the other at Mullan's Pass in the main division of the Rocky Mountains, were respectively 3,600 and 3,850 feet in length. The highest summit passed was 5,565 feet above the sea level. The western terminals of the Northern Pacific are at Portland, Oregon and at Puget Sound.

Another route is known as the "Thirty-fifth Parallel Route," and is composed of the Atlantic & Pacific, the Atchison, Topeka & Santa Fé, and the St. Louis & San Francisco Railroads. This road connects with the Southern Pacific in the southern part of California.

The want of a railroad across the southern portion of our continent was early felt by the people of that section and efforts were early made in that direction. A great convention was held at Savannah, Georgia, in December, 1856, at which resolutions were adopted to the effect that a railroad ought to be built from the Mississippi River along or near the thirty-second parallel to the Pacific Ocean, and even before this the State of Texas had granted a liberal charter through its domain, as well as aid by grants of land and a loan of $6,000 for each mile of road built. Under this charter forty miles of road were completed before the breaking out of the Civil War, which for the time effectually stopped the undertaking.

Nothing further was done toward the building of this line until the act of March 3, 1871, providing for the incorporation of a company to be known as the Texas Pacific Railroad Company, which was empowered to lay out and construct a continuous line of railroad over the thirty-second parallel of latitude from Marshall, Texas, to El Paso, thence through New Mexico and Arizona to the State of California, and to San Diego, California. Various changes and consolidations have since been made in this line, and at present the "Thirty-second Parallel Route" is composed of the Texas & Pacific, extending from New Orleans to El Paso, a distance of 1,162 miles, and of the Southern Pacific, which extends from El Paso to San Francisco, California, under the general direction of Mr. C. P. Huntington. The Southern Pacific, Atchison, Topeka & Santa Fé, Union Pacific & Central Pacific, Northern Pacific, Great Northern, with the Denver & Rio Grande and Oregon Short Line, constitute practically six great trunk lines across the great Western half of our country. These with their branch lines form a great network of communication devoted to the commercial development of that vast empire.

To the companies building these great Pacific Railroads, Congress has granted 19,015,977.69 acres, a greater number than are contained in the State of West Virginia. The whole number of acres granted to railroads in the United States is 57,025,532.50, or more land than is contained in the entire State of Minnesota. The sections where these grants were made naturally include only the Western and Southern States. The value of the land reserved was greatly enhanced by the building of the railroads.

Professor Henry C. Adams, in an article published in the "Review of Reviews" for August, 1894, says that the annual gross income to railways in the United States exceeds $1,200,000,000, being a sum greater by $285,000,000 than the aggregate income to the Federal, State, municipal and local governments. The business which gives rise to this income is represented by eighteen hundred corporations.

SIMON SNYDER, Major 5th Infantry.
Capture of Chief Joseph and Nez Percés, 1877.

G. W. BAIRD Adjutant 5th Infantry.
Campaign of Texas and Indian Territory, 1874.

LIEUT. ALLEN, Alaska.
Exploration of Alaska, 1883-84.

CAPTAIN LAWTON.
Geronimo's Campaign in Arizona, 1886.

CHAPTER XLIV.

CALIFORNIA.

SIZE OF CALIFORNIA — THE NAME "CALIFORNIA" — DISCOVERY — THE SPANIARDS — DRAKE — THE
COMING OF THE FRANCISCANS — THE MISSIONS — WEALTH OF THE SAME — THE INDIANS AND
THEIR CONDITION — CUSTOMS OF THE OLD TIME — FIRST IMMIGRANTS FROM THE STATES —
COMMODORE SLOAT AND GENERAL FREMONT — FIRST HOISTING OF THE AMERICAN FLAG
— DISCOVERY OF GOLD — SUTTER AND MARSHALL — RAPID INCREASE OF POPULATION
— THE CHARACTER OF THE PIONEERS — ADMITTANCE AS A STATE — GEOGRAPHY
OF CALIFORNIA — THE TWO NATURAL DIVISIONS OF THE STATE — CALIFORNIA
WONDERS — YOSEMITE, LITTLE YOSEMITE, KING'S RIVER CAÑON, ETC. —
THE SEASONS — VAST PRODUCT OF THE STATE IN FRUITS AND
CEREALS — MANUFACTURES — EDUCATIONAL INSTITUTIONS —
LOS ANGELES — SANTA BARBARA — SAN FRANCISCO —
THE VIGILANCE COMMITTEE — THE HARBOR.

ALIFORNIA, with her hundred million of acres, is larger in area than Massachusetts, Rhode Island, Connecticut, New Hampshire, Vermont, New Jersey, Delaware and Maryland, and the great States of New York and Pennsylvania, all combined. If it had been as thickly settled as these Atlantic States were in 1890, the census of that year would have given it twenty millions of inhabitants instead of one million two hundred thousand, while if it ever becomes as densely populated as the small but important manufacturing State of Massachusetts it will contain approximately forty-three millions of people, or more than thirty-five times its present population. On the other hand, if the busy little State of Rhode Island contained no more people to the square mile than California does, it would contribute less than ten thousand to the population of the Union. In size California is second only to Texas, and from north to south extends through ten degrees, or as far as from the latitude of New York to that of Florida. It is equal in territory to both Japan and Italy, each with their forty millions of people.

The name California is first mentioned in a romance published not many years after the discovery of America, that name having been given to an imaginary island situated near the equator. It was afterward applied in fact to the peninsula of Lower California, and eventually to an indefinite portion of country extending as far north as to the forty-second parallel. In the first part of the sixteenth century the coast was visited by various

Spanish navigators, and in 1579 Francis Drake sailed along the western shore of the continent to the latitude of forty-eight degrees, naming the country that is now California, "New Albion."

In 1679 the Franciscan monks founded a mission at San Diego, and secular immigration soon followed. Their first effort having thus proved successful, the priests continued to plant their missions along the coast up to the year 1823, by which time the revenues of the church from this source had become enormous. The Indians connected with these missions were taught agriculture and various trades, and in some cases even received a little education, but nevertheless they were held in a bondage that was nothing more nor less than a species of slavery. In 1777 the Spanish government began to establish pueblos or towns, a measure which was greatly opposed by the priests as being detrimental to their interests. The Mexican revolution of 1822 hastened the ecclesiastical downfall that was already begun. Four years later the Indians were released from their allegiance to the priests, and in 1834 the mission lands were divided, thus effectually terminating the church rule which had so long dominated in California.

The day of the old Spanish *regime* was a time of unbounded hospitality. It was even considered an offence for a stranger to pass by a ranch without paying a visit to its inmates. The hosts not only expected as a matter of course to supply fresh horses, but if their guest's financial status appeared to be somewhat low, a little pile of uncounted silver was left in his sleeping apartment, the idea being conveyed to him as delicately as possible that he was to take all he needed. The money was invariably covered with a cloth, and it was a point of honor never to count it, either before or after the guest went away. This money was known as "guest silver," and the quaint custom continued until a time came when it was so abused that the generous Californians were obliged to abandon it.

The first emigrants from the United States entered California in 1826; and though followed at intervals by others, there was still a comparatively small number of Americans in the country, when twenty years later, the United States, anticipating war with Mexico, and believing also that England had designs upon that part of the Pacific Coast, took steps to secure an alliance with California by promising assistance to the people in attaining independence in case of war, at the same time instructing the United States consul at Monterey, the then capital of California, to exert every possible influence in behalf of his country. Commodore Sloat, then in the Pacific, was ordered to occupy the ports of Monterey and San Francisco in case of an outbreak of hostilities. General Fremont who was at that time in the country in command of a small force, was ordered to coöperate with Sloat. But misled by reports of threatened violence to American settlers, he prematurely encouraged his countrymen to rise against the Mexican Government, and seizing Sonoma, June 14, 1846, he proclaimed a republic. On July 7, Commodore Sloat seized Monterey, and war with Mexico having been declared, the United States flag was raised at San Francisco, and the military department of California was then established under the command of General Philip Kearney.

With the discovery of gold in California in 1848, a new and wonderful era in its history begins. It seems somewhat singular that as far back as the early part of the sixteenth century the conquerors of Mexico were firmly convinced that the western coast of what is now the United States must be rich in gold, and sent out many expeditions to prove their theory, and that nevertheless the precious yellow metal remained hidden from the eye of man for three hundred years longer. For many years previous to the day that James Marshall picked the shining particles from the millrace at Coloma, the idea of gold being found anywhere in that country had been so entirely abandoned, that we read in the "Penny Encyclopedia" of 1836, "In minerals, upper California is not rich." This idea, though erroneous, was a very fortunate one for the United States, for had the hidden wealth of California been announced to the world a few years sooner we could never have secured from Mexico all the territory of which California is only a small part for the paltry sum of fifteen million dollars, and possibly we might not have been able to obtain it at all.

It seems strange that an event so important to California, to the United States, and to the whole world. should have been the result of a mere accident. In 1847 among the most prominent Americans in California was General John A. Sutter, who had acquired many acres of land there, and had taken up his abode at "Sutter's Fort" at the junction of the American and Sacramento Rivers. In the summer of this year, he began to perceive the necessity for a sawmill, and as there was no timber in the valley he was obliged to have this mill erected in the mountains. To build it he engaged James W. Marshall, who was to supply the skill and choose the site, while Sutter furnished the money, workmen and teams. Mr. Marshall selected a site at the spot afterward known as Coloma. and for four months he and his workmen remained in the midst of a primeval wilderness engaged in the construction of the mill. At the end of that time the structure was nearly completed, the dam had been made, the race had been dug, the gates had been put in place, the water had been turned into the race to carry away the loose dirt and gravel, and then turned off again, and on the morning of the 24th of January, 1848, Marshall, while taking his usual walk along the race after shutting off the water, was attracted by a small shining object about half the size of a pea. He hastily picked it up, and the results of his find are known to all the world.

Marshall himself received very little benefit from his discovery. Had notoriety been enough to satisfy him he might have been well content, for his name became widely celebrated, but, as he once naively remarked, that was "neither victuals nor clothes to any one." Owing to this neglect he gradually became embittered against all mankind, and after spending the last years of his life in poverty and privation, he died in 1885, at the age of seventy-three, and was buried at a spot within sight of the place where he made his famous discovery. His figure in colossal bronze has since been erected over his grave, and stands like a sentinel guarding the spot where the great event of his life occurred. It was an event which affected many lives for weal or woe, which turned the tide of emigration from all parts of the world to California, which caused the development of the neighboring States, and which finally made necessary the building of the great trans-continental railroads.

The impetus thus given to emigration, which was felt all over the globe, increased the scanty population of California to such an extent that by the end of 1849 there were more than a hundred thousand people within her borders. Naturally this was not a healthy growth, for there was much reckless speculation and extravagant living, which had its demoralizing influence upon the inhabitants. Life in California at that time was a kind of pandemonium. Thousands of men were constantly leaving and arriving; money was plentiful and freely spent; miners who had made their fortunes in a few days squandered them in a single night at the gaming table. There were but few women in the entire territory, and all good influences were chiefly conspicuous by their absence. The whole population of the towns and mining camps consisted of unkempt men clad in flannel shirts, patched clothing and heavy boots, and the hearts of all were animated by one great impulse — the thirst for gold. There was, however, a strong touch of sentiment in their rough lives; as for instance, when an intense excitement was one day created in a small town by a rumor that an invoice of women's bonnets had arrived — there was a rush from every direction to get a view of them. The sight of anything so intensely feminine as a bonnet touched the hearts of those rough men, and awakened in their breasts thoughts and feelings that had long lain dormant.

Although San Francisco was made a port of entry, no Territorial government was ever formed in California. As early as 1849 the people had succeeded in framing a constitution much resembling that of New York; and in September of the following year, California was admitted into the Union, being the thirty-first member of the great sisterhood of States. Two years of amazing prosperity followed, then speculation in all kinds of property ran riot, finally bringing about the financial crisis of 1855.

When the great Civil War came it was feared that California was contemplating secession, and she was therefore exempted from furnishing troops. But the Union party was stronger than had been imagined, and came to the front most nobly, not only contributing a million and a half to the national cause, but voluntarily sending a considerable number of volunteers into the field.

Since that time the State has been constantly developing new resources, and has rapidly gained in importance. It was the opinion of so impartial an observer as Charles Kingsley, when he visited that part of the country as far back as 1874, that California was destined to eventually become the finest country on the globe, and were he living now he would have no occasion to change his views. Between the northern and southern portions of the State lies a great transverse range of mountains, the lowest passes of which are from four to five thousand feet above the level of the sea. This range, with the division it makes in the lines of trade and travel, seems gradually forcing the two sections apart. The geographic, topographic, and climatic differences between the two parts are so radical that the indications are that sooner or later they must inevitably lead to a political division.

In California there are two great mountain ranges, the Coast Range and the Sierra Nevada; and in the latter it is estimated that there are at least one hundred peaks over ten thousand feet in height.

> " Afar the bright Sierras lie
> A swaying line of snowy white,
> A fringe of heaven hung in sight
> Against the blue base of the sky."

Among the most noted of these peaks are Shasta, Tyndall and Whitney, but there are others that almost equal them in height and grandeur. The largest and only navigable rivers, with the exception of the Colorado, are the Sacramento and San Joaquin.

An enumeration of the greatest wonders of the world would not be complete without mention of the marvelous Yosemite Valley. It lies in the Sierra foot-hills in the trough-like erosion, a mile in breadth and six

MOUNT SHASTA.

in length, with a flat bottom of irregular width. The visitor stands before the wonder of this place almost prostrated by the glory and majesty of his surroundings. Entering at the lower end, a general view of the valley is obtained. On the left rises the celebrated El Capitan, thirty-three hundred feet in height, while on the right falls the Bridal Veil, a cascade of gossamer a thousand feet from top to bottom. The floor of the valley is carpeted with the most beautiful flowers and blossoming shrubs, and is fringed with groves of oak, cedar and fir, while the Merced River winds and dashes its way along through this wonderful beauty, helping to form a scene of incomparable loveliness,

> " While we walk subdued in wonder
> In the ferns and grasses under
> And beside the swift Merced."

Farther up the valley is the obelisk-like Sentinel Rock, towering three thousand feet into the air, and just across from this, fed exclusively by melted snows, are the great Yosemite Falls, the most remarkable in the world when both height and volume are considered, they being fifteen times as high as Niagara and of indescribable grandeur. From the verge of a perpendicular wall the water springs and, swayed hither and thither by the wind as it falls, strikes an inclined shelf of rock from which it tumbles in a series of beautiful cascades six hundred and twenty-five feet more before it takes its final plunge of four hundred feet to complete its half mile leap, while every moment its deep continuous roar is heard reverberating through the cañon. Two miles above the Yosemite Falls the valley separates into three cañons. Choosing the one through which flows the Merced, you pass along beside two miles of cascades in which distance this dashing, foaming river descends over two thousand feet. Then follow more magnificent waterfalls, surrounded by scenery sublime and impressive beyond description.

Marvelous as is the Yosemite, it is only one of the numerous wonders of California. The Little Yosemite Valley is almost a counterpart of the greater on a smaller scale. The widely celebrated mammoth trees of California have not their like upon the planet. From a careful, minute and scientific examination by General Sherman with several eminent scientists, it was found that these giants of the forest were standing when Moses was an infant in the bulrushes, and for more than four thousand years they have defied the elements. Both the Columbia and Fraser Rivers have their fifty miles and more of stupendous gorges several thousand feet in depth, but grander yet is the King's River Cañon, with its hard granite walls from three thousand to seven thousand feet in depth.

Although there are two seasons in California, the wet and the dry, the former is so called rather because it is the only time when there is any rain than because it falls continually, for there are a great many delightfully pleasant days

GLACIER POINT. YOSEMITE VALLEY.

during that period of the year. It is scarcely possible to speak of the climate of the whole State at once, since there is a decided difference between the northern and southern portions. To the north of Point Conception the winds are such as to give the upper part of the State

M.—34

the exceedingly dry atmosphere for which it is noted.   The climate of the southern portion is most delightful, and is widely celebrated for its health-giving qualities.   Here the first rain falls anywhere from the middle of October to the middle of November, then come three or four weeks of pleasant weather to be followed by another rain, this time very likely accompanied by a snowfall in the mountains.   With the coming of the rains the land begins to renew its verdure, and shortly the plains are covered with the richest of green carpets.   Both the winds that regulate the seasons and those which control the daily temperature are exceedingly regular.

The commerce of California centers mainly at San Francisco, whose harbor ranks that city among the few great seaports of the world.   Below Puget Sound the best harbor on the Pacific Coast, with the single notable exception of San Francisco, is San Diego; but this seaport unfortunately labors under the disadvantage of lying on the southern edge of the great agricultural belt of southern California, thus giving to San Pedro, though

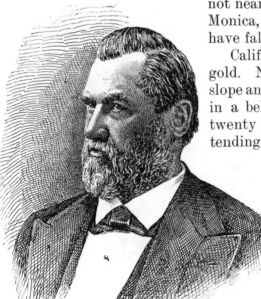

LELAND STANFORD.

not nearly so good a natural harbor, and Santa Monica, much trade which would otherwise have fallen to its share.

California still leads in the production of gold.   Nearly all the mines are on the western slope and in the foot-hills of the Sierra Nevadas in a belt of country about two hundred and twenty miles long by forty miles wide, and extending into Oregon.   Besides gold, a rich quality of silver and various kinds of iron are found; also tin, copper, zinc and lead.   The manufactures of the State include a great variety, and are rapidly growing in importance.

The most widely known of the educational institutions of California is the Leland Stanford University, situated at Palo Alto and formally opened in 1891.   It was founded by Mr. and Mrs. Leland Stanford in memory of their son, who died in 1884. It was a princely gift and probably the largest and most valuable donation ever given by one man for the benefit of his fellow men.   The Lick Observatory, erected through the

LELAND STANFORD UNIVERSITY, PALO ALTO, CALIFORNIA.
Roble Hall.   The Museum.   Encina Hall.

generosity of James Lick, is built on the summit of Mount Hamilton, near San José. It is over four thousand feet above the level of the sea, and it was necessary to remove seven thousand tons of rock from the summit of the mountain in order to get a level platform. This most powerful telescope is a refractor of thirty-six inches clear aperture.

The State University is one of the finest institutions of the kind in the country. The instruction in all the colleges is open to all persons without distinction of sex. Besides the university proper at Berkeley there is the Lick Astronomical Department at Mount Hamilton, and in San Francisco departments of Art, Law, Medicine, Dentistry and Pharmacy. The university was instituted by a law approved in 1868 and instruction was begun in 1869; and in 1873 it was formally transferred to its present site.*

In 1781, when the Franciscans established a mission in Los Angeles, it was already a thriving pueblo. On account of the beauty of its location, its charming climate and fertile soil, the Spaniards gave it a name which being translated means, "the town of the queen of the angels," which was afterward shortened to Los Angeles. It was not until Monroe was serving his second term that the first American entered the precincts of the beautiful town, and he was brought there by the Mexicans as a prisoner. However, he liked the place so much that he had no wish to leave, but married into a Spanish family and settled down as a citizen.

Two years later, in 1824, a Scotchman came to the town and opened a store on the American plan, and in 1831 the Santa Fé trail was opened, and by creating a new outlet to the East greatly developed trade. Four years later the town achieved the importance of being made the capital of California, and in 1846, when war had been declared with Mexico, Fremont marched into Los Angeles and raised the stars and stripes. Don Pio Pico, who was then the Mexican governor of California, escaped from the town at the time, but afterward returned and, though he would never acknowledge that the Americans had any right to California, became a registered voter, and at the time I had my headquarters there, though a very old man, he was still casting his ballot with all the regularity of a native of the United States. When Fremont was appointed Governor of California he

---

*In this connection I may add that by an act of Congress approved July 17, 1854, two townships of land were granted to the Territory of Washington for the purpose of establishing a university, but owing to the vacillation of the Territorial legislature, nothing was actually done towards erecting a building until 1861. In March of that year the stone of the university building was placed in position at Seattle. In September, 1895, the university was transferred to new quarters in a remarkably beautiful situation some distance from the center of the city. The University of Washington is maintained by the commonwealth and has also been richly endowed with lands by the government. With the exception of the department of music and law, tuition is free to all residents of the State of Washington, and is open to both sexes. The University of Oregon, established in 1872, is situated in Eugene and was endowed at the start with $50,000.

established his headquarters in the finest house in Los Angeles, for, as an old settler once remarked, "Fremont always would have the best of everything." His widow, the gifted Jessie Benton, resides there now.

The soil in this section is generally very rich, even the so-called "deserts" needing only irrigation to make them exceedingly prolific. The annual rainfall is quite sufficient to mature many of the crops, though there were 5,500,000 acres under irrigation in 1894. The agricultural fame of southern California is now world wide, yet twenty-five years ago its inhabitants imported all their vegetables, their flour, and everything else in the way of food except their meat, which they obtained from their flocks and herds. Now great train loads of these very products are shipped from there every day.

Upon many lands, after the winter-sown crop has been harvested without the aid of irrigation, another crop is produced with the aid of that important auxiliary, thus making the same land do double duty. The water used for this purpose is obtained from the rivers, small streams, and from artesian wells. The first oranges produced in that region were from trees planted at Los Angeles, and now the annual shipment aggregates many thousands of tons. Fruit culture of all kinds is exceedingly profitable, and the

IRRIGATING DITCHES.   ORANGE GROVE.

crops are simply enormous. Wheat, rye, barley and hops are largely produced.

Los Angeles, the chief city of southern California, and the headquarters of the Department of Arizona, is situated midway between the mountains and the ocean, the Sierra Madres towering up fourteen miles to the east, while the broad and peaceful Pacific lies the same distance to the west. It is the center of one of the finest agricultural regions in the world.

"Where the grape is most luscious, where laden,
    Long branches bend double with gold;
Los Angeles leans like a maiden,
    Red, blushing, half shy and half bold."

The first Protestant preacher arrived in 1850, with his entire earthly possessions contained in the ox-cart of which he himself was the charioteer. The first American child who could claim Los Angeles as his native town was born in April, 1851, and the birth of the town's first newspaper was chronicled a month later. By 1854 the population had increased to four thousand, though only five hundred were Americans.

Since the completion of the Southern Pacific Railroad, Los Angeles has made great progress, and now presents an odd picture of the combination of a sleepy old Spanish pueblo with a thriving, progressive American city. The Los Angeles River, which according to an old Spanish grant belongs to the city from its mountain source downward, runs through the town, and a large irrigating system is included in the municipality.

Los Angeles is an extremely cosmopolitan city, almost every nation under the sun being represented among her inhabitants. The city can boast many fine educational institutions, and numerous churches and philanthropic societies. Among the most unique of its charities is the Flower Festival Society, which each year gives a grand floral carnival the proceeds of which are used for the benefit of young working women.

Although not usually regarded as a manufacturing city, nevertheless Los Angeles contains a large number of extensive factories. Prominent among these are a number of iron foundries, several flouring and feed mills, a dozen planing mills, etc. The city is lighted by electricity, and there are cable and electric street cars which take one to every part of it. The chief exports to the East are dried and green fruits, wool, wine and vegetables. During the season the exportation of oranges is enormous. The climate of Los Angeles is delightful in both summer and winter, there seldom being a year in which there are half a dozen cloudy days from the middle of May to the middle of November.

Santa Barbara is another important and beautiful city of southern California, and is widely known as a health resort. Monterey is undoubtedly the most beautiful watering place on this continent, if not in the world. Nature and art have been lavish in its adornment. The great live oaks, the forests of pine, cedar and spruce, the remarkable groves of the cedars of Lebanon, the abundance of wild flowers, joined to what the skilled florists and architects have added, make it a most interesting and attractive place.

In northern California among the chief cities are Oakland, Sacramento, the capital, and most important of all, not only to that part of California but to the whole Pacific Coast, San Francisco.

When in the latter part of the seventeenth century the Franciscan fathers were making their little exploring expeditions throughout the southern portion of California, they christened the lakes, rivers and mountains they discovered in honor of their missions and various saints and

ORANGE GROVE NEAR LOS ANGELES.

angels. One of these priests was extremely solicitous that the patron of his order should not be neglected in this distribution, and to this end besought both God and the Virgin, but without avail. He then urged the matter upon the Visitador-General Galvez who bluntly replied: "If our seraphic father, St. Francis of Assisi, would have his name to signalize some station on these shores let him show us a good haven." This being the condition of affairs, when the little band of explorers after a weary journey along the rough sea coast suddenly found themselves on a high point overlooking a broad, peaceful, nearly land-locked sheet of water, dotted with green isles inhabited only by the seals and sea lions, with one voice they exclaimed : "Surely this must be the bay of San Francisco."

Here, during the very year which witnessed the signing of the Declaration of Independence on the eastern border of our continent, was planted the presidio of San Francisco, and near the Golden Gate a fort was erected. The present city began its growth at a little indentation of the coast three miles from this point, and the first name it received was the significant one of Yerba Buena — good herbs or grass. At the time when Mexico was throwing off the yoke of Spain, the soldiers of the presidio were faithful to their country even though, owing to the sad state of the finances of the home government, they received no wages.

In 1839 Yerba Buena was laid out as a city; a public plaza being first measured off, the remainder of the level ground was utilized as building lots and was divided by streets. In July, 1846, when the American flag was first given to the breeze on the plaza, there were probably two hundred inhabitants in the picturesque little village; but before the month ended the population was increased by a colony of Mormons from New York, who were a most diligent, progressive set of men, and among other benefits bestowed upon the little town its first newspaper. In January, 1847, Yerba Buena was transformed into San Francisco by order of the American alcalde, and the discovery of gold the next year wrought a complete transformation in San Francisco as well as in almost every other part of California. Thither flocked men of every race and clime on their way to the gold fields, and thither they returned on their way to their homes, some jubilant with their quota of the precious golden ore, and others bearing only disappointed hopes. But enough remained in the city to give it a population of twenty-five thousand by the end of 1849. Prices in the little town went up with a bound; one two-story house fronting on the plaza rented for $120,000 a year, while another of extremely small dimensions was hired for the exorbitant sum of $3000 a month. Carpenters who were getting twelve dollars a day struck for sixteen; forty dollars was the price of either a barrel of flour or a pair of boots; a small loaf of bread cost fifty cents and a hard boiled egg a dollar. The only currency was gold dust, which was rated at $16 per ounce, and was weighed out in scales which were to be found at every place of business.

At this period in San Francisco the arrival of the mail steamer, which occurred two or three times a month, was among the most important and exciting of events. The voluntary exiles who made up the principal part of the population could only hear from home and friends and all they held most dear through the medium of the mail. Thus the coming of each steamer was eagerly looked for, and became an important event in their toilsome, turbulent lives. The line before the postoffice window would begin to form from twelve to twenty hours before the mail was ready for delivery, and gradually lengthen until it numbered five hundred men with anxious hearts waiting for the letter, which, if it came, might either fill their hearts with joy or burden them with an additional load of sorrow. Sometimes a ragamuffin, who had early secured a place in the line, as he neared the window would be able to sell it for five, ten, or even twenty dollars. It is said that one young man whose friends proved neglectful correspondents, hit upon a plan of writing to three or four of the gossips of his town, asking the price of land and stock and what advantageous investments could be secured. This expedient was so successful that thereafter never a mail arrived without an epistle for him.

The streets of San Francisco, ungraded, unpaved, cut up by heavy teams, and used as a dumping ground for all the filth and rubbish of the town, made transit at all times difficult and disagreeable; but when they were transformed by the winter rains into a perfect swamp, they became almost impassable. Loads of brushwood and branches of trees were thrown into these quagmires, and boards and boxes were utilized as crossings; but in spite of all precautions, lives were sometimes lost by suffocation in the mud. Saloons were plentiful, and gambling was the occupation of many and the recreation of all, with almost no exceptions. Those were the days when "might made right," depredations and assaults were common offenses, and there was absolutely no one to enforce law and order. Murders were committed by the hundred, but never a murderer was hanged. A gang of young men calling themselves "regulators," but more commonly known as "hounds," paraded the town by day, and by night raided the stores and saloons and taverns. At last patience was exhausted and in July, 1849, a meeting of "all good citizens" was called to devise some means to put a stop to this state of affairs, and this was the forerunner of the celebrated Vigilance Committee of 1851.

Still affairs did not improve. Fire after fire desolated the unfortunate city, the last one, which occurred in May, 1851, so far exceeding the rest that it was known as the "great fire." The whole business portion of the town was a mass of flames, the reflection of which is said to have been visible a hundred miles away, and nearly everything was destroyed. It was the firm belief of many that the fire was due to incendiarism. Another conflagration occurred in June, and those who were suspected of being the cause of it were arrested, but it was impossible to secure their conviction, and robberies and murders became more and more common, until at last it was the general feeling that forbearance had ceased to be a virtue. Then the famous Vigilance Committee was formally organized "to watch, pursue and bring to justice the outlaws infesting the city, through the system of the courts if possible, through more summary processes if necessary." The committee did such extremely effective work that at the end of thirty days it was able to quietly disband. It was afterward reorganized, and was equally efficacious in 1856, when the city was threatened with similar dangers. And once more in 1877 this unique force came to the front in the interests of order and justice, but this time under very different auspices.

Although San Francisco was almost entirely destroyed by the terrible fire of 1851, the enterprising citizens were by no means discouraged, but straightway went to work to rebuild their city, and by 1852 there were few characteristics of a Spanish town remaining in San Francisco. It had now assumed a more regular aspect, and substantial houses took the place of the huts of former years, though most of the structures were of wood,

MARKET STREET, SAN FRANCISCO.

as brick and stone were so hard to obtain, and there was a general dread of earthquakes.

The modern city is a strangely foreign-looking place, especially when viewed from the harbor. The business portion of the town lies at the foot of several hills on which most of the residences are built. These dwellings are even now more commonly built of wood, but, fear of earthquakes having somewhat abated, brick and stone structures have commenced to go up. The cable cars were first invented and used at San Francisco, and when the hills on which the city is built are considered, a better mode of transportation could not be devised. Market Street, a stately thoroughfare of which the residents are very proud, runs southwest from the bay and divides the older from the newer portion of the city. It finds an almost level way through the city, despite the hills, and on either side rise great buildings like the Palace Hotel, one of the most perfect buildings of its kind in the world, the Chronicle Building and many others. Here the crowds gather in the greatest numbers, and remind one somewhat of Broadway, New York. Among the new public buildings may be mentioned the City Hall, a fine structure that cost $4,000,000. There is also a branch of the United States Mint here. As natural in so progressive a city, San Francisco has many fine educational institutions, as well as numerous churches; the church buildings recently erected have shown a marked improvement in architectural design, and the same may be said of many of the new residences. Few cities are more delightfully or more healthfully located than San Francisco, facing as it does the beautiful harbor and the Golden Gate, and being built upon high dry ground. The scenery around it is most picturesque and inspiring. From homes overlooking the harbor, you can drive out through the Golden Gate Park, which is one of the most beautiful parks in the United States, and combines the picturesque splendors of tropical climes with the fragrance of the live-oak, fern, pine and cedar of the temperate zone; and thence through fields adorned with trees and flowers, shaded avenues and glens, lakes and fountains, you come directly to the bold surf where the waters of the Pacific are dashed against the rocks of the great cliffs, and where the seals are seen sporting in the foaming billows or basking in the sun upon the rocks, the whole giving one a picture vividly contrasting the wildness and grandeur of natural scenery with the art and culture of an enlightened community.

It was Andrew Jackson who said, "upon the success of our manufactures as a hand-maid of agriculture and commerce depends in great measure the prosperity of our country," and San Francisco has not been unmindful of this wise axiom, for its manufactures are yearly increasing in importance and variety. It has great foundries and immense flouring mills, and boasts the oldest cordage factory on the Pacific Coast. This factory was established in 1859, and now covers sixteen acres. The Union Iron Works have built several ships of war, including the "Charleston," "San Francisco" and "Monterey."

The great Midwinter Fair, opened on the first of January, 1894, was held in the Golden Gate Park — a most beautiful spot. There were three hundred buildings, said to have cost $1,500,000, in the grounds.

The fair was a decided success financially, and was of great benefit to the city in tiding it over the period of extreme dullness in trade and stimulating many branches of trade. Its benefits were not merely local, for it had a good influence that was felt along the entire coast.

It is as a commercial center that San Francisco is best known. Through the Golden Gate, or Chrysopylæ, come vessels from all parts of the world to anchor on the broad bosom of the harbor of San Francisco. This beautiful bay is seventy miles long, from ten to fifteen in width, and narrows to a channel only one mile wide at the entrance. In this harbor may be seen vessels from China, Hawaii, Japan, Australia and Panama. Huge Chinese junks, the queer feluccas of the Maltese and Greeks, and the great war ships of the United States, Great Britain, France, Russia and other powers, all help to lend variety to the beautiful scene.

At the upper end of the bay is located, on Mare Island, the United States Navy Yard, a most important and valuable national establishment, landlocked and well protected. Here we see floating on its waters the "Comanche," the "Swatara," the "Omaha" and the "Pensacola; also the wooden battle ship "Hartford," once the flag ship of the greatest Admiral of his time, Farragut, the sight of which almost prompts one to raise his hat in reverence for the heroic deeds of this ship of war and the skill of its indomitable commander who defied not only the destructive engines beneath the surface, but also the batteries on land and sea which sank part of his fleet and crashed through the rigging where he was lashed. There also is the "Miantonomah," one of the famous ships of the Monitor class.

At Hunter's Point is a great dry dock four hundred and fifty feet in length hewn out of the solid rock. San Francisco will naturally become the center of a great ship-building industry, not only because of its position, but because there is scarcely another place on the continent whose climate is so suitable for the purpose at all seasons of the year, and because in some respects the ship timber of that region is the finest in the world.

San Francisco is still ahead of any competitors on the Pacific Coast, though there are large towns of importance fast growing up which force her to look well to her laurels. It was the opinion of William H. Seward, that in the future the Pacific Ocean with its eighty millions of square miles, "will be the scene of man's greatest achievements." And if that be so, there are scarcely any limits to the great possibilities of San Francisco's future, situated as it is on a harbor unequaled in that quarter of the world.

"Serene, indifferent of Fate
Thou sittest at the Western gate;
Upon thy heights so lately won
Still slant the banners of the sun;
Thou seest the white seas strike their tents
O, Warder of two continents !"

The people of the Pacific Coast, are as a rule most enterprising, intelligent and ambitious, and they are exceedingly generous and hospitable. It is a mistake to suppose that the West is crude or uncultivated. The strongest, most resolute, enterprising and ambitious of our men have gone West.

They have either carried with them or have returned for those cheerful companions who are prompted by love and devotion to accompany the pioneers to their Western homes. While their material interests have been in the Western country, their fond memories and attachments have remained in the East, and in the frequent journeys they have made back to

A SCENE IN SOUTHERN CALIFORNIA.

the old homesteads and the Eastern centers of business and civilization, they have brought their children with them. In this way the youth have become familiar with our entire country, as well as with the section to which all are naturally most attached as being the place of their birth. As these children have grown up, and after passing through the primary and high schools, they have been sent East to complete their education at the great colleges of Harvard, Yale, Princeton, Bowdoin, Wellesley, Smith, Vassar, and many other important educational institutions. Then, returning to their Western homes, they have in many cases made a tour of travel and observation, often passing out at the Golden Gate, or the Straits of Juan de Fuca, and making the round of the world. So we find the native population that has grown up on the Pacific slope as refined, intelligent, and quite as well informed, especially concerning their own country, as those of the Eastern States.

The long and interesting journey across the continent has been completed; a journey fraught with many vicissitudes and many interesting incidents. It has witnessed many historic scenes. It has had many dark hours of great anxiety and uncertainty, mingled with forebodings of evil for the future condition of our country. It has witnessed the terrible ordeals and sacrifices of war, as well as the fascination and exhilaration of victory and the restoration of perpetual peace. It has known the disappearance of the cause of disaffection and hostility, and the reunion of the elements in a stronger, more perfect, purer, grander, nobler bond of union. It has seen the building up of waste places, and the restoration of fraternal feeling; the return of the most generous magnanimity and the most bountiful charity. It has beheld the transformation of the wild wastes and the desolate, unproductive regions of our country to the scenes of vast industries, progressive civilization and universal prosperity. It has followed the gradual march of civilization toward the western horizon. Westward the course of empire has taken its way, and the center of population now creeps Westward to the region beyond the Mississippi. What the future destiny of that great Western portion of our continent shall be, no one can foretell or prophesy. No one can forecast what great interests, local and national, will center around the Mediterranean of the Pacific slope, the Hudson of the West, and the Golden Gate of California; or what proportions the commerce of these great Pacific States may assume; or what naval battles shall yet be fought for the defense or possession of that great coast.

With much reluctance I bid my Western friends and their most interesting country adieu. I hope that I may again visit that coast, going by quite a different route than by those seven railway lines by which I have been accustomed to cross and recross the continent. I trust that great enterprise will be soon undertaken and speedily completed that shall divide the great isthmus, yet unite in still stronger bonds of interest and friendship the two great geographic divisions of our country.

Should the readers of these pages find themselves any better informed concerning our Western country and people than before reading them, and should they find enough in them to kindle a patriotic emotion or awaken a becoming pride concerning their own great country, my efforts and ambition will have been amply rewarded; and I wish every happiness and prosperity to attend my *compagnons de voyage* from New England to the Golden Gate.

GOLDEN GATE, SAN FRANCISCO.